KU-487-078

The
COUNTRYSIDE
COMPANION

Wynford Vaughan-Thomas

Hutchinson/Webb & Bower

To Lotte

Frontispiece: Autumn sunlight on a woodland
stream in Devon

A *Webb&Bower* BOOK

Edited, designed and produced by
Webb & Bower (Publishers) Ltd
9 Colleton Crescent, Exeter, Devon EX2 4BY

Designed by Vic Giolitto
Picture research by Anne Horton

Hutchinson & Co. (Publishers) Ltd

An imprint of the Hutchinson Publishing Group

17–21 Conway Street, London W1P 6JD

Hutchinson Group (Australia) Pty Ltd
30–32 Cremorne Street, Richmond South, Victoria 3121
PO Box 151, Broadway, New South Wales 2007

Hutchinson Group (NZ) Ltd
32–34 View Road, PO Box 40-086, Glenfield, Auckland 10

Hutchinson Group (SA) Pty Ltd
PO Box 337, Bergvlei, 2012, South Africa

First published by Hutchinson & Co (Publishers) Ltd 1979
First published as a Hutchinson Paperback 1983
© Webb & Bower (Publishers) Ltd 1979

The paperback edition of this book is sold subject to the condition
that it shall not by way of trade or otherwise be lent, resold,
hired out, or otherwise circulated without the publisher's
prior consent in any form of binding or cover other than that
in which it is published and without a similar condition including
this condition being imposed on the subsequent purchaser

Typesetting and monochrome origination by Keyspools Ltd, Warrington

Printed and bound in Aylesbury, Buckinghamshire, Great Britain by
Hazell Watson and Viney Ltd

British Library Cataloguing in Publication Data

Vaughan-Thomas, Wynford
    The countryside companion.
    1. Country life—Great Britain   2. Great Britain—Descriptions
    and travel 1971–
    I. Title
    914.1'04858   DA566.2

ISBN 0 09 151071 6

Contents

Introduction

Forget six counties over-hung by smoke,
Forget the snorting steam and piston stroke
Forget the spreading of the hideous town,
Think rather of the pack-horse on the down,
And dream of London small, and white, and
    clean
The clear Thames bordered by its gardens
    green. . . .

A hundred years have passed since William Morris – poet, artist, craftsman and pioneer Socialist – wrote this celebrated and fervent plea to his fellow countrymen to put back the clock and return to a largely imaginary but still unspoilt and beautiful mediaeval Britain. Since his day, the town has spread even wider. The motorways and the industrial estates bite into the green fields and over the once lovely hills. One might think, from some of the laments and cries of alarm, that the countryside of Britain had become, as Morris feared, a totally lost cause.

Yet, for those with eyes to see, and who are prepared to walk or climb, the astonishing fact about the British countryside is that so much of it is still there – and that it remains in such amazing beauty. In very few parts of the Earth's surface is so much variety of landscape in so small a space. Other lands are composed of vast and homogeneous units which impose a sameness of scenery over wide areas. The great steppes of Russia or the deserts of North Africa have their own beauty but it is not one of contrast or variety. The landscape of Britain is totally different. It gets its effect by continual change. Travel a mere 50 miles in any direction and the countryside takes on a new character, a fresh delight.

I recently drove westward from London towards Wales and marvelled at the way Britain contains 50 smaller Britains in the course of a mere six hours' journey. First come the rich plains of the Thames Valley, with the river making its slow and noble curves amongst the lush water meadows – a landscape that still keeps the charm that William Morris found a hundred years ago. Then the road takes you up into the chalk ridges of the Chiltern Hills, where the valleys hold magnificent groves of ancestral beeches. You suddenly come to the escarpment edge, and, from the open downs, you look out over the upper Thames valley – a quilted pattern of vividly green fields. Travel 50 miles through the pastures and lanes of Oxfordshire and again the landscape changes. You enter the ever-rising, open country of the Cotswolds, where the enchanting villages are built of a warm, honey-coloured stone and the streams run clear in their shallow valleys. From the high edge of the Cotswolds you have a heart-lifting view over the Severn valley, with its strange, isolated hills such as the poet's celebrated Bredon or the elegant, volcanic summits of the Malverns set in the rich, agricultural lands formed by Britain's longest river. But all the time, beckoning you forward from the far horizon are the romantic hills of Wild Wales. These, too, offer a subtle variety of form as you drive in amongst them – rounded and gentle at first, then getting wilder and more lonely the further you penetrate their fastness, until you reach the savage cliffs and jagged peaks of 3,600 ft high Snowdon, the highest and boldest mountain in southern Britain. You can stand on the summit and look down on the precipices, the forbidding screes, the lakes and tarns of the lower slopes and remember that this exciting almost Alpine splendour is exactly 252 miles from the traffic swirling around Piccadilly Circus in London.

What is the secret of this surprisingly varied landscape? How is it possible for a small island to

Hay-making in the Buckinghamshire Chilterns

6

change and renew itself so often and so swiftly? The first secret lies under the outward surface of fields, moors and downs in the rocks, the hidden bones of the countryside, the strong framework that holds everything together. Here Britain has been fortunate indeed. Few patches of the Earth are composed of such a varied selection of rock formations. Every possible rock is here, from the Precambrian of unimaginable age – over 500 million years old – to the latest deposits of boulder clay left behind as the ice retreated. And they are laid down in a remarkably subtle pattern. In the south and east of the country are the newest rocks – the chalk, the clay, and oolitic limestone that lie in comparatively undisturbed series, one over the other. They give the landscape a rich, settled look. This is the country painted by Constable and sung by Tennyson – the classic England of time immemorial and unchanged. North and west of the line drawn from the Humber to the mouth of the Severn lie the far older rocks, torn and twisted over the long centuries of geological time. Above them the landscape can be wild and dramatic. This is the Britain whose natural painter is Turner, and whose poets are the Wordsworth of the Lakes of Cumbria and the bards and seers of Celtic Wales and Scotland. The rocks – the skeleton beneath the flesh of the landscape – are here hard, bold and resolute. And again amazingly varied. Take a geological map, printed in such splendid colours by the Geological Survey, of any part of western Britain and hang it on your wall. The strange patterns the rocks have created are works of art in their own right.

The second moulder of the landscape of Britain is man himself, and again we come across this secret variety, which is the key to the beauty of the country. Wave after wave of invaders have flowed across Britain, each one helping to shape the scenery we enjoy today. The old megalithic builders of the cromlechs and stone circles began to tame the wilderness and clear the uplands 4,000 years ago. The Celts left their mark in the small fields and stone walls of the west. The Anglo-Saxons worked the heavy clay of the lower ground. The Normans gave us hunting forests. Each generation of farmers, merchants, soldiers and churchmen has worked on the land, shaping it to their needs. There is not a part of Britain, even in the wildest hills, that has not, at one time or another, been touched and altered by the hand of man. Our landscape is an artificial one. On the original rocks and raw earth left by the retreating glaciers, the early inhabitants of Britain carved the signs of their possession.

Many of these signs are still there, if you know where to look for them. Archaeologists can trace the pattern left by the fields of Neolithic farmers on the chalk downs. You can walk along trackways first made by herdsmen 3,000 years ago. The lanes that wriggle amongst the high hedges may have been laid out by the old monks in the Middle Ages. Some of the crafts practised by those ancient farmers have surprisingly survived all through the changing centuries. The reeds are harvested from parts of the Fens just as they were in days of the Roman invasion when the Iceni rose in revolt under Queen Boudicca in AD 61. The crofters in the Outer Hebrides cut their peat in a way which would be familiar to St Columba when he settled in Iona in the Dark Ages. The salmon-fishermen, on the Teifi in West Wales, paddle the coracles that were used by their remote Celtic ancestors long before the Romans arrived in Britain. And who can say from what remote pagan origins come those strange rituals and dances they still practise once a year at places like Helston or Abbots Bromley?

There is a third factor in the making of Britain – and maybe it's the most important of them all – our climate. There are moments when we cry aloud in our vexation at the utter unpredictability of the weather, and long for the endless, cloudless days of the Mediterranean sunshine. We do our climate grievous wrong. Again its very variety helps to create the amazing variety of our landscape. Take September. Within that month in Britain you can have hot sun beating down on the yellow sands and glittering limestone cliffs of the Gower Peninsula in South Wales until you feel you are on the Costa del Sol. Suddenly the weather changes and now snow lightly sprinkles the high summits of Ben Nevis and the Cairngorms. Three days later, the mists are creeping across the waters of the Fen country and the high tower of Ely Cathedral rises above them in a ghostly outline of Gothic beauty. The wind changes and great white cloud balloons go sailing over the sunlit downs and the grass shivers and ripples like silk in the water-meadows along the Avon at Shakespeare's Stratford. Our landscape needs our capricious climate to keep it eternally young and green.

And in this rich framework of fields, moorland and meadows, the wild animals and birds of Britain still live their secret life alongside the pulsing industrial activity of modern man. The survival of our wildlife, and again its surprising variety, is the fourth secret factor in the making of the landscape of Britain. The wily fox still slinks amongst the dustbins of greater Manchester. A badger can be caught in your headlights as you drive home at night in a Wiltshire lane, the great flights of wild duck settle on the sandbanks in the Wash and the gannets rise in a swirling white cloud off the lonely island of Grassholm like the snow-plume blowing from the top of Everest.

All these natural and man-made delights lie before you as you travel over the surface of Britain. Our book is designed to celebrate them, and to give you a new awareness of the landscape of these islands. We will watch that landscape change month by month as the seasons change – each season bringing a new pleasure to our countryside. We start our journey in the green freshness of Spring.

For each month that follows around the calendar I have selected a part of the country which seems to me to be particularly suited to the mood of that month. This is a personal choice. I do not claim that high Summer is more splendid amongst the woods of the Weald than on the dunes of the Norfolk coast, or that the autumn tints above Tintern in the valley of the Wye rival the vivid colour of the dying bracken on the high fells above Grasmere. But of the infinite richness of the countryside of Britain, I have simply taken the places where I, myself, have enjoyed the passing of the seasons, and I have been fortunate to see a great deal of unspoilt Britain.

To my own evocation of the place and the month, I have added a small collection of quotations from the English poets. The poets of Britain always seem to me to be more firmly rooted in the landscape around them than most of the European poets. I cannot conceive of a French Wordsworth or an Italian John Clare! Poets may not be precise guides around a countryside, but they have the enviable gift of swiftly creating a picture in memorable words – which leads me on to the actual pictures in this book. They are, perhaps, the most important part of it. No amount of description can replace the impact of a landscape on the eye of the beholder. I have placed some of our master-painters in a prominent position in this Countryside Companion, but I have not been afraid to place alongside them the work of our modern photographers, who on occasion can share a little of the quality of a Turner or a Constable.

So, through the selective eye of the painter and photographer, and the penetrating words of the poet, we now travel around unspoilt Britain in the wake of the changing seasons. We start our journey in the freshness of early Spring – in March.

March

March, says the old proverb, comes in like a lion and goes out like a lamb. That is the secret of its charm. You can have cold, even vicious days any time during this month, but behind any change in March weather you are conscious that Spring really is on the way. February – uncouth, unfriendly February – will not return. Every new March day brings promise of far better things to come. The primroses are out on the hedgerows. The first shy violets appear. In my native Wales we all wear a daffodil on March 1st, St David's Day, for with boundless Celtic optimism, we always hope that March will see the first daffodils in our own gardens. Usually our daffodils have to come from the Isles of Scilly where they can always depend upon lamb-like conduct from March. In any case, Welsh purists always insist on wearing a leek for this was the first acknowledged national emblem in Wales and goes back to the early days of the Hundred Years' War.

The long-bow was invented in South Wales, and his Welsh archers were Edward III's secret weapon at Crécy – they loosed their arrows from their bows with the speed of machine-gunners! The story goes that, before the battle, the Welshmen had to march through a field of leeks to take up their position. They picked the leeks and placed them in their hats in order to distinguish themselves from the French. After that famous victory at Crécy, the Welsh always sported the leek on St David's Day as a badge of honour. But, tactfully, the town-dwelling Welshmen of the 19th Century changed from the powerfully smelling leek to the gentler perfumed daffodil. Frankly I do not regret the change. I feel that I am officially welcoming Spring once I place

A carpet of daffodils in early Spring

that bold yellow trumpet of a flower in my button-hole. Shakespeare was right, as usual, to talk of the daffodils

> '. . . that come before the swallow dares
> And take the winds of March with beauty.'

There is a second sign of Spring that I welcome with the daffodils in March. The first lambs appear in the hill country. In southern England, with its gentler climate, lambing can be earlier, but up on the higher ground farmers cannot risk too early an arrival of this most attractive of young domesti-cated animals. In the really high mountains lambing can be as late as April and early May. When I was young I used to lament that they ever grew up into such unprepossessing creatures as sheep; although when I started to walk the high hills I developed a respect for the old ewes, that know every yard of their mountain pastures and every trick of survival in rough weather. But it was the first lambs of the year that were important to us. If we saw them with their heads towards us, we were certain we would have good luck for the next 12 months.

My third March delight is the song of the skylark. Many other birds start to come into fuller song in March after the restraint of the Winter, including the blackbirds and thrushes in my garden. But the skylark's song seems to have a greater delight, a more reckless abandon to the challenge of Spring. And the best place to hear it in March is on the rolling chalk downs that cover so much of southern England. Climb up on to the South Downs where they rise above the ancient town of Lewes in Sussex. You will first be walking over the track taken by Simon de Montfort 700 years ago in 1263 as he manoeuvred his men to surprise the Royalists in the town below. The battle of Lewes, we were taught (not altogether ac-curately, as later historians have been at pains to point out), led to the firm establishment of parliamentary government in England. You reach the summit of the Downs and follow a trackway that goes back a thousand years before Simon de Montfort. The bare treeless downland rolls away before you. The March wind sends the white clouds sailing through the boisterous sky. When I last walked there, I climbed up over a grassy brow and came across a group of hares in the grip of their March 'madness'. They were so intent on their extraordinary courting display that they took not the slightest notice of me. The does sat around like spectators at a boxing match while the males stood on their hind legs and sparred with one another, or suddenly raced around in circles, kicking as they ran. Mad as March hares they seemed indeed, but there was method in their madness. The maddest male got the most females.

Over all, as I walked, the larks were singing their hearts out. It was then that I first felt that March and the sweeping chalk hills of the south country were the perfect match. Ever since, the chalk has seemed to me to be a light-hearted, spring lark-song of a rock. I know that it is absurd to attribute human qualities to anything in Nature. Ruskin called such an irrational proceeding 'the pathetic fallacy', and read poor Tennyson a stern lecture for the poet's rhapsodic invitation to Maud to come into a garden where passion flowers shed splendid tears and the casement jessamine obligingly stirred to the sound of flute, violin and bassoon! But rock is something about which you cannot be totally indifferent. Consciously or unconsciously, you associate certain rocks with seasons, emotions and past experience. For me, the dark Pennant sandstone, that crops out between the upper and lower coal-measures in South Wales and frowns down on the deep gash of the Rhondda, is a sad rock, linked with rain, depression and long dole-queues. On the other hand, the Old Red Sandstone of Hereford-shire is a warm, holiday sort of rock, when the first shoots of corn are pushing up their small green spears from the rose-coloured ground and I am drinking cider in some friendly inn overlooking the Wye. The limestone is a clean rock that glitters after rain. The volcanic crags of Ordovician rocks in Cumbria are sterner – challenging rather than welcoming rocks. I could go through the whole gamut of British rocks, from Precambrian to the latest glacial deposit, and assign a personal emotion to each one of them, but I shall always return to the chalk as the most light-hearted of rocks. I remember Augustus John once laying down the law in one rather bibulous gathering. 'Chalk,' he thundered, 'That's a rock you must always paint in water-colour!'

From where does the chalk get this exceptional whiteness, that sets it apart from all other rocks? Geologists tell us that it is formed of shells. 10% of it comes from the shells of microscopic organisms called Foraminifera, and about 50% from very fine-grained calcium carbonate probably derived from the disintegration of larger shells. It was deposited between 120 and 90 million years ago in the clear shallow seas that then covered southern Britain and a great deal of the northern European plain as well. The chalk is not uniform. Some beds are harder than others; some are laced with flints made of silica. But it is the foraminifera that seize the imagination – falling gently through the countless years like a white snowstorm in the shallow sea. Under the chalk lie beds of clay and sands that come up to the surface in the Weald of Kent where the chalk has been worn away from the summit of a dome. Below the sands lie the vast beds of oolitic limestone that crop out to form the Cotswolds. As you travel westwards from London you realize that southern England is constructed of regular layers of rock, placed one on top of the other and gently sloping eastwards. It is in extraordinary contrast to the western and northern parts of the country where the far more ancient rocks are twisted and contorted to an extraordinary degree. No wonder that early geologists fastened on the South as they laboriously laid the foundations of their science. One of the most famous of them, William Smith, worked as an engineer in the construction of canals. In the canal cuttings he had ample opportunity to observe how regularly the rock beds succeeded each other. 'Slices of bread and butter laid on a plate,' he called them. He also noticed how each could be differentiated by the fossils it contained, and so laid down one of the basic principles of geology. Nick-named 'Strata' Smith, he became the father of stratigraphy.

Although he made his first studies further west at the foot of the Cotswolds, the regularity of the chalk must have delighted him. But chalk has

The skylark, whose song can be heard on fine spring days high above the countryside of southern England

another curious quality besides regularity. It is a remarkably porous rock, and water sinks down through it as if it were a sponge. Some of the valleys in it are quite dry and you wonder how they were formed, until you remember that there was once a time when the great glaciers crawled down over England almost to the line of the Thames. The chalklands south of the glacier tongues were in the grip of the 'permafrost' – the ground below the surface remained permanently frozen, as it does today in the tundras of Siberia and northern Canada. The torrents pouring away from the ice-face could cut down quite easily into this frozen ground. When more genial conditions returned, the rock became porous again and the water-table sank. There came a time – long, long after the Ice Age – when the shepherds found the downlands ideal for sheep, but less than ideal when it came to the water supply. They solved the problem by constructing 'dew-ponds' – shallow excavations in the chalk, puddled with clay that collected and kept the rain, as much if not more than the dew. Legend has gathered around them. The country folk maintain that if ever a stream is allowed to fall into one, it will surely fail thereafter. Kipling, who lived in later life in the shadow of the South Downs at Burwash could write:

> 'We have no water to delight
> Our broad and brookless vales –
> Only the dew-pond on the height,
> Unfed, that never fails.'

The dew-ponds are man-made, but the chalk has another curious formation which looks man-made but is entirely a natural product. In a few parts of the downland and especially in the area that stretches from Malborough towards Avebury you will find a bed of hard sandstone lying on the surface of the chalk. Over the ages, it has weathered into great blocks called sarsens. The name comes from the word 'Saracen', which was used in the 17th Century to describe anything exotic and foreign-looking. The sarsens are certainly strange and mysterious objects to find on the smooth grassy downland. Near Fyfield Down, you can wander through a quiet valley full of them, and as you walk through the rocks scattered under the low trees, they seem like a flock of sheep gently lying down at close of day. You appreciate the aptness of the other name given them by the country folk: 'the Grey Wethers'.

It is the sarsen stones that stand in such majesty at Stonehenge and Avebury to remind us that the chalk uplands have played a key role in the early development of civilization in Britain. All over the gently sloping downs we see the handiwork of our earlier farmers and stock-keepers – trackways, barrows, strange figures carved in the chalk, long avenues of grey stones standing against the skyline. The chalk country is a vast open-air museum of our pre-history.

I felt this strongly when I climbed up on to the open downland to see the West Kennet Long Barrow in Wiltshire. This is classic pre-history country. The great stone circle of Avebury is not far away. At the foot of the down is Silbury Hill, the biggest prehistoric mound in Europe. With its majestic sarsen stones, its entrance avenue and the little mediaeval village placed in the middle of the huge ditch that surrounds the stones, Avebury disputes with Stonehenge for the title of the most impressive archaeological site in Britain. The builders of the huge barrow of West Kennet – and a barrow is simply a burial chamber heaped over with earth or stones – had an eye for country. The whole landscape is spread below you. The barrow has been carefully restored and the great stones replaced in position, to guard the entrance to a long, mysterious tunnel leading deep into the heart of the grass-covered mound. I groped my way along the tunnel and found small chambers opening on either side. These are the burial chambers, where perhaps 4,000 years ago our remote ancestors came to lay their dead. What strange ceremonies did they perform before those quiet stones that form a forecourt to the mound? Who lies buried here, and what power did they hold to make their fellow men go through the immense labour of dragging the heavy stones into place in a world where everything had to be done solely by the muscle power of man?

Even the modern archaeologists can give only a partial answer. They tell us that the first farming people who entered Britain, those early husband-men who left their mark here in the chalklands, were the heirs to the Neolithic Revolution, that remarkable change in the way man gained his food which began in the Middle East around 7000 BC. A series of inventions changed him from a hunter into a farmer, able to produce a steadily increasing surplus of food. These Neolithic farmers entered Britain some thousands of years later and found the chalklands to their liking. These lands were more open and the farmers could move freely across them. Of course, the downs may not have been so treeless then as they are now. We can still enjoy the noble beech-woods which are the glory of the Chiltern Hills and glimpse a picture of what other parts of the chalklands looked like before man cleared them. But the soil could be tilled by light ploughs and the farmers conquered the downs.

The first comers did not remain in sole possession. Wave after wave of invaders crossed the Channel – Windmill Hill Folk, Beaker Folk, Urn Folk and plenty of others. Archaeologists have had a happy and sometimes an acrimonious time distinguishing them all. No-one can defend himself with such verbal venom as an expert accused of ascribing an artefact found in dubious circumstances to the wrong sub-section of a certain culture. I rather enjoy these battles, because they are fought between men who feel deeply about their subject and are passionately concerned to get at the truth. I will not forget the reverence with which Dr Glyn Daniel placed in my hand the polished piece of rock with which the late Dr H.H. Thomas had proved in 1923 – by an extraordinary piece of scientific detective work – that the blue-stones in one of the circles of Stonehenge had come from the distant Preseli hills in far West Wales. And that brings me to the most impressive prehistoric moment in the whole world of the chalklands and even in Europe itself, Stonehenge.

Above: The Cuckmere River, behind Cuckmere Haven on the Sussex South Downs, a typical chalkland river meandering through the rolling downland

Below: The West Kennet Long Barrow. The entrance tunnel gives access to small chambers on each side where the Neolithic chalk-dwellers buried their dead

Even today, when there is an army camp on one skyline and car parks have perforce been built near it, (but full marks to the Ministry of the Environment, not too near) Stonehenge remains extraordinarily impressive. Here the sarsen stones have been used with genius, shaped and morticed with stone hammers alone. They stand, joining giant hands in an outside ring, within which huge trilithons make doorways into mystery. No-one who sees it for the first time can fail to be excited and moved by it. King James I, while out hunting from Wilton House with the Earl of Pembroke, became so intrigued with the noble stones that he instructed his architect, the great Inigo Jones, to make the first plan of them and also to add an explanation. Jones made the first of the many wrong guesses as to their origin when he ascribed Stonehenge to the Romans, who, he declared, had erected it in honour of the god Coelus. Later came that most attractive if somewhat muddle-headed of biographers, John Aubrey, who claimed that Stonehenge was a temple of the Druids, thereby starting a connection with these Celtic mystery-men which is irrevocably fixed in the popular mind, no matter how the experts may protest. His comment on the stares (starlings) that once nested in the holes between the tenon and the mortice on the lintels of the great trilithons, is so charming that we are obliged to quote it: 'The high stones of Stonehenge are honeycombed so deep, that the Stares do make their nests in the holes. Whether these holes are naturall or artificial I cannot say. The holes are towards the tops of the jambe-stones. This did put me in mind, that in Wales they doe call Stares Adar y Drudwy, sc Aves Druidum. The Druids might make these Holes purposely for their Birds to nest in. They are loquacious birds and Pliny tells us of a Stare that could speake Greeke. Why not?' Why not indeed!

To this day, the modern Order of Druids, clad in their white robes and led by their Chief Druid, resplendent in gold torque and head-dress, march solemnly into the circle as dawn breaks on June 21st, the summer solstice, and lay their offerings on the so-called Altar Stone. When I last saw them do it, the effect of the ceremony was a little diminished by the fact that these reverent heirs to the mysteries of the Druids all arrived at Stonehenge in buses. No matter. They felt, as all visitors to Stonehenge feel, that they were directly in communication with our most distant past.

Gradually, as in the case of geology, archaeology moved out from the twilight of romantic speculation into the state of a serious scholarly discipline; and most of the pioneers of the new study were men of the chalk country. After all, they had around them the greatest collection of barrows, avenues and prehistoric monuments in the whole of Britain. Among the pioneers was the attractive figure of Sir William Colt Hoare, the author of 'Ancient Wiltshire'. He made his mistakes as all pioneers must do, for he lived at a period, the first years of the 19th Century, when country gentlemen still invited their neighbours to join them in 'cracking a cromlech', and one well-known amateur was reputed to sit on top of a barrow clad in an enormous cloak, while he pretended to contemplate the view. Beneath the cloak, he was recklessly digging down into the burial mound for anything he could find. Colt Hoare demanded more scientific methods. In 'Ancient Wiltshire' he wrote: 'We speak from facts not theory. I shall not seek among the fanciful regions of Romance for the origin of our Wiltshire barrows.'

But the man who really placed the whole business of archaeological excavations on a sound basis was General Pitt-Rivers. In 1880 he inherited a great estate in Cranborne Chase and in fact changed his name from Lane-Fox to do so. He had an inquiring and scientific mind which had brought him distinction in his army career, and he tackled the excavation of the many barrows on his estate with military thoroughness. He insisted on the most meticulous records being kept, with every object found, however humble, being noted in the exact place where it was discovered. As a result, his records can still be used by modern archaeologists. He had money as well as enthusiasm and operated

Avebury in Wiltshire, one of the most important sites of sarsen stones in Britain, was set up by Bronze Age men c. 1800 BC. About 100 of the stones still stand

A view of the Chiltern Hills in Buckinghamshire

on the grand scale. On a 'digging day', he assembled his specially trained assistants on parade, and after inspection, he would mount his dog-cart drawn by fast high-stepping horses. His assistants, wearing straw boaters decorated with ribbons in the general's colours, would get on penny-farthing bicycles, and away went the procession through the startled countryside, singing a chorus specially composed for the occasion. Eccentric the general might have been, but once arrived on the site, Pitt-Rivers and his team were models of scientific precision. His finds have been carefully preserved in Oxford and in his own museum at Cranborne. Everything is arranged in correct sequence.

Nothing was discarded. When the Pitt-Rivers methods were at last applied to sites like Stonehenge and Avebury, we began to see them at their true worth. These are no Druidical temples. They were built and rebuilt over many centuries in the 2nd millennium BC and the men who ordered their building were the leaders of a powerful Bronze Age society. Were they built as temples or even astronomical observatories? Who can tell? We look at Stonehenge, as the evening light caresses the mellow-coloured sarsen stones and the great trilithons are outlined against the sky, and feel, with the authority on Stonehenge, Dr J.R.C. Atkinson, that this monument 'so far transcends all other European monuments of its age that it can justly be counted among the highest achievements of the human spirit in the prehistoric past'.

The chalk can show other memorials to our

distant past which may not have the splendour of Stonehenge and Avebury, or the impressive positions of the great barrows, but which are fascinating and mysterious in their own right. The great Bronze Age princes and potentates of the Stonehenge period fade into the dark night of history and long after come new invaders of Britain, bearing all-conquering iron swords. Britain is now Celtic, but like their ancient predecessors, the Celts also felt the lure of the chalk. They built their vast forts out of it, for the Celts, and especially the latest Celtic invaders, the Belgae, were warlike. The centuries immediately before the Roman invasion saw Britain filled with the tumult of battle between the small tribal states. These Celtic forts on the chalk are impressive and one of the biggest is in the heart of the Hardy country just outside Dorchester in Dorset. Maiden Castle is a stupendous fortress, with triple ramparts over 100 ft high and covering an area two-thirds of a mile long and one-third of a mile wide. It has been well said that this is the work of a fine intelligence, a Vauban of the Iron Age. When the Romans made their Great Invasion of Britain in AD 43 on the orders of the Emperor Claudius, the 2nd Legion was under the command of the future Emperor Vespasian. As the invasion progressed over a period of years, this legion fought its way westwards until at last it stood before Maiden Castle and looked up at the high ramparts crowned with wooden palisades and manned by hordes of the formidable Belgic slingers.

1,800 years later, the famous archaeologist Sir Mortimer Wheeler started scientific excavations at the eastern approach. Through the work of his spade we can now know what happened next. Sir Mortimer found big 'ammunition dumps' of sling stones, and scores of shallow graves in which lay huddled skeletons of men and women, their bones scarred by sword cuts or pierced by the neat holes made by the pilum, the deadly Roman throwing spear. Sir Mortimer had uncovered the first British war cemetery. Everywhere around the eastern entrance lay the iron Roman ballista-bolt – fired from the formidable ballista, a sort of early spring-gun. As he dug, Sir Mortimer could see, in his

mind's eye, the scene as the experienced, tough yet humane Vespasian gave the order for his legionaries to make the final assault. The ballista-bolts showered down on the devoted defenders, but the disciplined Romans linked their shields and, like a human battering ram, crashed through the more lightly armed Celts. Then came the frenzy of killing, the dark coils of smoke from burning huts mounting into the Dorset sky at the end of that hot, tragic summer's day. Next morning Vespasian moved on westwards. He had taken another step on his journey towards the splendours of the Imperial throne.

The great Celtic forts can yield vivid pictures of the past to the archaeologist's spade. There are other remarkable patterns made by the Celts in the chalk that do not 'abide our question' but remain puzzling and challenging. Not far from Wantage the chalk downs reach a height of over 800 ft. From their edge you have a heart-lifting view over the wide green expanse of the low-lying valley of the Thames and its tributaries. Here on the bare steep slope high above the pattern of fields far below, a stylised portrait of a horse has been cut out of the chalk. Its economy of line – suggesting graceful movement with a few brilliant strokes – gives it a strange affinity with modern art. It was cut on a big scale, 365 ft long and 130 ft high, and its outlines were carefully cherished by the peasantry through the long centuries with regular 'scourings'. A fair was held on the downs, with rural sports and jollifications and the revellers ended up by standing in the eye of the horse and making a special wish, which, through the magic power of the White Horse, was bound to come true.

The unshakeable devotion of the country folk to their local imagery which surely goes back to the pagan world of the early Celts, may account for the survival of two remarkable human figures carved in the chalk – the Long Man of Wilmington, and strangest of all, the Cerne Abbas giant. The Cerne Abbas figure shows an enormous nude man brandishing a club, and takes up a whole hillside. But the most extraordinary thing about the Cerne Abbas figure is its frank depiction of the giant's most intimate possessions. This is phallic art on an

Right: Stonehenge, the best known Neolithic monument in western Europe. It consists of an outer ditch round a double circle of standing stones, with a large bluestone, the Altar Stone, in the centre

Below: Silbury Hill in Wiltshire, the largest prehistoric mound in Europe. The reason for its building is still an unsolved mystery

heroic scale. It survived all the assaults of the churchmen in the Middle Ages and the disapproval of the Puritans. Year after year the local men staunchly kept the outline of their giant cut in the chalk in all his naked splendour. When the late Queen Mary was taken on a tour of the Cranborne Museum by the son of General Pitt-Rivers, she was somewhat startled to see a similar figure preserved from the past. She looked at it steadfastly and pronounced her verdict: 'A debased people, Mr Pitt-Rivers, a debased people.'

But attitudes change over the years even in the highest circles and today the Cerne Abbas giant has attained a new popularity. I stopped at the friendly inn not far from the figure. The landlord is sure it must rank as the smallest in England and it got its licence from King Charles II in return for a drink

offered to him on a particularly hot day in the midst of what was then an alcoholic wilderness. We had a splendid half hour of rich country talk about the giant, and when I set off to inspect him they offered me a word of advice, accompanied by happy rural laughter as I walked out through the door. 'Our giant, Mr Thomas – don't be discouraged after you've seen him!'

So, over the centuries the chalk country keeps its traditions. There is even a possibility that the most traditional of English games, cricket, might have originated on the downs. The wicket – theorists say – was originally the wicket gate forming an entrance to a sheep-fold, and the shepherds practised defending it with their crooks. The attacker bowled stones towards the defender, who hurled them away with the curve of his crook.

Who knows? It might be possible. The early bats were curved like the end of the shepherd's crook. And didn't Samuel Pepys, in a charming passage, describe how he once walked in high Summer on the downs and met a shepherd with his little son in a lonely sheep-fold? The shepherd showed Pepys the trick of using the curve of the crook to fling flints far from the fold, 'which,' says Pepys, 'pleased me mightily.'

It would also please me mightily if cricket really had started on the chalk downs, for they have been the place of origin of so much that has been woven into the fabric of English life – including the scene that has become almost the symbol of England abroad, the White Cliffs of Dover. Behind the port, the North Downs come dramatically to the sea, and until the advent of the aeroplane, their cliffs were inevitably the first view of England offered to the visitor from the continent and the sight of Dover was a particularly emotional moment for the armed forces returning from active service in the World Wars. The Channel crossing can sometimes be very rough indeed, which may account for much of the emotion aroused by this glittering backdrop of chalk, standing high above the welcoming arms of the great breakwaters that lead you at last thankfully into the smooth waters of Dover Harbour.

To the west, immediately behind the harbour, rises the sheer face of Shakespeare's Cliff, so called because, by tradition, it was the scene of that moving passage in 'King Lear', where Edgar guides his blinded father, Gloucester, to the cliff edge and vividly describes the plunge of the cliff:

'How fearful
And dizzy 'tis to cast one's eyes so low!
The crows and choughs that wing the midway air
Show scarçe so gross as beetles. Half-way down
Hangs one that gathers samphire – dreadful trade!
The fishermen that walk upon the beach
Appear like mice . . .'

Gathering samphire dangling on a rope half-way down Shakespeare's Cliff must have been indeed a dreadful trade, since there were surely easier ways to get it, even in Elizabethan days. The marsh samphire grows on the mud marshes that are washed over by the sea, and I have eaten the fresh, young green stems in East Anglia, where some people pickle them. In the old days marsh samphire was burnt to produce the soda needed in glass manufacture. Perhaps Shakespeare's daring dangler was after some specially valuable variety. But Shakespeare knew about their sheer verticality.

The sea cuts away at the soft foot of the cliff like slicing cheese, and the blocks fall clear to leave a sheer or almost sheer face. Shakespeare's Cliff is by no means the highest. The South Downs also come

down to the sea between Eastbourne and Brighton and form Beachy Head which is over 500 ft high. Beachy, with its lighthouse far below the almost vertical face, is one of the show-places of the chalk, and beyond lies Seaford Head and the strangely regular Seven Sisters Cliff. Here you can see how fiercely the sea has been biting into the chalk. Originally the seven shallow valleys went down gradually to the shore, but the waves have driven the cliff line back and the valleys, as it were, hang in air. Still further westward, the chalk continues to make impressive cliffs wherever it comes down to the sea. The Needles guard the entrance to the Solent and the chalk makes its final appearance along the Dorset coast with impressive isolated stacks and deep-cut coves.

But somehow it is always to Dover I return when I think of the chalk. And to the cliffs that front those narrow and difficult waters that separate us from France. I remember how recently, in geological time, Britain became an island and the rising sea cut the umbilical cord of chalk that still linked us to Mother Europe. Even 15,000 years ago, the

Opposite : The Uffington White Horse, near Wantage, which can be seen from several miles away, looking as if it is galloping across the downs

Below : The Cerne Abbas Giant near Dorchester, one of the most spectacular chalk carvings of the downlands. The figure is 180 ft tall and dates back about 1600 years

hunters following the great herds of game as the ice retreated could have walked across. By 3000 BC, the first Neolithic farmers in their frail hide-covered coracles had to cross the newly made channel where the tides raced furiously. They must have been profoundly glad to see the white cliffs looming at last out of the mists. The channel tides were still strong when Caesar crossed and landed a little further west than Dover. He was lucky to get back safely to the continent after a channel storm had almost wrecked his fleet. The Spanish Armada in 1588 wisely kept clear of Dover and sailed through the bottleneck of the channel on the Calais side. Napoleon looked across to the white cliffs when he encamped his Grande Armée near Boulogne. But the Royal Navy firmly held the channel. Napoleon built a splendid column to his own glory on the chalk cliffs above Boulogne and swung his army away towards Vienna and his crowning military masterpiece at Austerlitz. Nearly 100 years later another even more formidable dictator, Hitler, looked across to the White Cliffs of Dover and also decided not to risk it. Instead the

big guns he installed on Cap Gris Nez sent their shells whistling across the channel, and our own big guns on the cliffs above Dover barked back in reply. Down below Dover Castle, the cliff is honeycombed with passages in the chalk which hid the military headquarters. So the white cliffs went boldly to war, but this was not the first time the chalk country was involved in modern warfare.

In the heart of southern England lies Salisbury Plain, a wide stretch of open chalk downland which was an irresistible attraction for the military. Just as the Lunebergerheide, the vast sandy heath in North Germany, became the training ground of the old Imperial army in the days of the Kaiser, so Salisbury Plain complemented Aldershot as the First World War loomed. Generations of British soldiers got to know the character of chalk intimately as they dug trenches in it, drove tanks over it and sighted their guns on the bare ridges rolling away to the horizon. And in the days before the army mechanised itself and men marched to war, the dust of the plain lent point to the old soldiers' chorus :

> 'One day we had manoeuvres on dear old
>   Salisbury Plain,
> We marched and marched and marched and
>   marched and marched again.
> I thought the Duke of York a fool but he
>   wasn't in the van
> With us who marched and marched and
>   marched and marched back home again.'

I, too, have reason to remember certain features of the chalk. During the last war I was engaged in an exercise of walking behind a moving barrage. The brisk young captain in charge told us that the guns were going to put down such an accurate line of fire that they would 'shoot you into the objective'. 'Now men,' he exhorted us, 'have confidence in the gunners. I want you to lean against the barrage.' We set off in a long line of tin-hatted khaki-clad figures slightly hesitant behind that moving cloud of smoke and dust ahead. 'Lean against it, lean against it,' shouted the captain in my ear, when there was a startling shriek and a big chunk of the barrage dropped again – right behind me! I looked around desperately. It was then I realized how

bleak and bare a chalk down can be. I only wish Hilaire Belloc had been with me. I'd have told him what to do with that verse of his: 'And along the sky the line of the Downs, So noble and so bare.' They were the barest bit of Britain at that moment. Ahead of me was a low mound. I dived for it, and when the next shell burst, I was safely huddled behind it. And when silence came and I stood up again, I realized that my providential mound was the remains of a small bell-barrow. I had been saved by a structure built to bury one of those old warlike iron-sworded Celts 2,000 years before. So the chalk keeps its history intact. Every scratch or ditch or mound, made by man through the ages, seems to have survived on its smooth surface.

Salisbury city lies a little apart from the plain but as you drive south-eastwards from the open country you will see from afar off the thin pencil of that marvellous cathedral spire soaring up over the downs. Constable painted a great picture of this most homogeneous of Gothic masterpieces, but then he dashed off an equally brilliant water-colour of Stonehenge, complete with rainbow. As far as I know he didn't paint any part of the Avon valley, the limpid stream that runs down from the plain through Salisbury to the sea – a typical river of the chalk country, its clear waters running through the long lines of trailing water-weeds. The Avon and its neighbour the Test are great trout streams, but they must harbour some of the most expensive trout in Britain. Every fly cast on these exclusive waters can hook your bank-balance before the fish.

The chalk rises to its highest point in England a little north and east from Salisbury Plain, high

Opposite: Constable's painting of Salisbury Cathedral, a fine example of Early English Gothic architecture. The spire is the tallest in England

Right: An adonis blue, one of the rare species of butterfly found in the chalk country

though the plain seems to be when you are marching over it on a chill day. Not far from Newbury, Walbury Hill and Inkpen Beacon are only 50 ft or so short of that magical 1,000 ft mark. This area forms, as it were, the central hub of the chalk formation in southern England. But we must not forget that the chalk is not the exclusive property of places like Sussex just because the poets have sung about it there.

A long chalk arm extends northwards from the Thames into the fine edge of the Chilterns that looks out over the wide Oxfordshire plain. I cherish the view from Sherburn Hill. You stand here over 800 ft, although the highest point of the Chilterns lies some miles further north-east near Wendover, where the long escarpment reaches the respectable altitude, for southern England, of 859 ft. But to my mind Sherburn has the finer view, although I must admit that the best time to be here amongst the beech woods is October not March and early spring. It is then that you get the full golden glory of the Chiltern woodlands and realize why England's furniture industry started in the Chilterns. When I first visited the Chilterns in the 1920s, bicycling along roads that never seemed to know a motor-car, you could still meet individual craftsmen called 'bodgers', who had ancient rights to fell beech trees. They shaped the wood roughly into chair arms and legs and then sent their work to the factories of High Wycombe to be finished. I wonder if their roughly shaped arms and legs were the origin of that rather unkind phrase 'a botched job'. The bodgers I met were all proud of their job or at least of their independence.

The Chilterns sink from prominence beyond Luton, although the chalk formations run east of Cambridge all the way up into Norfolk. At

Newmarket it is the chalk that nourishes the famous gallops and race-courses that made this pleasant little town the centre of horse-racing in England from the days of Charles II. There is no more attractive sight on a clear March day than to see the long-legged, brisk-stepping thoroughbreds in a great trainer's 'string' going out for the morning's walk-out over the close-cropped turf. The larks sing overhead, and they are probably doing the same thing at Lambourne – Sir John Betjeman's 'leathery Lambourne' – over a hundred miles away at the far south-western end of the chalk country of England, where rival trainers' 'strings' are also moving out on to the high downs for their trial gallops. And 'never the twain shall meet' until the 'Flat' racing opens in the end of the month. Some will feel the triumph of success and others the bitterness of seeing the whole of their winter's work 'also ran'.

The long northern extension of the chalk also has its ancient trackway, the Icknield Way, which ran along the edge of the Chilterns, on past Newmarket and up into the heart of Norfolk. And prehistory follows it, as it does the old trackways on the downs of southern England. Near Thetford, on the edge of the vast forest which was first planted by the Forest Commission as far back as 1922, you can visit the remarkable site of Grime's Graves. Here, far back in the late Stone Age, around 2000 BC, miners sunk 40-ft shafts through the surface sand and clay to reach the chalk, which held a layer of high quality flint known as floorstone. You can still see the tunnels driven out from the bottom of the pits by the ancient miners using picks made of red deer horns. In one of the tunnels they found a skeleton under a rock-fall. This poor Stone-Age miner died as the result of the first known accident in British industry. And at nearby Brandon the flint that he died to extract is still shaped and cut by modern 'flint knappers'.

But although the chalk is present in Norfolk it is often over-lain by later clays and sands. It makes low cliffs at Hunstanton before it is breached by the Wash. It crops out again in Lincolnshire, where it forms the gently sloping Wolds. The chalk finally reappears north of the Humber in the Yorkshire Wolds. Here the rock is harder and almost approaches limestone in consistency. The Wolds rise over 800 ft and seem to have a different character from the great downs of the south country. The slopes can be more abrupt and the valley-bottoms more richly cultivated, but where the Wolds come to the sea at Flamborough Head the rock maintains its true character to the end. Under a more gently sloping top of boulder clay, the headland cliffs drop with a vertical plunge worthy of Beachy Head. Flamborough can even supply a final characteristic chalk link with pre-history in the Dane's Dyke – far more ancient than the Danes. Rather it is an Iron-Age construction dug perhaps 2,000 years ago to turn the whole of Flamborough Head into a big defensive camp.

I confess I have never heard the lark trilling above Flamborough Head for I have never been there in March. But as I stood near the lighthouse on a warm day in early September I could not help thinking of how the chalk has linked together so many widely separated parts of England and almost given them the same character. Its only rival in this respect is the oolitic limestone, which outcrops further west than the chalk, and curves up from the Cotswolds up through the heart of England to form that curious feature, the Lincolnshire cliff. It is not much of a cliff – it rarely rises more than 150 ft. But it forms a sort of spine to the county, for it is remarkably straight – a quality much appreciated by the Romans who drove their Ermine Street along it. The oolitic limestone ends on the Yorkshire moors.

Splendid though these moorlands can be, my thoughts at Flamborough Head kept returning to the chalk – so white and clean, so linked with the history of England. And to the southern down-lands with their rare butterflies like the chalk-hill blue, the adonis blue and the silver-spotted skipper, their unique orchids – yes, and to their snails, for these chalk hills harbour a greater variety of snails than anywhere else in Britain. The biggest one, the so-called Roman snail, is edible. The experts claim that it was brought to Britain by the Romans with the sole purpose of giving variety to their cuisine. I have eaten them myself, but that was outside the chalklands, at the Miners Arms at Priddy in the Mendips. Maybe the chalk-bred snails have a special flavour.

As indeed has everything connected with the chalk. We shall let Kipling have the last word, as he looked out from the South Downs to the more richly wooded Weald and gave his word of praise for the sparse, spare, taut quality of the country built by those countless multitudes of Foraminifera over 100 million years ago:

'No tender-hearted garden crowns
No bosomed woods adorn
Our blunt, bow-hearted whale-backed Downs.
But gnarled and writhen thorn –
Bare slopes where chasing swallows skim,
And through the gaps revealed
Belt upon belt, the wooden, dim
Blue goodness of the Weald.'

March with the Poets

The hard blue winds of March
shake the young sheep
and flake the long stone walls;
now from the gusty grass
comes the horned music of rams,
and plovers fall out of the sky
filling their wings with snow.

Tired of this northern tune
the winds turn soft
blowing white butterflies
out of the dog-rose hedges,
and schoolroom songs are full
of boys' green cuckoos
piping the summer round

LAURIE LEE

Leathery limbs of Upper Lambourne
Leathery skin from sun and wind,
Leathery breeches, spreading stables,
Shining saddles left behind –
To the downs the string of horses
Moving out of sight and mind.

Feathery ash in leathery Lambourne
Waves above the sarsen stones,
And Edwardian plantations
So coniferously moan,
As to make the swelling downland,
Far-surrounding, seem their own.

SIR JOHN BETJEMAN

Nothing is so beautiful as spring –
    When weeds, in wheels, shoot long and lovely and lush;
    Thrush's eggs look little low heavens, and thrush
Through the echoing timber does so rinse and wring
The ear, it strikes like lightnings to hear him sing;
    The glassy peartree leaves and blooms, they brush
    The descending blue; that blue is all in a rush
With richness; the racing lambs too have fair their fling.
What is all this juice and all this joy?
    A strain of the earth's sweet being in the beginning
In Eden garden. Have, get, before it cloy,
    Before it cloud, Christ, lord, and sour with sinning,
Innocent mind and Mayday in girl and boy,
    Most, O maid's child, thy choice and worthy the winning.

GERARD MANLEY HOPKINS

April

April in Britain is the most fickle, inconstant yet enchanting of months. The true delight of Spring lies, after all, in its very uncertainty, which was summed up in a memorable piece of bad verse by one of the many contenders for the title of England's Worst Poet, William Watson. Watson produced two lines on April which stick in the mind:

'April, April, laugh thy girlish laughter
Then the moment after, weep thy girlish tears.'

We chuckle and remember! T.S. Eliot may have apostrophised April as 'the cruellest month, breeding lilacs out of the dead land', but he was philosophising and April is no month for philosophy. I remain with William Watson and rejoice in its swiftly changing moods. Behind all the April showers lies the exhilarating feeling of life returning again after the long suspended death of the Winter. There are days of warm delight when you first realize that the leaves are bursting forth on the trees in a fresh green spray. The Spring is here with all its promise, and the voice of the cuckoo is heard in the land. To me, the cuckoo is the real symbol of returning Spring, with his glad, confident shouting of his deceitful double-note in the depth of our valley. He is not the most moral of birds. He early mastered the modern art of living at other people's expense. But he is bold and enterprising and I make an annual ritual of going to listen for the first cuckoo in the little churchyard at Nevern, in West Wales.

Nevern Church, surrounded by its dark yew trees and rich in inscribed stones from the Dark Ages, gives an impression of memorable, mysterious age, and is dedicated to St Brynach. I cannot claim that St Brynach is one of the best known of British saints and somehow I feel that this most modest of hermits would never wish to be. He settled in the remote country of North Pembrokeshire, where the Preseli Hills, like the Mountains of Mourne, sweep down to the sea. In common with all the old Celtic saints, he seemed to have a particular affinity with birds and animals. Perhaps they were the only living things that could stand a three-hour sermon in Welsh every day! Above all, St Brynach sympathised with cuckoos, and cuckoos were devoted to him. After he died, on every St Brynach's Day in late spring, the first cuckoo of the year arrived to perch on St Brynach's Cross, which still stands in Nevern churchyard in all the beauty of its intricately twining Celtic patterns. As soon as the cuckoo arrived, the Mass in honour of the saint could begin. But one stormy saint's day, reports old George Owen, the delightful Tudor historian of Pembrokeshire, the congregation waited and waited but there was no sign of the bird. At last, as dusk was falling, the bird appeared. He had fought his way gallantly through the furious gale. Then, gathering all his remaining strength, he managed to gasp out a faint 'cuck-oo' – and fell dead. But he had kept faith! 'This religious tale,' says George Owen, 'you may either believe or not, without pain of damnation.'

But, as with many birds, legend has gathered so thickly around the cuckoo in Britain until, even without pain of damnation, the layman is indeed uncertain what to believe about him. He is a favourite theme with our poets, but poets are notoriously untrustworthy when it comes to ornithology. At school I learnt Wordsworth's lovely lines about the song of the 'cuckoo bird':

'Breaking the silence of the seas
Among the farthest Hebrides.'

But my English master, who was Dylan Thomas's father, maintained – with what justice I am still

Spring green of a beech wood in April

uncertain – that the cuckoo never visited the farthest Hebrides! Similarly Welsh poets in North Wales have been eloquent in praise of the song of the nightingale in the quiet of the summer night. But the nightingales sing most thrillingly in southern England and never penetrate further west into Wales than the Vale of Glamorgan.

The birds and also the flowers thus have boundaries in Britain beyond which they do not spread. These boundary-lines have only been accurately plotted on the map in comparatively recent times after centuries of patient work by ornithologists and botanists. The early folk who settled in Britain, and then slowly and painstakingly came together to form the united country of today, also had their boundaries, but while we have been busy discovering the limits of the settlements of plants and birds, and even minutely charting the rocks on our map, we have been forgetting many of the human boundaries which were once so

Above: A young cuckoo, still demanding constant feeding from its foster parents

Left: Evening feed for a flock of ewes with their lambs in the last days before the new season's grass grows

important to our forefathers. Hunting for lost boundaries is a fascinating business and as exciting as looking for rare plants, for the map of Britain is a palimpsest on which the new names and borders overlie the old. It can need expert knowledge, for example, to trace the limits of the Danelaw, the eastern part of England held by the Danes in the 10th and 11th Centuries. Historians can track it by looking at the place names which end with the Scandinavian endings of 'thorpe' or 'by' which you

find in profusion in places like Lincolnshire and Yorkshire.

There is also a firm linguistic boundary between the English-speaking and Welsh-speaking parts of Pembrokeshire. It lies not so many miles south from that churchyard of Nevern, where I go to wait for my first cuckoo in Spring.

Anglo-Normans conquered the whole of the southern half of the old county, which became 'Little England beyond Wales', and the two nations

Above: The Cheviot Hills from Coquet Head on the Northumberland-Roxburghshire border, looking towards the Cheviot, the highest point at 2,674 ft

Opposite: Tintern Abbey in Gwent on the west bank of the Wye. The abbey church was founded in 1131 by the Cistercians

confronted each other across a border called the Landsker which was a very real one within living memory. People born in farms on the Welsh side of the line always married north of the Landsker and referred to the folk on the south side as living 'down below'. Similarly the River Tamar is not only part of the county border between Devon and Cornwall; it is in a very real sense a strong demarcation line between the Cornish, still fiercely proud of their Celtic ancestry, and the English Devonians.

All these borders were once dangerous for the uninitiated to cross. They are not now officially marked on the map, but remain very real still to those who live near them. There is of course one border in these islands which is a true border in the political sense of the word, the border between the Province of Ulster and the Republic of Ireland; a

rather tragic border at the present time. It has the regulation frontier posts and you can be searched for arms as you cross it. You are very conscious today that this is the firm limit set between two nations, two religions and even two attitudes of mind. Who knows how it may change in the future?

There are two other principal borders in Britain which do not have customs posts, but are also as clear-cut as the Ulster border when it comes to attitudes of mind: the Welsh border and the Scottish border. Unlike the Landsker or the Cornish border, these are marked on the map. For many centuries, they were the scene of warfare and border raids. Poetry and romance still cling to their castles. In the old days, April and Spring were not welcome times of the year in the border country. They were the seasons when war was in

Offa's Dyke at Springhill near Clun in Shropshire, looking
south to Llanvair

the air. In the Middle Ages, and in the days of the
Civil War, armies and raiders could only move
when the earth had dried after the snow and rain of
Winter. It was then that the wardens of the pele
towers in Northumberland or of the castles of
Shropshire and Herefordshire strained their eyes to
look west or north to catch the first flash of the sun
on the armoured men marching down from the
hills to burn and plunder in the lowlands. Strange
indeed that these parts of Britain, which were once
so dangerous and turbulent, are now amongst the
most peaceful and unfrequented. You can walk on
the moors around the Cheviot Hills, and look from
Woden Law across to where the salmon-rich waters
of the Tweed flow down between the woods, and
no murmur will come to you now of the 'old,
forgotten far-off things, And battles long ago'. As
for the west border, doesn't Housman declare that:

'Clunton and Clunbury,
Clungunford and Clun,
Are the quietest places
Under the sun.'

Indeed of the two border countries, the Welsh
border still seems more peaceful and settled than the
Scottish – and for one good reason. The Welsh lost
their political independence first. Edward I swept
away Llewellyn ap Gruffydd in 1282, and in spite of
Owain Glyn Dŵr's spectacular revolt in the early
15th Century, Henry VIII felt able to incorporate
Wales legally and politically into England. He was
a Tudor, and the Welsh felt that, with the Tudors,
the old prophecies of Merlin were fulfilled. King
Arthur had come again. There was now no need for
the English along the border to quote the old
warning:

'Beware of Wales; Christ Jesus must us keep
That it makes not our child's child to weep.'

The Welsh nobles were too busy making their mark at the King's Court to go back to the old-fashioned business of border raids. So the Welsh border settled down into the charming, out-of-the-world place it is today – a land of lost hills, quiet rivers, rich woodlands, and ruined castles perched on tree-clad mounds in secret valleys. This whole varied landscape is linked by a strange feature that runs from south to north, over hill and dale, like a 160-mile long serpent – the remarkable earthwork known as Offa's Dyke. The Dyke doesn't coincide with the present political border; it runs alternatively into England and Wales. And there are gaps in it, especially in Herefordshire, where the forests may have been so thick in the old days as to make the dyke unnecessary.

There can be no question that it was built by command of Offa, the great King of Mercia in the 8th Century. It shows great engineering skill in its lay-out, and whoever planned it had a masterly eye for defensive country. But the Dyke was not intended as a permanently manned line like Hadrian's Wall. Rather was it an attempt to mark the boundary for all time. Maybe penalties might be inflicted on anyone found on the wrong side of it, although the theory that any Welshman found to the east of it would have his hand cut off seems to date from 12th-century chroniclers. There is no doubt, however, that the Dyke was accepted by both sides as a firm demarcation line. The Welsh, to this day, speak of going to England as 'crossing Offa's Dyke'. The place-names show its effectiveness. On one side we find the names of English villages ending with 'ham' and 'ton', on the other the Welsh villages beginning with 'Tre' and 'Llan'. In its central section, where it is exceptionally well preserved, it is a memorable sight as it climbs out of the valley bottoms and over the rounded hills. Late April is a glorious time to follow the officially marked Offa's Dyke path which now runs through the whole length of the Welsh border country. The hawthorn and the wild cherry are beginning to cover the hedgerows with the snow of their blossom and the lark's song fills the clear air.

The Dyke begins dramatically at the mouth of the River Wye. The Wye enters the Severn estuary in a series of noble curves under high limestone cliffs. The whole of this area, from the ancient castle of Chepstow up to the graceful ruins of Tintern Abbey, is a 'beauty spot' in the genuine sense of the word. The poets have always praised it. Wordsworth talked of the beauty of its hedgerows, 'hardly hedgerows, little lines of sportive wood run wild'. Tennyson caught the strange effect of the tidal stretch of the lower Wye when he wrote:

'Here twice a day the Severn fills;
The salt sea-water passes by,
And hushes half the babbling Wye
And makes a silence in the hills.'

The Dyke runs along the tops of precipitous limestone cliffs and as you tramp from point to point you get a series of heart-lifting views – back, to the wide flood of the Severn crossed by the daringly graceful Severn Bridge with its 400-ft high towers; onward, to the curving Wye, a silver thread far below amongst the deep woods; away to the west, where the great hills of Wales lift to the Black Mountains and the Wye enters England.

After this lower Wye section, the Dyke ceases to be our close companion as we follow up the border. The Black Mountains may have looked barrier enough as they frown over the lower country, and the Wye breaks out of them near Hay-on-Wye to flow down to the towered city of Hereford. Here we are on classic ground associated with the attractive figure of Parson Kilvert, keeper of the now famous diary. Until 1938, Kilvert was totally unknown, but then his diaries from the 1870s were edited and published by Dr William Plumer, since when this gentle Victorian country clergyman has taken his place with Pepys, Evelyn and Dorothy Wordsworth as one of the most attractive of our English diarists. He gives us a vivid, unrivalled picture of country life in the late 19th Century in Clyro, the little village on the Welsh side of the border near Hay, to which he came as a curate in 1870. Later in life he was appointed Vicar of Breadwardine on the Herefordshire side, so that in his diary he appears

The River Wye near Hay-on-Wye. It rises on Plynlimon and flows through exceptionally beautiful scenery into the Severn estuary near Chepstow

very much a man of the border. As he sat at his desk in his lodging at Clyro, opposite the local inn and with the church just round the corner, he poured out his stories. Everything is here, from the parishioners' decorating the graves on Palm Sunday until the churchyard looked like a glorious garden, to a walk to see the lonely eccentric Vicar of Llanbedr, who lived in his hut on the hills, and was once an Oxford graduate. 'The people who met him touched their hats to his reverence with great respect. They recognised him as a very holy man and if the Solitary had lived a thousand years ago he would have been revered as a hermit and perhaps canonised as a saint.' Kilvert not only had the novelist's gift of creating character, but the eye of a poet when it came to describing scenery and weather.

'As I came up the steep, snowy hill to Bethel I pursued the fast retreating and ascending wan sunshine of the still winter afternoon. I overtook the sunshine just before I got to the lone house on the bleak windy hill top. All the valley and plain lay bathed in a frosty rosy golden glow, and just as I got to Cae Perthy the sun was setting behind the lone level snowy blue-white line of the Black Mountain and the last rays were reddening the walls and the chimney stacks of the solitary cottage.'

We read that entry and we feel we are back at that very moment of setting sun on 16th December, 1878. Kilvert died at Breadwardine at the early age of 39, but through his diary he has made this part of the border 'Kilvert's Country'.

Between the point where the Wye breaks out of Wales to the spot where the Severn does the same thing lie 40 miles of withdrawn but beautiful country that has hidden itself, until recent years, from the tourist's gaze. The modest rivers wriggle quietly down from the high Radnor Forest past little towns, once important, which have dropped out of history for their own happiness – Knighton, Kington, Presteigne as well as Clun – 'the pleasantest places under the sun'. The capital of this

37

country – if a small but enchanting town of mellow red brick can be given such a grandiose title – is Ludlow. The River Teme encircles it and the ancient castle and splendid church give a hint of its old glory, for after Wales had been legally and politically drawn closer to England, especially under the Tudors, Ludlow became, for over 100 years, the real capital of the country. Here sat the powerful Council of the Marches which dealt with all the legal disputes that did not need decision in London. Welsh geography is peculiar in that all the great rivers flow eastward or south- and north-eastward out of the country. Communication between North and South Wales had always been difficult. The mountains cut the country into two separate blocks and it was easier – until the advent of the motor-car – for Welshmen who sat on committees to meet on neutral ground. In the railway age Shrewsbury was the favourite spot. Under the Tudors and early Stuarts the true capital of Wales was Ludlow.

North of Ludlow lies the fascinating county of Shropshire. To me it's the most typical of all border counties, and the most varied in its landscape and geology. Here you can imagine the sea of the great central plain of England washing against the rugged coastline of the mountains of Wales and being thrown back in a series of waves. The wooded wave of Wenlock Edge runs from Craven Arms to Much Wenlock almost unbroken for mile after mile. Around Church Stretton the waves are more complicated and some of the most ancient Precambrian volcanic rocks in Britain come welling to the surface to form the shapely summit of Caer Caradoc. The border country is full of these strange upsurges of igneous rock, from the Wrekin that dominates the landscape near Shrewsbury to the Breidden Hills which guard the valley through which the Severn flows out towards the wide English plains. All these border hills and ridges have strange surprising features and monuments. The Breiddens are crowned with Rodney's Pillar, a Doric column surprisingly set up by local farmers in honour of the great admiral. Rodney had no connection with the area, but this part of the border supplied many of the great oaks for his ships. The

strangest oak, the Prince's Oak, lies at the end of the nearby Long Mountain and commemorates the only visit ever paid to this principality by George IV when he was Prince of Wales. He rode over the border while staying in Shropshire, received the respectful homage of the gentry of Powys – and then rode off as fast as he could to the cosier comforts of Brighton and Mrs Fitzherbert. Prinny came too early to see the border's noblest grove of trees – the great Californian redwoods planted in the 1850s by the owner of Leighton Hall in a protected hollow on Long Mountain. They have grown through the passing years until they are all now well over 100 ft. When the sunlight strikes down through the high branches you are in a cathedral of the woods, with the red tree-trunks soaring upwards like splendid Gothic columns. I know no more thrilling sight in all the woodlands of Britain.

Eastward from the Long Mountain lies Corndon Hill and beyond, the Long Mynd, all over the 1,000 ft mark. These Shropshire hills can be seen from a long way off and the distant view of them cheered, in his boyhood home in North Worcestershire, the poet whose name is now bound up with them. A. E. Housman was no 'Shropshire lad'. He was a distinguished classical scholar who never worked on a Shropshire farm. But he found the names of the places and the lines of the landscape perfect raw material for his nostalgic verse, with the result that no-one can walk through the hills and valleys of this most unknown of counties without quoting Housman's 'Shropshire Lad'.

'On Wenlock Edge the wood's in trouble
His forest fleece the Wrekin heaves;
The gale, it plies the saplings double,
And thick on Severn snow the leaves.'

North of Shrewsbury the border has had no poet to sing the landscape into fame. Offa's Dyke now goes into the foothills of Wales and the high ridges of Shropshire fade away into the Cheshire plain.

This plain, however, is not without its charm. When the ice retreated it left a maze of moraines and little hollows in the boulder clay to form the country of small tarns set amongst gentle wooded

A view of Wenlock Edge from Packerstone Hill, an outlier of the Long Mynd in Shropshire, with the hamlet of Minton in the foreground

hills that they call the Cheshire Lake District. The Welsh mountains are your constant companions on the western horizon as you journey over the plain to come at last to the ancient town of Chester. Offa's Dyke continues away in the hills to the west to reach the sea – if indeed the great earthwork was actually completed – somewhere near Prestatyn. For most people, however, Chester marks the end of the true border of Wales. The Romans certainly felt so. Here they built a great military base, manned by the 20th Legion, and from it the roads were driven into the wild mountains to the west to bind the Celtic tribes to the will of Rome. Far to the south, some miles west of the other end of that long walk up Offa's Dyke path, lies Caerleon, the other great anchor of Roman power in Wales. It was the Romans who, after all, first created the Welsh border. All the land eastwards, the lowlands of southern England, were peacefully settled not so

very long after the conquest. The inhabitants accepted the rule of Rome and were happy to Romanise themselves and supply lucrative corn to the Imperial City. The Welsh remained defiant and the country remained a military zone. Offa's Dyke simply confirmed the limits set by the Romans between the men of the fertile low country and the Celts clinging to freedom in their sparse mountains.

You get the same impression when you follow the Romans north along the Pennines for 200 miles into Northumberland and Cumbria, and into our second border country. Striding across the land, from the Solway Firth to the Tyne, goes Hadrian's Wall, the most impressive of all the boundaries marked on the map of Britain. The modern motorists driving into Wales see a polite notice on the wayside marking the border with 'Croeso i Cymru', Welcome to Wales. Crossing at the present Scottish border at Carter Bar, again you are firmly informed by a notice that you are in Scotland. But there are, of course, no border posts. To find the actual border line you must get out and

Above: Ludlow Castle on the River Teme. Built in the 11th Century, it was the seat of the Council of Marches in Tudor times and has had a long and violent history

Below: Bamburgh Castle on the Northumberland coast opposite the Farne Islands. Built by the Normans, but much restored, St Aidan died here in A D 651 and Grace Darling is buried in the churchyard nearby

Left: The Black Mountains in Brecknockshire, a range of Old Red Sandstone intersected by deep valleys

41

trace it on the map. You will have no such difficulty with the northern boundary of Roman Britain in areas north of Corbridge or near Housesteads in Northumberland. There before you is a strong wall, marching firmly across wild country. This was the 'limes', the line drawn between the civilization of Rome and the barbarian world beyond. To the old Romans it was the line drawn between darkness and light. You can stand in one of the 'mile-castles' on a crag at Housesteads and look northwards, as did the Roman guardians of the Wall. The lonely country rolls away before you – with small woodlands, open moors and tiny tarns tucked under the cliffs. It cannot be very different in appearance from the time when the brilliant but cynical historian Tacitus reported on the campaigns of his father-in-law, Agricola, who had carried the Roman arms still further north into Scotland in AD 83–84: 'They made a desert and called it peace.'

The Wall ran for 73 miles but not all of it is intact. A long stretch was destroyed by General Wade to make a road for his troops and guns, rushing across to try to intercept Bonnie Prince Charlie as he came south in the rebellion of 1745. Enough remains to give you the spirit of the period – this was the North-west Frontier of the Roman Empire! The Roman military engineers took advantage of a remarkable natural feature that geologists call the Whin Sill.

This is a lava flow, injected from below, after the rocks of the Carboniferous period had been formed. This dolerite rock crops to the surface at many places across this neck of England as it bends towards Scotland. Wherever it outcrops it gives rise to dramatic scenery. Bamburgh Castle, the greatest of the Northumberland mediaeval strongholds, stands on it. The lonely seal-guarded Farne Islands are formed from it. The splendid waterfall of High Force in Upper Teesdale tumbles over it. To me, its noblest manifestation occurs along the course of the Wall, not far from Housesteads Fort, where it lifts the long sinuous line of the Roman fortifications over Highfield Crags with the still waters of Craig Lough far below. I can picture the levies from Spain or southern France slapping their

chests to keep themselves warm in the mile-castle forts on Cuddy's Crag, as they looked towards the dangerous north. It can be chill here even in April, 'the month before the month of May', for, as Coleridge said, 'the Spring comes slowly up this way'. They could count themselves lucky that the Emperor Hadrian, during his last two months' visit to Britain in AD 122, had ordered the construction of a wall along this line. 20 years later, the Romans were carried away by success and decided that they could hold a line much further north. In the reign of Antonius Pius, the governor Q. Lollius Urbicus built a wall across the narrow isthmus between the Firth of Clyde and the Firth of Forth. You can trace its 37-mile long line today and I remember seeing a stretch of the turf ramparts near the New Kilpatrick golf course, and again in the open country near Rough Castle. My old friend, the late Leonard Cottrell, who took me there, claimed that this stretch rivalled Hadrian's Wall. With due respect, I had to disagree. The Romans themselves found the Antonine Wall too exposed to defend. By AD 200 they had sensibly decided to withdraw, and for the rest of the history of Roman Britain, Hadrian's Wall was the boundary between the wild tribes of Scotland and the snug, civilized south.

Far away, 300 long miles to the southwards, the retired governors and the centurions on leave could be taking the cure in the luxuriously appointed warm, healing springs of Bath; the rich client-king might be ordering mosaics for the floors of his new palace at Fishbourne in Hampshire; the merchants of London might be complaining of the costs of a new temple to be tactfully erected to the glory of the new emperor. They all went about their business for over 300 years – longer than the British Raj lasted in India – because here, up on these bleak northern moorlands, the soldiers of the legion took their turns of duty to march along the wall from mile-castle to mile-castle all through the cold, mist and snow of the harsh border Winter. How glad the legionaries must have been when they saw the frail, hopeful April sun bringing life back to the moorlands; and as we think of the tribesmen gathering in strength in their northern hills ready to use the Spring for the next trial of strength, how frail Hadrian's barrier seems. Its wall was 18 ft high and 10 ft wide. The ditch in front of it was 30 ft across, but it ran for over 70 miles and the whole length could only be held by resolute, well organised men.

Alas, there came a time when the resolution of the guardians faltered; or were there not enough of them to face the gathering storm from the north? The Empire was starting to crumble at the centre, and not even the magisterial Gibbon, in his 'Decline and Fall of the Roman Empire', can tell us all the causes of the collapse. Here, on the outward fringe of the once all-powerful imperial structure, the tribes swarmed over the Wall and the Dark Ages had begun. When they ended, the frontier had long ceased to be that tidy line, drawn with Roman straightness from the Solway Firth to the Tyne. The Anglo-Saxons had seized most of England and were steadily advancing up the north-east coast. For centuries afterwards the line fluctuated until at last it stabilised in a generally acknowledged border that sloped from Carlisle and the Solway Firth in the west, where the anchor-end of the Wall remained intact, away in a north-easterly direction to end at Berwick at the mouth of the Tweed. This is the border today, a place of lonely moorlands, new forests filling the remote valleys, sheep-walks, peaty summits and the high Cheviots looking down over it all. The main roads and railways have to climb high to cross it, or go round its eastern edge along the narrow coastal plain fronting the North Sea. But nowhere is the crossing easy.

You look across the moors from Carter Bar and you suddenly realize why Scotland remained independent so long, in face of its powerful neighbour to the south. As we explored the Welsh border, we came across a whole series of wide valleys – the Dee, the Severn, the Usk and the Wye – leading deep into the mountains. An invader using them has a comparatively easy passage into the heart of the country. Invading Scotland demands crossing lonely moors where the rain can demoralise sun-loving southerners. On the narrow coastal strip north of Berwick small bodies of resolute men can hold up armies. In 1650 Oliver Cromwell himself was skilfully cornered by the veteran Scots

commander, David Leslie, who lay on the high ground and had the English at his mercy down on the low plain. But the Committee of the Estates, dominated by the Covenanting ministers, were convinced that the Lord was on their side. Unwisely they ordered Leslie to move down into the lower ground. Cromwell attacked them at dawn. The Lord had changed sides overnight, and as Cromwell reported exultantly to Parliament, the Scots 'were made by the Lord of Hosts as stubble to their swords'. Not for the first time was a nation ruined by a committee!

Over the whole of this border country hangs a sense of ancient tragedy, and the countryside is full of the names of sad connotation in Scottish history. The Cheviot is the highest point on the border at 2,676 ft. It is a dome of igneous rock formed in the Devonian period and the Carboniferous rock has been washed away from it. The high summits are rounded and peat-covered, lonely rather than striking but with fine views back over the moorlands of Northumberland. Here rises the river Till which curves back northwards over the border to join the river Tweed. Up the valley of the Till in 1513 marched King James IV of Scotland with the flower of Scottish chivalry on an invasion of northern England, against the better advice of his councillors but undertaken to aid the 'auld alliance' with France. At Flodden, near the village of Branxton in Northumberland, he was defeated by the Earl of Surrey. He and the majority of his nobles were slain in the worst military disaster in Scottish history. The grim border verse sums it up with ghastly brevity:

'Tweed said to Till,
"What gars ye rin sae still?"
Till said to Tweed,
Though ye rin wi' speed
And I rin slaw,
Yet whese ye droon ae man,
I droon twa."'

With this legacy of invasion, war and feuding, no wonder that the border country is a country of castles. The biggest ones must inevitably be found on the English side for this was where the money lay. Alnwick, Bamburgh, Carlisle and Berwick

itself still possess impressive fortifications, but the most characteristic defence structures of the border country are the pele 'castles', the single towers that gave refuge to a minor nobleman and his family from the ever-present dangers of a hostile world. Around them cluster the stories related by the Border Ballads, stories of feuds, revenge, bold defiance of authority, love and sudden death. The heroes are daring raiders like Johnnie Armstrong or Kinmont Willie or strange, fey personages like Thomas the Rhymer, brave lovers like Clerk Saunders or Fair Annie of Lochroyan. This wild country suits them. Until the 18th Century the ballads were being sung or recited in the chimney-corners of the lonely farms on winter's nights, until they came to the ears of the young Walter Scott, who published them in 1802 in 'The Minstrelsy of the Scottish Border' and laid the foundation of his literary reputation. It was to the border country that Scott returned at the height of his European fame to build his dream castle at Abbotsford on the Tweed and live the life of an old border nobleman, while turning out a stream of novels. 'The Wizard of the North' and memories of him still dominate the border.

The Tweed is the great border river and Scott

Above: Hadrian's Wall near the mile-castle of Housesteads. The completed wall reached from Wallsend in Northumberland to Bowness on the Solway Firth, a distance of 73 miles

Opposite: The Scottish border near Galashiels and the Tweed Valley

was wise to settle on its banks. It only forms the actual boundary for the last 15 miles of its course, and it rises far back in the Southern Uplands; but its southern tributaries all come from the long border ridge of the Cheviot Hills. The Tweed Valley itself is good agricultural land, as are many of the dales further to the west like Eskdale and Liddesdale. The high moors may have been debatable ground, but along the valleys the kings of Scotland founded abbeys like Jedburgh, Melrose and Kelso, in the hope, it is said, that they would be respected by the invader as places of refuge as well as for their sanctity: a pious hope which was often deceived. They also gave grants of land to the corporations of the little border towns to encourage the inhabitants to defend them. In places like Langholm, the citizens still celebrate these grants in the holiday atmosphere of a 'riding', when they traverse the old

boundaries. Today this is an occasion of fun and ceremony. Even 300 years ago it could have been a matter of life and death.

There are other great 'ridings' in the border country, all linked with its history. At the Hawick Common Riding, which takes place annually in June, they link this 'beating of the bounds' with the commemoration of Flodden and a small victory won soon after by the local men which wiped out the memory of the greater disaster in their eyes. The leader of the riders, the elected cornet, receives from the provost a replica of the banner captured by the Hawick Gallants at Horneshole. Sonter's Day takes place at Selkirk soon after the 'riding' at Hawick. Here a single horseman races ahead along the boundaries carrying a banner. This is believed to be the banner – or at least a descendant of it – carried back from Flodden by the single survivor of all the many young men who rode out of Selkirk on that fatal day. History still dies hard on the border.

On the moors the sheep graze, with an immunity from danger that they would never have dared feel in the days of Johnnie Armstrong – who complained that:

'Liddesdale has layen lang
There is na' ryding there at a';
The horses are a' grown sae lither fat,
They downa stir out o' the sta'.'

and then promptly went a' raiding over the English border to sweep back into Scotland every sheep in sight. These would have been the ancestors of the famous breed of Cheviot sheep; short-legged and hardy, giving good mutton and fleeces that started the woollen weaving industry in towns like Hawick. The whole of the Southern Uplands of Scotland is great sheep country, and two other breeds, the Swaledales and the Scottish Blackface join the Cheviots to remind us that, next to New Zealand, Britain has the highest density of sheep population in the world – on average 200 to the square mile. There are a quarter of a million of them in the Northumberland National Park alone.

In recent years the sheep are having to share the moorlands with the forest. The Forestry Commission has indulged in large-scale planting in the Cheviots and there are great forests around the headwaters of many of the streams, including the huge Kelder and Wask Forest in Northumberland. Opinions differ about the whole policy of tree-planting on this scale, not only on the Scottish border but over the rest of the highlands of Britain. There are battles as fierce as Flodden or Otterburn over the economic and certainly the aesthetic value of continually putting the moorlands under the serried ranks of the firs. But there they stand, and like Scott's description of the Scottish ranks at Flodden:

'The stubborn spear-men still made good
Their dark impenetrable wood,
Each stepping where his comrade stood
The instant that he fell.'

The forests are now a permanent feature of the border landscape.

With devolution in the air, both the Welsh and Scottish borders are also likely to remain as permanent as the forests on the map. You will still have the curious thrill of driving north over the flats of the Eden and the Solway Firth to cross the Scottish border into Gretna Green, and of seeing the notices of 'Land in Feu' instead of 'To Let', and looking at the 'original' blacksmith shop (or are there two?) where they celebrated run-away marriages. It reminds you that Scotland did not give everything away in the Act of Union and become the 'end of an old song' as the opponents of the Act lamented. It still has its separate Law system and educational structure and, who knows? – a great deal of power may yet return across the border.

And on the Welsh border, as you drive through Oswestry, past the great earthwork of the Old Town – where the story goes that the old Celtic hero Caractacus made his last stand before being betrayed to grace the conqueror's triumph in Rome – you have not many miles to travel before you come to villages where they all speak Welsh, and you can feel you are in a foreign land only 100 miles from the centre of Birmingham.

This is the magic of the borders – long may it continue!

April with the Poets

Is the night chilly and dark?
The night is chilly and not dark,
The thin grey cloud is spread on high,
It covers but not hides the sky.
The moon is behind, and at the full;
And yet she looks both small and dull.
The night is chill, the cloud is grey;
'Tis a month before the month of May,
And the Spring comes slowly up this way.

S. T. COLERIDGE

Here, with green Nature all around,
While that fine bird the skylark sings;
Who now in such a passion is,
He flies by it, and not his wings:
And many a blackbird, thrush and sparrow
Sings sweeter songs that I may borrow.

W. H. DAVIES

Stay, spring, for by this ruthless haste
You turn all good to waste;
Look, how the blackthorn now
Changes to trifling dust upon the bough.

Where blossom from the wild pear shakes
Too rare a china breaks,
And though the cuckoos shout
They will forget their name ere June is out.

ANDREW YOUNG

Ettricke Forest is a feir foreste,
In it groes manie a semelie trie;
There's hart and hynd, and dae and rae,
And of a' wilde beastis grete plentie.

There's a feir castelle, bigged wi' lyme and stane;
O! gin it stands not pleasuntlie!
In the forefront o' that castelle feir,
Twa unicorns are bra' to see;
There's the picture of a knight, and a ladye bright,
And the grene hollin abune their brie.

OLD BORDER BALLAD

May

May in Britain is traditionally a joyous month, when people recognise that Spring has reached its climax and Summer is just around the corner. May 1st is now formally designated as a Bank Holiday, but this evocative date was eagerly celebrated by country folk long before politicians, in their belated wisdom, decided to make it official. We forget how serious an ordeal Winter could be in the old days before the 18th-century agricultural revolution, when all extra cattle had to be slaughtered around November after the pasture had run out. Throughout the Middle Ages and on through Tudor times, countrymen longed for the first signs that life was returning to a world that had lain dead or dormant under its burden of cold rain or snow. By May, there was proof everywhere that the world was indeed renewing itself. The fresh green leaves were bursting out on the branches, the corn was starting to spring after the early sowing, the birds rioted in song in the woodlands. The whole community felt the need to express its joy. The Church never officially sanctioned a May festival. Perhaps the clergy suspected that much of the old pagan fertility ritual was being carried over into the May Day festivities. No matter: the celebrations went on, and still go on in places all over Britain.

At Padstow an extraordinarily shaped hobby-horse leads the revels, accompanied by black-faced followers, and dies his ritual death at regular intervals through the streets, happily only to rise again. At Helston in Cornwall on May 8th, the whole town dances through the streets and in and out of the houses, to the lilting tune of the Helston Furry Dance that has gone around the world. They do the same thing at the May Fair at Torrington.

The River Avon at Stratford

Little Gaddesen has retained the actual dance around the Maypole, and everywhere pretty young girls still get elected as May Queens.

The poets, naturally, have a field day. So much so, that Dylan Thomas once described May to me as the 'platitude month'! But even our greatest poets were moved to yield to the mood of this happiest of months. The Elizabethans were especially good at that type of spring verse which sounds as artless as lark song or cuckoo call, but which can only be produced by the highest technical skill. You think of Shakespeare's 'lover and his lass', wandering the Warwickshire lanes in 'spring-time, in spring-time, the only pretty ring time'; of Nashe announcing gladly that 'Spring, the sweet Spring, is the year's pleasant king'; of Herrick urging his Corinna to 'wash, dress, be brief in praying', for this May beauty is fragile and transient:

> 'So when or you or I are made
> A fable, song or fleeting shade,
> All love, all liking, all delight
> Lies drown'd with us in endless night,
> Then when time serves and we are but
>   decaying,
> Come, my Corinna, come, let's go a-Maying.'

The only time, I admit, that I went a-Maying was long ago at Oxford. At dawn on May Day morning, the white-surpliced choir of Magdalen College climb to the top of the chapel tower and sing their May Day hymn, as depicted with Pre-Raphaelite detail in the painting by Holman Hunt. In those days, there was no traffic and the voices sounded sweet in the clear air. Then we walked through Christ Church meadows where certain lady undergraduates from St Hilda's declared they were going to test the old May Day custom, that 'dabbling in the dew keeps the milkmaids fair'. As far as I can remember, the experiment was not a success.

Perhaps the little verse I heard one May morning, in a country lane near Colwall at the back of the ancient and graceful Malvern Hills, got nearer to the old, elemental pagan spirit of the festival. A young lad passed me, hands in pockets and singing quietly to himself:

> 'First of May, First of May,
> Hedgerow loving starts today.'

I was bound for the summit of the Worcestershire Beacon, which rises to nearly 1,400 ft and is the highest point of this most attractive range. I was going to pay tribute to another poet whose work was poles apart from that perky little ditty I'd just heard in Colwall. John Langland lived in the second half of the 14th Century and his view of life was more sombre than that of his contemporary, the captivating extrovert Chaucer. But if you want to penetrate the mind of the mediaeval English peasant, who, after all, was the forefather of the men who work on the land today, you should try to read Langland's 'Piers Plowman'. I say try, because Langland's English looks very foreign indeed to a modern reader, who may also be puzzled by the verse form of stressed syllables. I think, however, that there's a certain quality of almost magical incantation in the original manuscript orthography. Even if you don't understand half the words, Langland, in his opening lines, takes you back to that far-away May morning when he climbed the Worcestershire Beacon, wrapped himself in his cloak, and fell into a deep sleep, in which he had a vision of labouring England.

> 'In a somere seyson · when softe was the sonne,
> I shop me in-to shrobbis · as I a shepherd were . . .
> Ac on a may morwening · on Malverne hulles
> Me byfel for to slepe · for weyrynesse of wandryng.'

I felt that Langland was close to me as I stood on the summit of the Beacon and looked away eastwards to the wide-spreading Severn plain 20 miles away across that marvellous pattern of fields, tall trees and winding rivers, the long ramparts of the Cotswolds, dropped sharply down to the level ground. This whole landscape was the result of century after century of patient work by generations of uncomplaining Piers Plowmen, who had treated the soil with care and reverence, always putting in far more than they took out from it. This great view is their noble memorial.

The Severn plain is a dividing line. To the west you get the older, more contorted rocks of the Welsh borderland and the mountains. To the east, starting with the Cotswolds, are the younger rocks, laid down in regular beds. Underneath the later boulder clays and gravels of the plain itself, lie beds of rock of the late Triassic and the early Jurassic periods. They, too, are as regular as the oolitic of the Cotswolds and underlie it, dipping like the Cotswold rocks gently towards the east. This has

The market town of Evesham on the River Avon in Worcestershire, the centre of the fruit-growing and market-gardening industry of the Vale of Evesham

led many geologists to visualise a time, millions of years ago, when these regularly layered belts of rock like the oolitic limestone and even the chalk extended far further west and may have overlain the foothills of the Welsh mountains themselves. Down this gentle slope the rivers flowed into the

valley of the Thames. But the ancestor of the Severn had already started work, cutting back steadily into these softer rocks and eventually cutting right across the course of these eastward flowing rivers. This great vale spreading below me on that Malvern May Day is a classic case of what the geographers call 'river capture'. When I looked at the extent of those green fields and rich river meadows spreading away to the blue hills on the far horizon, I found it impossible to calculate the unimaginable amount of material the river must have swept out to sea in order to form this Severn plain. No wonder geology has to operate in terms of millions of years.

I noticed another far more recent feature as I stood where once John Langland had fallen into his deep and fruitful sleep. The fresh green of the great plain was speckled with flecks of white, rather like

Above: Blossom time in the orchards of the Vale of Evesham

Opposite: The Malvern Hills, looking across the Severn plain

the later landscapes of Constable, when the great artist gave sparkle to his painting by small flicks of his palette knife – Constable's 'snow' they called it; but the white flecks I saw were the snow of the orchards, apple, pear and plum blossom still in their white and pink splendour. April is usually the month when you expect the orchards of southern Britain to cover themselves with frothy glory, but this was a year of late Spring; and the delights of the flowering orchards were still to be seen far below on that, for me, most memorable May Day on the

Above: Working in the hop fields of Kent, which cover more than 10,000 acres

Below: Cider-making using an old hand press to squeeze the juice from the pulp. Most of these presses have been replaced by power-driven machinery

summit of the Malvern Hills. Ever since that moment of vision I have associated May with the garden counties of Britain.

Once the blossom is out, I always go on pilgrimage across the Severn plain into the valley of the Avon – Shakespeare's Avon. I drive through timeless towns like Pershore and villages of red brick as mellow as Pershore plums. Then suddenly I find myself in the middle of a landscape which is just a mass of white blossom. As far as I can see, the neatly spaced fruit trees are flaunting their fragile and delicately tinted petals or tossing them lightly in the gentle breeze. It is not often that agriculture can produce a sudden visual sensation. Its effects are generally gradual, like the steady ripening of the green stalks of the wheat through July into late August and September gold. The change grows gently on your eyes. But orchards seem to me to do the whole dazzling transformation act in a matter of days. I am always stirred by this swift change from green to foaming white. No other farming operation can compare with it.

Beauty, however, must be paid for. The price of

the glory I admire so intensely in high Spring in the Vale of Evesham is the eternal vigilance of the fruit farmers. April and May can bring dangerous night-frosts that can nip beauty in the bud. The anxious owners used to bring out the oil-fired 'smudge pots' and place them under the trees. The fires would twinkle away through the night as if an army had encamped in the orchards. The Evesham farmer used to inherit his tenancy of the land by what was known as the Evesham custom, by which he got a property in the improvements he made and had the right to nominate his successor. Where he nominated his son he was able to pass on his long accumulated wisdom, for successful fruit-growing has secrets as well as demanding high technical knowledge. Like everything else in our agricultural world, improvements in fruit-growing go back to the 18th and 19th Centuries. Great names like Richard Cox and Thomas Laxton go marching on to our own day. Thomas Andrew Knight, who died at a ripe old age in 1838, was the genius of apple hybridising; and I keep a warm place in my heart for that enterprising cleric, the Reverend John Lawrence, rector of Yelverton in Northamptonshire, who began improving our pears as far back as the reign of Queen Anne. I like the title of the book he published in 1717, 'The Clergyman's Recreation' – an extremely fruitful recreation indeed for most of us. The Victorians were very enterprising in the world of fruit and introduced a whole series of new varieties. You could get most of them in the fruiterers of my youth, but as in every aspect of modern agriculture, fruit-growing has changed under the impact of high-class technology, big combines and the drive for greatly increased production. Inevitably this must mean a certain amount of standardisation. I seem to be buried under a deluge of Coxes, russets and even of Granny Smiths! I long for an old-style Ribston Pippin.

There has always been specialisation, however, in the various fruit-growing areas of Britain. If you want the best cider apples you go to Herefordshire or Somerset. The finest strawberries I've tasted came from Hampshire. They grow the champion black-currants in Norfolk and Essex. And eating apples? Who dares decide? But perhaps I should vote for Kent. It was the apple orchards of Kent which helped the county to gain the proud title of 'the Garden of England', and it is the only other part of the country, besides the Vale of Evesham, to which I have gone on pilgrimage in Blossom Time. I have memories of the spring glory of the cherry orchards around Sittingbourne, even though today the competition from imported Italian cherries has reduced the acreage under cherries in Kent. Yet Kent still possesses those advantages which gave it its original pre-eminence in fruit-growing – a dry, warm climate and light, fertile soil in sheltered areas. Some parts of the county, however, have heavy soils, which had to be tilled by the specially large Kentish plough, drawn by a team of 16 oxen. There are early photographs of such teams at work. They have a wonderfully monumental look about them, but, of course, all this is far removed from the elegance of fruit-farming.

Kent has another string to its bow besides fruit. I used to make my spring pilgrimage with a somewhat portly friend who was quite prepared to admire the apple blossom but after a morning of inspecting orchards would roundly declare, 'Enough of this. On to the most important part of this county.' And he drove straight to the hop fields! Now I must admit I am not an avid beer drinker, but I will also admit that hop fields have a strange beauty of their own. It comes from the mathematically complex arrangement of the hop poles and the artistic trellis-work that keeps the poles upright. You look at the vast amount of work involved, much of it performed from the top of tall ladders, and you understand why they tell you in Kent that hops are the most expensive crop to grow in England.

The use of hops to flavour beer is a comparatively recent practice in Britain. The hop plant has always grown wild in southern England, and in the 16th Century country people started growing it in their gardens to give a bite to their rather wishy-washy ale and to make it keep better. The rise of the big brewing interests in the growing industrial towns made it worthwhile for some farmers to specialise in the business of hop-growing. Kent,

with its proximity to London and its long-established traditions of fruit-growing and market gardening, was the natural place for the hop to be cultivated on a big scale. Hop-growing is a highly skilled, almost finnicky business. There are both male and female plants, but only the female flowers develop into the cones which are used for brewing. The young hop plants twist themselves eagerly upwards in the Spring and the poles that support the elaborate cages of twine have to be 12 to 14 ft high. The hop gardens are renewed by transplanting root cuttings and demand lavish manuring and constant spraying.

The great moment of the hop world comes not in Spring but in the harvest which starts in late August. Until the last war, thousands of East Enders would leave London in special trains for the annual 'hopping'. I was lucky enough to spend a day with one Kent farmer, who had the same families coming to his farm for generations. Everyone worked in the hop fields. Father helped to bring down the long, tangled hop vines; mother

Above: The village of Lower Slaughter, a much-visited beauty spot of the Cotswolds

Opposite: Bredon Hill in Worcestershire with a view of Bell Castle, an 18th-century Gothic folly on its upper slopes

and daughters picked the hops; the little boys ran busily back and forth to the rapidly bulging bags. Even grandma and grandad did their bit of picking or looking after the baby in a corner of the field. They all camped out in the great barn. There was singing in the evening, and the whole thing was one glorious Cockney holiday. How all has changed in 30 years! The old East End disappeared in the Blitz. The Cockneys now spend their holidays in the Costa Brava and machines do the hop-picking in half the time.

Even the oast-houses are changing. These curious and attractive structures, with their pointed cowls perched on their squat red brick circular towers, were mainly built in early and mid

Victorian days, when the brewing industry was booming. They add charm to the whole landscape of Kent. At the bottom of the tower is a kiln and above it the drying floor on which the hops are spread. The conical roof is capped by a wooden cowl which acts as a ventilator and is driven round by a wind vane. Sometimes the kiln towers are picturesquely grouped around the rest of the red-bricked buildings in which the hops are bagged and stored for transport to the brewery. Few oast-houses are working today. Electric drying has surplanted the kilns and the old 'oasts' are being converted into desirable country residences.

Kent has no monopoly in oast-houses. When I looked westward from my May Day summit on the Malvern Hills I could pick out the little village of Bosbury behind Colwall, which has hop kilns among its delightful black and white houses. A few miles beyond it you cross the Herefordshire border and enter a county that rivals Kent in its devotion to the hop. Again you meet with the fields, patterned with hop poles supporting the cages of twine on which the hop plants tangle themselves like lithe green snakes. Around each field are the tall hedges that protect the tender plants from the slightest breath of harsh wind in May and the growing season.

Herefordshire also rivals Kent in a second way. It, too, is a great apple county, only Herefordshire apples are not mainly for eating. They usually end up in the cider press. The old-fashioned method of making cider has not yet been completely over-whelmed by the mass-produced stuff, although the day has gone by when every farmer prided himself on his own cider press. Noble works of art they were, with their great oak beams and cast-iron spoked wheels and screws. It took men of power to work them or else a patient old horse going round and round as the heady juice ran out into the vat. Fermentation was wrapped in mystery and each farm hugged its own secret recipe to itself. I've heard hair-raising tales of some of the objects which were thrown into the vats – from old socks and boots to cattle bones – to give the cider a bit of body. No matter, I'm sure fermentation always killed all the germs, although I must confess some of the rougher home-made varieties I've tasted, especially the ones they call 'scrumpy', had a kick like a mule.

After that slightly alcoholic paean of praise for Herefordshire, perhaps I had better look eastward again to that long line of hills that marks the eastern horizon of the Severn plain – the Cotswolds. This is one of the show places of Britain which the tourist agencies insist all good Americans must see even if the visit has to be tacked on to the statutory trip to Stratford. In this case, the tourist agencies are right. Once you have seen the great view from Birdlip Hill over the Severn plain – it's the Malvern Hills view in reverse, with the sun setting in the west for good measure! – or your first Cotswold village, perhaps Bibury with its houses of golden stone and the little stream of the Coln running clear in front of them, in the way that made William Morris hail Bibury as 'the most beautiful village in England' – once you have seen all this you are wedded to the Cotswolds for life. But before we go into the rhapsodies proper to anyone describing this unique country, let us take a coach ride through the Cotswolds with the Rev Sydney Smith. The time is the 1830s and although Byron called him 'Smug Sydney', Smith was a doughty champion of reform, a man of sterling honesty and kindness but, above all, a great wit. And perhaps it was in his capacity as a wit that he wrote this description of his journey through the Cotswolds out to the edge of the escarpment.

'You travel for twenty or five-and-twenty miles over one of the most unfortunate desolate counties under heaven, divided by stone walls and aban-doned to the screaming kites and the larcenous crows; after travelling really twenty and to appearance ninety miles over this region of stone and sorrow, life begins to be a burden and you wish to perish. At the very moment when you are taking this melancholy view of human affairs and hating the postillion and blaming the horses, there bursts upon your view, with all its towers, forests and streams, the deep and shaded Vale of Severn.'

Sydney Smith was right about the splendour of that view. If you walk the Cotswold Way, which runs along the edge of the escarpment and reaches over 1,000 ft at Cleve Cloud above Cheltenham, you will have the lush Severn Vale stretching out below for over 25 blissful miles. But he was also right about the Cotswolds' being a region of stone (but not sorrow!). It is the stone that made the Cotswolds' fortune. The Cotswold rocks are usually referred to as oolitic limestones. They are Jurassic in age, much younger than the Carboniferous limestones that we find further west and north in Britain. But they, too, were laid down in clear, warm, shallow seas. The soil they produce is not obviously rich and easily cultivated. It is shallow but strong and is known locally as 'brash'. The climate, too, is harsher on these uplands than in the low-lying Severn valley. Down on these rich plains the farmers used to talk of their crops in unfriendly years as being 'as long coming as Cotswold barley'. But like the chalk the oolite provided high, dry and open ground on which prehistoric man found it easy to move his flocks. The Severn valley may appear overwhelmingly fertile and attractive today when you look down from the Cotswold escarpment. Neolithic man, and his successor the Celt, must have shuddered when they saw its tangled woods far below with the Severn struggling through the unreclaimed swamps. They wisely stayed 800 ft up on the high bare ground and have left notable memorials of their passage. The Rollright Stones near Chipping Norton approach Avebury proportions. The chambered long barrows of Belas Knap and the charmingly named Hetty Peggler's Tump are amongst the finest in the country.

In the Middle Ages and in Tudor times, the Cotswolds became great sheep country. The thin soil supplied good open pasture, and a new prosperity came to the little towns tucked in the upland valleys. When the time came to enclose the landscape, the Cotswold stone again provided a bonus. Certain beds of it split into flattish pieces which are extremely convenient for wall-building. One old Welsh hill farmer from the wild country of the Rhinog mountains in Merioneth, where they had to construct their walls out of heavy, massive rocks placed into position by almost prison-like hard labour, looked at them incredulously and then said to me, 'Duw, the boys here have had it easy for 200 years.' Not too easy, however, since the flat pieces tend to fit so closely that the rainwater can be held back in the wall. The Cotswold waller therefore takes care to lay his flat stones on a slight tilt out from the centre to make certain he gets rid of the water.

The walls are only one example of the skill of the Cotswold builder. Everything he constructed, from barns and farm-houses to gateways and, above all, the villages, seems naturally to turn into things of quiet beauty. Of course, he inherited a tradition established at a lucky time for building styles. Money came into the Cotswolds in the Tudor and early Stuart period – a pleasant period for domestic architecture. It went away with the Industrial Revolution, when the wool trade was increasingly captured by Yorkshire. The Cotswolds had no more cash to rebuild, and so stayed happily out of date. The oolitic limestone, so easily quarried and so encouraging a rock for the stonemason to work in, now revealed a further unexpected quality. It weathered with serene confidence. Wander where you will in the Cotswolds – to Upper and Lower Slaughter and Upper and Lower Swell where the tourists tend to go, or into the less publicised byways behind Stow-in-the-Wold – and you will find the old houses all honey-coloured and tranquil. The stones out of which they were built with such skill and love, are strokable. They have sunlight sleeping in them.

The Cotswold rivers are as sleepy as the stone. They are not large and have plenty of time to meander through valleys that always look too big for them, but they make up for size with lovely, liquid names like the Windrush and the Evenlode. The Thames is present, of course, but here it is in its infancy and distinctly uncertain about its origin. Where in the Cotswolds does it actually start? You can take your choice. At Seven Springs the little river Churn rises and this is the longest tributary of the Thames, if it is not the main stream. Or you can go to the spring behind Cirencester which boldly calls itself Thames Head. In any case the streams from both these points unite and flow eastwards out of the actual Cotswolds on to the wide

Oxfordshire plain, passing through lush water-meadows and almost under the windows of Kelmscott Manor. Here William Morris came in 1871 and set up the Kelmscott Press, as part of his long struggle to restore the virtues and values of mediaeval craftsmanship in an increasingly industrialised world. He lost the battle in so many areas that I think he would be pleased if he could revisit the Cotswolds today. There have been changes, inevitably, but at heart the Cotswolds have remained what they always were – the one part of Britain where man has perfectly matched his building with the spirit of the landscape.

Another writer comes to my mind when I think of the Cotswolds; assuredly a greater one than Morris, as the generous Morris would be the first to admit. Did not Shakespeare himself know them well? How else could he have made young Henry Percy, in 'Richard II', pick out Berkeley Castle so confidently as he looked out from the Cotswold

Left: Eastleach in Gloucestershire, a village in the heart of the Cotswolds between Burford and Lechlade

Below: A farmhouse near Cheltenham, built out of the distinctive Cotswold limestone and in a typical setting of orchards and wooded slopes

edge? 'These high, wild hills' he called them, and so they must have been in his day. But he must have loved them because he took care to have Falstaff come to Gloucestershire on his robustious recruiting expedition and call on the garrulous, doddering Justice Shallow. And Shallow's house was surely built of the warm Cotswold stone. As for his orchard, in which the fat knight sat drinking with Master Silence, I picture it still with the apple trees in flower, the spring evening ending and the lights appearing in the scattered cottages on a hillside – shall we say behind Broadway?

But there is no need to let our imagination run riot on a Shakespearian scene in the Cotswolds. For the hills run north-east to come at last, in their final dramatic upsurge, to a point that looks out over Shakespeare's own county of Warwickshire, and over little towns and villages that we are certain Shakespeare knew. This point is Edge Hill, famous in its own right as the scene of the first confused battle of the Civil War. You can see the mock Gothic tower put up in 1750 to mark the spot where King Charles is supposed to have raised his standard. You go down the steep road over the Edge and you come to the battle site amongst the green fields by the same route as Prince Rupert led his men on that October day in 1642. Some weeks after the battle in which both sides claimed the victory, shepherds in the fields looked up into the sky and declared that they saw the whole fight being re-enacted there, complete with the sound of guns and the groans of the dying. They were so positive, and so many reputable people came forward to support them that the King sent a special commission to investigate, and the commissioners published a pamphlet coming down, on the whole, on the side of the shepherds. The whole thing sounds rather like a 17th-century version of our modern UFO reports.

At Edge Hill you are only 12 miles from Stratford itself and you are already in the Shakespeare country. Stratford is the heart of it and this attractive town has performed the remarkable feat of becoming the centre of a big tourist industry and yet remaining at heart a market town, wrapped up in the solid business of agriculture. The country all around is real country, as solid a piece of England as you could wish to see. You wander through places like Hampton Lucy, or Charlecote with its Tudor manor house, deer park and the unreliable story that here the young Shakespeare was hauled before Sir Thomas Lucy for deer-stealing. You look at the incredibly tall maypole that still stands proudly on the village green at Welford-on-Avon, or stop to drink at the Falcon Inn in Bidford and remember that Shakespeare – how the legends gathered round him once he became a National Monument! – is supposed to have woken up under a crab-apple tree after a thick night in the inn and tossed off an impromptu rhyme summing up the character of the local villages:

'Piping Pebworth, Dancing Marston,
Haunted Hillborough, Hungry Grafton,
Dodging Exhall, Papist Wexford,
Beggarly Broom, and Drunken Bidford.'

There's no need to believe this particular piece of village character-assassination or that Shakespeare ever wrote it, or that the Bard ever got pickled under that crab-apple tree. Similar rhymes were repeated about other villages all over England as part of an ancient folk tradition. But at least all these stories remind you how deeply Shakespeare was a man of the countryside. So many of his images come from country sources, and have nothing to do with town experience – they are lines that could have been written only by someone deeply imbued with country lore. H. J. Massingham points to a passage in 'The Tempest', where Ariel refers to the grief of old Gonzago, the faithful courtier, and says quite naturally:

'His tears ran down his beard, like winter's drops
From eaves of reeds.'

Shakespeare must have seen hundreds of thatched cottages in Warwickshire and plenty of them remain, but no-one but a true countryman would have used the word 'reed' for a thatch on a Warwickshire house. He knew that thatchers always refer to wheat-straw as 'reeds', and in his day red wheat furnished the long straw for the thatch. No wonder Justice Shallow was so anxious to have his land at Nibley carefully planted with red wheat. Today the long-stalked wheat has disappeared and reed, indeed, must be used for the thatched roofs we still admire in Warwickshire. A small detail, perhaps, but it's these curious small details that link Shakespeare so firmly to his native county. And it must be somewhere near Stratford, on the banks of the placid Avon, that we should end this May journey that began in the Malvern Hills. We look at the lush country around us, bursting green with the new hope of high Spring, and are grateful for the lucky chance that ordained that England's greatest poet should have been born in the lovely Warwickshire countryside that Henry James, that perpetual American tourist, saluted as 'the core and centre of the English world ... unmitigated England'.

May with the Poets

This is the weather the cuckoo likes,
    And so do I;
When showers betumble the chestnut spikes,
    And nestlings fly;
And the little brown nightingale bills his best,
And they sit outside at 'The Travellers' Rest',
And maids come forth sprig-muslin drest,
And citizens dream of the south and west,
    And so do I.

THOMAS HARDY

Beneath these fruit-tree boughs that shed
Their snow-white blossoms on my head,
With brightest sunshine round me spread
    Of spring's unclouded weather,
In this sequestered nook how sweet
To sit upon my orchard-seat!
And birds and flowers once more to greet,
    My last year's friends together.

One have I marked, the happiest guest
In all this covert of the blest;
Hail to thee, far above the rest
    In joy of voice and pinion!
Thou, Linnet! in thy green array,
Presiding Spirit here today,
Dost lead the revels of the May;
    And this is thy dominion.

W. WORDSWORTH

The fields breathe sweet, the daisies kiss our feet,
Young lovers meet, old wives a-sunning sit,
In every street these tunes our ears do greet:
Cocukoo, jug-jug, pu-we, to-witta-woo!

THOMAS NASHE

Now the lusty spring is seen;
    Golden yellow, gaudy blue,
    Daintily invite the view;
Everywhere on every green
Roses blushing as they blow,
    And enticing men to pull,
Lilies whiter than the snow,
    Woodbines of sweet honey full;
    All love's emblems, and all cry,
'Ladies, if not plucked, we die.'

JOHN FLETCHER

June

June is a rich, satisfying month. Some say that the name comes from Juno, the mother of the gods in classical mythology. Others claim that it was named during the consulate of Junius Brutus. It may simply signify fertility. The year reaches its centre at the Summer Solstice on June 21st, and ripeness starts to spread across the land. The hay harvest begins in southern Britain. The cuckoo prepares to change his tune; soon he'll be singing a slightly stuttering note like 'cue-cuckoo'. The skylark is in splendid form on the open uplands. The whole country is moving happily towards high Summer and my thoughts turn westwards, away from the mainland and out over the calm sea, to the largest of the islands that form this strange cluster off the coast of Europe that we call the British Isles – to Ireland.

I live in a house that looks out over Cardigan Bay and the harbour of Fishguard. June brings long calm to the restless sea and the red-funnelled ferry boats go busily out around the breakwater past the bold gnarled crags of Strumble Head, where the French landed in 1797 in the Last Invasion of Britain. It wasn't a particularly desperate affair. The French high command had only intended it as a diversion, and the commander, an American named Tate, surrendered after a few casualties had occurred on either side, and one Frenchman had been tipped down a well by an irate Welshwoman. Most of Tate's men had got extremely drunk on the Portuguese wine they had found in the Welsh farmhouses, from a ship which had been providentially wrecked on Strumble Head a little time before. You can still see the table on which it is claimed the surrender was signed in the Royal Oak Hotel in the pleasant square at Fishguard. But what

Lough Caragh, one of Co. Kerry's most popular fishing lakes

on earth had possessed the French Government to launch this somewhat farcical army in the first place? The answer lies in the attraction of Ireland. In December, 1796, only ill luck had prevented the French from landing a large force in Bantry Bay and thus setting all Ireland on rebellious fire. In February, 1797, the Directory might still hope that a diversion on Welsh soil would fan the smouldering embers of revolt in the nearby island. Not for the first time was the sea-girt peninsula of West Wales drawn closely into the complex and often tragic history of Ireland.

15 miles to the south-west along the rugged coastline from my Fishguard home – like Dylan Thomas's boathouse at Laugharne, 'a sea-shaken house, on a break-neck of rocks' – lies the pilgrim 'city' of St David's. This pleasant cluster of modest buildings around a village green is nevertheless a city for it holds the magical cathedral dedicated to the patron saint of Wales. David came to this Land's End of Wales in the 6th Century and there could be no place more out-of-this-world for a saint looking for convenient retirement. Beyond the 'city' the rocks of the peninsula break down into a string of small islands. The biggest is Ramsay where the seals breed in Autumn, but the seas around are scattered with lesser islets and savage, gull-haunted rocks, the Bishop and the Clerks, which as old George Owen, the Tudor historian of Pembrokeshire, remarks, 'preach deadly doctrine to their winter audience and are commendable in nothing but for their good residence'. The whole of this Pembrokeshire coastline is now deservedly a National Park. It rivals Cornwall for great cliffs, sandy beaches and inlets holding forgotten fishing hamlets.

The great church of St David, with its strong Norman tower and glorious Tudor roof of Irish oak, hides out of sight in a rocky valley, and must be the only cathedral in Britain which has a small trout-stream flowing past the West Door. The stream runs down for a gorse-brightened mile to the little creek of Porth Clais, guarded by its small stone pier. The stories have gathered thickly around this tiny 'port' of St David's, and all seem to lead you eventually to Ireland. Here the legendary wild boar, Trwrch Trwyth, came ashore from Ireland to be hunted by King Arthur and his Knights, as related in the great collection of mediaeval Welsh folk-tales, the Mabinogion. St Patrick himself, so the stories go, sailed to and fro from Porth Clais in his long task of converting the Irish, and before Patrick the Romans are supposed to have built the first pier here. We know from Tacitus that after his great victory over the Scottish tribes at Mons Grampius in AD 84, Agricola ordered his fleet to circumnavigate the island of Britannica, but it is doubtful if they went the whole way around. The Romans were basically a land power and were never renowned for their seamanship. I cannot see them navigating the wild Atlantic seas off the west coast of Ireland, but I would like to think that some of the fleet got as far as Porth Clais before they turned back. In any case the Romans never tried to annexe Ireland. They knew all about it, for the main features of the island were clearly marked on Ptolemy's celebrated map drawn in the 2nd Century BC, probably from information supplied by the more daring Phoenician navigators. They were also well aware of the lead and gold to be mined in the Wicklow Hills. Agricola had an exiled Irish prince all ready as a plausible excuse for intervention and calculated he could scoop up the whole island with one good legion and auxiliaries, in all about 10,000 men. Not the first time, or the last, that a military adviser put an over-optimistic proposal to his government. The Emperor Domitian turned it down, through jealousy, as Tacitus hints, but it was more likely that he took the 'global view' and saw that the Empire's resources were already overstretched.

So the old Celtic civilization remained undisturbed in Ireland. With the Highlands of Scotland, it was the only part of western Europe that never underwent the stern but educative discipline of Rome. The petty kings ruled in their stone-girt forts, with their warlike exploits celebrated by their bards in long epic poems, and their wives and warriors decorated with the wonderfully wrought metalwork which is the glory of the old Celtic craftsmen. When the Roman Empire finally collapsed, the Irish were ready to take advantage of

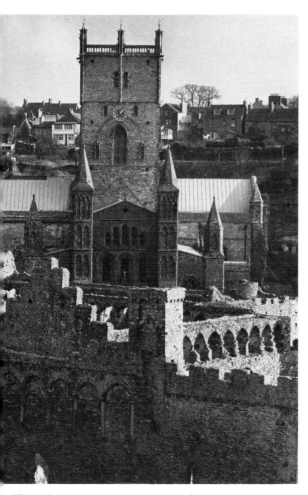

The 12th-century cathedral of St David on the Pembrokeshire coast

strange script invented in Ireland in pre-Christian days, in which the letters are represented by strokes cut on the edges of stones.

600 years later there came a time when the invasion roles were sharply reversed. After the Norman Conquest of England these formidable and rapacious freebooters advanced through South Wales, pushing the Welsh back into the hills. By the middle of the 12th Century they were firmly established in Pembrokeshire and were ready to look for further loot elsewhere. When Dermot II of Leinster clashed with the High King of Ireland, Rory O'Connor, he fled to Henry II of England, who gave him permission to recruit volunteers. One tough adventurer immediately offered himself, Richard de Clare, Earl of Pembroke, nick-named Strongbow. He left his stronghold on the shores of Milford Haven and in 1170 he followed up his advance guards with a force of 200 armoured knights and 1,000 men-at-arms, mostly Welshmen and Flemings. With the landing of Strongbow, the old Gaelic Ireland began her long journey towards becoming, as the old song put it, 'the most distressful country that ever yet was seen'.

Curiously enough you can see Ireland from Pembrokeshire. On an exceptionally clear day last June, when the whole western sky had been swept clean of cloud after rain and the horizon was a sharp line drawn against the pale blue, I climbed Carn Ingli, the 1,000-ft outlier of the Preseli Hills. These rolling moorlands hold secrets among the scattered rock outcrops that rival the tors of Dartmoor in their impressive shapes. From one of them came the blue stones that form the heart of Stonehenge. Great cromlechs like that of Pentre Ifan lie on the lower slopes. Everywhere you feel the presence of the megalithic tomb-builders, of the Iron Age warriors who piled the stones for the great hill-forts and of the kindly and absent-minded old Celtic saints. Deep below Carn Ingli runs the wooded valley of the Gwaun, where they have resolutely refused to accept the reform of the calendar in the 18th Century and joyously celebrate the New Year 11 days later than the rest of Britain. In all this, I see a faint anticipation of Ireland.

I climbed over the tumbled walls of the Carn

the departure of the legions – especially in Pembrokeshire. Gildas, that eloquent but querulous monk who disapproved so violently of the petty princes who filled the power gap left by the Romans in Wales, gives a vivid description of the Irish invaders, 'whose hulls might be seen creeping across the glassy surface of the main like so many insects awakened from torpor by the heat of the noonday sun and making with one accord for some familiar haunt'. Pembrokeshire early became one of these haunts; so much so that the Irish took the whole place over in the 5th and 6th Centuries. The county thus contains a great percentage of the ogam inscriptions in Wales – ogam being that

Right : The 'Green Bridge of
Wales' on the limestone coast
of the Castle Martin peninsula
in Dyfed

Opposite : Glenmalure in the
Wicklow Hills south of
Dublin, the scene of several
early attempts by the Irish to
resist English rule

Below : The Upper Lake of
Killarney, with
MacGillycuddy's Reeks
in the background

Ingli fort with a tingle of excitement. The conditions were just right for the long views and Carn Ingli and the Preselis are perfectly placed for those great visual leaps which stir the imagination and which you can only get on the isolated high hills of western Britain. I calculate that you can cover the whole of England and Wales from five viewpoints. From the summit of Bodmin Moor in Cornwall you can look to Land's End, and then north-east to Exmoor. From Exmoor you can pick up Preseli top over the Bristol Channel. From Preseli you can look across the wide Cardigan Bay to Snowdon. Snowdon is high enough to give you a series of choices. I have seen the hills of the Lake District from Snowdon summit but I've also picked up the outline of the Isle of Man – that most romantic of islands with its own government owing direct allegiance to the Crown and its own Parliament, the Tynwald, which is claimed to be the oldest parliament in the world. It is a land, not just of holiday resorts like Douglas, but of lonely glens, prehistoric monuments, fine castles and the little islet of the Calf of Man off its southern tip, now a nature reserve. The highest point of the island is Snaefell, just over 2,000 ft, reached by a tramway – when I was last there – which was the delight of connoisseurs of ancient traction. Snaefell gives you a clear line to the Southern Uplands of Scotland and completes my five-man visual link-up. No doubt you could see some part of Scotland from the summit of Scafell Pike in the Lake District but I'm not as sure of this as of Snaefell in the Isle of Man. Naturally, with the British weather being what it is, I would never expect to make this link-up on one particular day. It is pleasant, however, to think that it is possible.

But was the link-up with Ireland possible from Carn Ingli on that exceptionally clear June day with the green farms of North Pembrokeshire stretched below me like a map encircled by the sea? I turned my binoculars to the north-west and there, rising up over the very edge of the world, were the outlines of another land, a mysterious country like the fabled Celtic Tir-nan-Og, the land of eternal youth where no snow falls and life passes in an everlasting golden June. Prosaically, I had to look

on the map. These mystic shapes must simply have been the southern end of the Wicklow Hills. Ireland, after all, was firmly anchored in reality. I remembered my old geography master telling us, 'Ireland is like a saucer. All the high land is around the edge.' What I was seeing wasn't Tir-nan-Og after all; it was just part of the saucer's rim.

Dublin, the capital city of the Republic of Ireland, lies on a convenient gap in the rim, and from the city's suburbs you can look south to one of the highest points of it, the Wicklow Hills. These are grand moorland wastes to find so near a busy city centre. Manchester and Sheffield can claim to lie closer to the Pennines and Glasgow has the beginning of the Highland splendours within an hour's ride; but from none of them do you sense the presence of the hills so closely as in Dublin. The graceful cones of the Sugarloaf introduce you to the higher hills – and, indeed, the Wicklows are high. The highest, Lugnaquilla, tops the 3,000-ft mark. There are three other mountains in Ireland that exceed that magic number: Galtymore, surprisingly placed high over the rich pastures of Tipperary; Mount Brandon, rising superbly from the western sea on the Dingle peninsula; and the noblest summit of them all, the highest point in all Ireland, Carrantuohill (3,414 ft) in County Kerry. Lugnaquilla thus stands in worthy company. The Wicklows hold deep glens, including the famous one of Glendalough. Maybe it is overrun at certain seasons, but it contains all the classic features the visitor demands from an Irish landscape – a great crag mirrored in a still lake, a round tower, a ruined church, legends galore about St Kevin and a convenient hotel.

The Wicklows introduce you to the rim, and you have only to drive 50 miles westwards from Dublin to come to the centre of the saucer, the Bog of Allen. On your way you can pass the Curragh, the largest stretch of unenclosed grassland in Ireland, breezy, open country and as a result the head-quarters of Irish racing. The Bog of Allen is another matter. It hasn't exactly got the feeling of dead level flatness you get, for example, in the English fen-country; but it is certainly flat for Ireland, and in the flattest part near Allenwood in

A winding road among the Wicklow Hills

County Kildare is a curious industrial plant, a peat-fired power station. It symbolises one of the oldest problems of Ireland, her chronic lack of really big sources of power. There are coal-measures, but on such a tiny scale as to be unimportant. Peat has been the traditional source of heating, but how long can such a formation survive mass-exploitation? As a character said in Michael MacLiammior's play, 'Ill Met by Moonlight', 'They're burning poor old Ireland sod by sod.' Water power has been developed, as in the famous Shannon scheme. Ireland's biggest river runs a little west of the centre, taking its time to loiter down through a string of wide, fish-filled lakes of which the noblest is Lough Derg. It enters the sea, as befits Ireland's longest river, through the longest estuary in a country that specialises in estuaries. All around the coast you will find them, from Lough Foyle and Lough Swilly in the north to a whole string of winding waterways in the south that bring the sea far into the land.

But as you drive westwards beyond the Shannon, or leave it at Limerick to wander back south-eastwards through the Golden Vale of Tipperary into the farmlands of Kilkenny, Waterford and Wexford, you become impressed with another basic aspect of Ireland. It is still, fundamentally, an agricultural country. Both sections of the island are now in the Common Market and the Republic of Ireland has certainly benefited by its membership. Industry has grown around the big towns. There has been much American and even Japanese investment, and the old patterns of life are changing. But to a visitor used to the vast urban conglomerations of Western Europe and Eastern USA, Ireland, in both parts, still seems a land which takes its rhythm, its whole philosophy of life, from the needs and long traditions of the farmer. There is still a blessed indifference in rural Ireland to the tyranny of the stop-watch, enshrined in a whole series of classical epigrams – 'sure, the men who made time made plenty of it' – and the celebrated story of the Irishman who, when asked by a Spaniard what was the equivalent of 'mañana' in Irish, replied, 'I don't think that we have any word which conveys the same sense of urgency.' Once you are outside the orbit of Dublin and Belfast, the roads are surprisingly free of traffic. In the top end of County Cork they can still play their special game of bowls along the side roads, with the champions hurling a heavy metal ball the size of a tennis ball for miles, occasionally taking the risk of 'lofting', or cutting corners, followed by a crowd of supporters busily betting and cheering. No wonder that as you come from a side road to a main road in the Republic the signs carry only one powerful word, 'Yield'. It is clearly a case of 'may the best man win'.

There is time for talk, too, especially in the country pubs. I remember the bar-tender in one little country town in Clare, near that strange landscape of bare limestone rocks they call the 'Burren', saying in reply to my question about what happened in the place, 'Well, nothing that you might call happening. You look into the main street at 10 o'clock in the morning and all you'll see are Tim Murphy's cows coming back from the milking and two old bodies going to the Mass.' Then he sighed, 'It's a long day in an empty bar.' I talked with an old man at Dunquin at the very end of the wild Dingle peninsula in Kerry. I was waiting to go across to the Blasket Islands, which were then still inhabited and a stronghold of Irish speaking. Below me, on the rocky landing place, the islanders were loading their black, high-prowed canvas boats – 'they'll dance over the waves like white gulls.' The old man looked longingly across at the islands. 'I'd go with you with the best of them but for the cramp that's coming over me now. Ah, if I'd only have my

The Mountains of Mourne at Newcastle in Co. Down

MacGillycuddy's Reeks in Killarney, a hill range in some of the most beautiful scenery in Ireland. One of the peaks in the range is Carrantuohil (3,314 ft), the highest in Ireland

middle age again, I'd be as airy as a lark.'

Of course, you will not hear such lilting words in every pub in Ireland. There are places where they are as level-headed and as silent as they are in Norfolk – although I must say you have to look hard for them. But the visitor has been pre-conditioned to expect vivid talk in Ireland by long reading of the great Irish poets and writers who put Ireland on the international literary map in the first quarter of the 20th Century and have kept her there ever since. You discover, with a sense of delighted surprise, that the tower about which Yeats wrote in 1923, is still there, some five miles from the pleasant market town of Gort in County Galway. The poet converted the tower of Ballylee and placed a dedicatory inscription on it:

'I, the poet William Yeats,
With old mill-boards and sea-green slates
    And smithy work from the Gort forge,
Built this tower for my wife George;
    And may these characters remain
    When all is ruin once again.'

Yeats abandoned the tower in 1929 and ruin did come again, although the place is now restored as a Yeats museum. I stood before it with a well-known Irish writer after it had been deserted for many years. 'Yes,' he said, 'this is how it should be. Ireland, after all, is a country of lovely ruins.' You meet them everywhere, and all of them are tangled up with the equally tangled history of Ireland. 'Irish history!' a wit once exclaimed, 'if only the English would remember it and the Irish forget it.' But how can they when at every hand they see reminders of their romantic and often tragic past. The country began to provide fascinating ruins from the moment it first emerged from the mists of pre-history. There are cromlechs and burial tombs in profusion and the greatest lie at Newgrange in County Meath. Here the huge burial chambers, which must date back at least 4,000 years, have mysterious carved stones that seem to anticipate the later Celtic craftsmen in their display of intricately carved patterns. Much later the old Celtic saints left moving memorials to their faith in their simple beehive cells and tiny churches at places like Galleras near Ballyferriter and, even more

Above: Gathering seaweed on an Irish beach

Opposite: The Giant's Causeway near Bushmills, an extraordinary basalt lava formation on the Antrim coast in Northern Ireland

impressively, on the wild Skellig islets off the west coast of Kerry. Here the gannets breed, and a cluster of tiny beehive huts clings to the 700-ft pinnacle of the Greater Skellig. This must be the most remote early Christian settlement in Europe. On the Aran Islands, far out in Galway Bay, the famous ring forts with their massive walls remind us of the Celtic world of independent princes and heroic warfare celebrated in song and legend. At the opposite end of the country, the great Rock of Cashel holds the well-known collection of ruined churches, Romanesque chapels and round towers which make it almost a text book for the development of Irish ecclesiastical architecture. All

through the country, ruined Franciscan priories testify to the rigours of Queen Elizabeth I's Irish policy. Our own time has added its quota in the police barracks and great houses burnt out during the 'Troubles'. Over all, time has cast its cloak of consoling green that grows so quickly over ruins, if not over memory, in the encouraging damp of Ireland.

The Emerald Isle, however, becomes progressively less emerald the more you journey to the far west. On the coast of County Clare the limestone shows through and makes a spectacular 600-ft plunge into the sea at the cliffs of Moher. Then, northwards into Connemara and County Mayo where the stony earth gives the landscape a strange, spare beauty. The mountains rise above lonely lakes, and the tiny fields are ringed by stone walls that look as if they had been built around each individual grazing cow or donkey. When the visitor reaches the great cliffs of Achil Island or stands on Glen Head in Donegal he feels he has reached the very edge of the western world.

Here – and in a section of County Kerry – lies the Gaeltacht, the area where Irish is still the medium of everyday speech. The language was once spoken throughout the whole island, but has progressively been driven westwards to seek refuge in the lonelier and poorer parts of the country. The Great Hunger – the famine of 1845–7 – led to the emigration of thousands of native Irish speakers. The Government of the Republic is now firmly behind the preservation of the language but Irish, like Welsh, is having to fight hard to survive in a world increasingly dominated by television and mass entertainment. But the battle is not yet lost, and even if this western coastline remains poor, the people seem to preserve a certain quality of life which may have disappeared from the more prosperous rural areas. Above Clew Bay in County Mayo rises the 2,510-ft white quartzite cone of Croagh Patrick, Ireland's Holy Mountain. From the summit there are magnificent views over some of the loveliest country in the west. St Patrick is claimed to have fasted 40 days on the top, and every year, on the last Sunday in July, thousands of pilgrims set off before dawn to reach the summit:

by no means an easy climb, for the final ascent goes up the bare rocky scree of the upper cone. The pilgrimage to Croagh Patrick is a moving demonstration of faith.

It may seem logical to come down from the summit of what is in essence a Catholic mountain and then drive eastwards out of the Gaeltacht until you cross the border with Northern Ireland, where the first town of any size you come to is Enniskillen, an old Protestant stronghold and thus a symbol of the separation of the six counties of Northern Ireland from the rest of the island. The town itself is beautifully placed between the wide reaches of Lough Erne and the sister lake of Upper Lough Erne. The countryside around has features that would make the fortune of many an English resort but remain comparatively unknown outside Ulster. There is a strange limestone area near at hand complete with underground cave systems and, near the intriguingly named spot they call Boho, Noon's Hole, reputedly the deepest pot-hole in Ireland. But all the time I was there, I confess to have been conscious of the important role played by Enniskillen in Ulster's history. The town held out against the Irish in 1641, and was again a major Protestant rallying-point in 1689–90 when King William III arrived to win the Battle of the Boyne. It was bound to be so, for Enniskillen was on the western border of the great 'plantations' that began at the end of the reign of Elizabeth I, and reached their ruthlessly efficient climax after Cromwell's 'purification' of Ireland in 1649. A large proportion of the settlers came from the Lowlands of Scotland and the tie thus created between Scotland and Northern Ireland has remained strong to this day. The net result of the 'plantation' of Ulster was the creation not just of a Protestant Ascendancy as in the rest of Ireland, but of a Protestant peasantry and farming community as well. This deep identification of Ulster with the Protestant cause was intensified when Belfast, with its great shipyards and linen mills, became the most heavily industrialised part of Ireland by the end of the 19th Century. The Orange Order was there to keep the faith strong and bright. Inevitably, the six counties of the north went their own way when the

settlement of 1922 established the Irish Free State.

The visitor will thus not be surprised to find in Northern Ireland all the problems that attend separation – and the wise visitor will not offer a solution to them. What will surprise him, however, is the unexpected, unspoilt beauty of the countryside. Away from the industrialised towns you travel on comparatively uncrowded roads. Again you are in a landscape shaped by farming and the mountains rise from a pattern of lush, green fields. The Sperrin Mountains rise well over 2,000 ft and hold lonely, unfrequented valleys. They lie beyond Ireland's biggest lake, Lough Neagh. Then there are the Mountains of Mourne which obey the well-known song and really do 'sweep down to the sea'. But the Ulster tourist show-piece is probably that scenic Coast Road that links the Glens of Antrim. The glens themselves are deep valleys cut into a high tableland roofed in places by beds of basalt. They are alive with waterfalls and clear running streams and separated by impressive headlands. Inevitably, the tourist goes on from the glens to that remarkable curiosity, the Giant's Causeway.

You can approach it through the little town of Bushmills. You will have already heard the name not only in Northern Ireland but around the world,

Left: Yeats's 'lake isle of Inisfree' on Lough Gill in Co. Sligo

Below: The cathedral on Iona, where St Columba founded his monastery in the 6th Century

for it is associated with Ulster's finest whiskey – which you must take care to spell with an 'e'. Whisky is the product of Scotland, and Bushmills reckons it can hold up its head as a malt whiskey with the best of them. The whole approach to the Causeway is thus a splendid build-up. Not many miles away the much-photographed Dunluce Castle stands on its wind-beaten headland. Then on to the Causeway itself, which astonishes you however often you see it. A great flow of volcanic rock called basalt has been suddenly cooled and thus formed into forests of polygonal columns, from three- to nine-sided, and looking as if carved by the hand of man. It is hard to believe that Nature could behave with such disciplined regularity. But the formation is not unique. It reappears across the sea 100 miles to the north on the tiny Scottish island of Staffa, off the coast of Mull. Here the great multi-sided basalt columns, like the pillars of a huge Gothic cathedral, support the 200-ft high roof of Fingal's Cave, while the sea surges in with a rhythm that inspired Mendelssohn's famous overture. Staffa and the Giant's Causeway link Northern Ireland and eastern Scotland as firmly geographically as they already are socially and historically.

If you want to see the Scottish hills from Ulster, there is no need to do as I did down in West Wales and climb to the top of the Preseli Hills and pray for a day of exceptional clarity. From the noble 600-ft prow of Fair Head on the Antrim coast the Mull of Kintyre in Scotland is visible on any reasonably clear day, for the North Channel between the two countries is under 15 miles across. It is not much wider down at Donaghadee, around the corner from Belfast Lough – a little port with a harbour built by the great Scottish engineer Sir John Rennie and where you can sample 'dulse', the local delicacy made from seaweed.

This close proximity of the two coasts led to continual comings and goings between them across the narrow channel through the long centuries. Along the Antrim coast in the 4th and 5th Centuries lay the little kingdom of Dalriada, inhabited by the original Scots. Their rulers had ambitions and crossed the channel to carve out another kingdom for themselves amongst the Western Islands and the lower Clyde. They drove back the Picts and, as time passed, gave their name to the whole country. Ironically, it is thus the Irish who were the first true Scots and they brought the Irish language which is the Gaelic still spoken in the Highlands and Islands. They brought more than the language. In the 6th Century, Christianity came to western Scotland through the devoted work of the Irish missionary saints. The greatest of them was Colmcille, 'The Dove of the Church', whom we remember as St Columba. Columba was not only a missionary; he was also a statesman who helped to revive the kingdom of Scottish Dalriada after a defeat by the Picts. He supported rulers with titles like Eochaid the Venomous, surely the most curiously named king in the history of Britain and obviously a dangerous man to cross.

Columba left his most lasting memorial in his monastery on the little island of Iona, again like Staffa off the coast of the larger island of Mull. This was his base for his long and arduous journeys to spread the gospel through the wild Highlands. During one of them he came to Loch Ness where, according to legend, he encountered the Monster and thus became the first publicist for this much-loved tourist attraction. The cathedral at Iona became the burial place of the early Scottish kings and has been restored through the devoted work of the Iona community under the Rev George MacLeod. Iona has a remote, deeply moving atmosphere of its own. Here we stand by the intricately carved St Martin's Cross and end our long June journey, that has taken us through the Celtic lands from West Wales, on across Gaelic Ireland to end here on this lonely sea-guarded isle, which 1,400 years ago was the most northerly of all Christian communities. On Iona in June the nights are merely short interludes between dusk and dawn, and the sunsets can have a long lingering glory as the colour floods the western horizon and outlines the myriad islets scattered over the sea. It was such a sunset that surely moved sturdy, common sense Dr Samuel Johnson to break his 18th-century restraint and write, 'the man is little to be envied ... whose piety would not grow warmer among the ruins of Iona.'

June with the Poets

O these lakes and all gills that live in them,
These acres and all legs that walk on them,
These tall winds and all wings that cling to them,
Are part and parcel of me, bit and bundle,
Thumb and thimble. Them I am, but none more
Than the mountains of Mourne that turn and trundle
Roundly like slow coils of oil along the shore
Of down and on inland.

W. R. RODGERS

When we were little childer we had a quare wee house,
Away up in the heather by the head o' Brabla burn;
The hares we'd see them scootin', an' we'd hear the crowin' grouse,
An' when we'd all be in at night ye'd not get room to turn.

The youngest two She'd put to bed, their faces to the wall,
An' the lave of us could sit aroun', just anywhere we might;
Herself 'ud take the rush-dip an' light it for us all,
An' 'God be thanked!' she would say, 'Now we have a light.'

MOIRA O'NEIL

If all the young maidens were blackbirds and thrushes,
Blackbirds and thrushes,
Sure all the young men would go beating the bushes!

If all the young maidens were grouse on a mountain,
Grouse on a mountain,
Sure all the young men would seize guns and go shooting!

If all the young maidens were salmon so lively,
Salmon so lively,
The devil a man would eat fish on a Friday!

OLD SONG

What can I but enumerate old themes?
First that sea-rider Oisin led by the nose
Through three enchanted islands, allegorical
    dreams,
Vain gaiety, vain battle, vain refuse,
Themes of the embittered heart, or so it seems,
That might adorn old songs and courtly shows;
But what cared I that set him on his ride,
I starved for the bosom of his faery bride?

W. B. YEATS

July

July, so-called because the great Julius Caesar was born at this time, must be everybody's favourite month. We are now into high Summer. The sun beams down on a land drowsy with heat. The scent of the new-mown hay still hangs in the country lanes and the hedgerows flower in full glory. This is how we always picture July and how we generally find this happy month. But this is Britain, and even on the hottest July day, we keep a wary eye on the sky. We don't forget that 15th July is St Swithin's Day. We uneasily repeat the old rhyme:

'St Swithin's Day, if it do rain,
For forty days it will remain.
St Swithin's Day, if it be fair,
For forty days 'twill rain nae mair.'

Swithin doesn't seem to have been much of a saint. He was Bishop of Winchester in AD 852, and counsellor to King Egbert and King Ethelwulf of Wessex. They buried him outside his church and his uneasy spirit resented the rain falling on his grave. The authorities took 100 years before they removed the saint's bones back 'into the dry' inside the cathedral, so we are lucky to have escaped with only forty days' malevolence.

Meteorologists, as usual, declare that there is no foundation in fact for the St Swithin's superstition. We are always likely to have some wet Julys. We can, however, console ourselves with the thought that nothing we've experienced can beat the dreadful July, and indeed the whole Summer of 1879, when the hay was too damp to cut and simply rotted in the fields. My memories of July when I was a boy are surely nearer to the true spirit of the month. I can only remember endless blue skies and warm mothy evenings, when the swallows darted from under the eaves of the great barn on the farm where we used to go in early July for the end of the hay harvest. In those days the farm had not yet

become a mechanised food factory. We led the old horse slowly down between the windrows of the cut hay, while the brawny farm lads pitched it up on to the wagon. We drank the bitter-sweet buttermilk to quench our thirst, and came back in the cool of the evening, riding high on the hay. In the farmyard the little pony stepped delicately around in a circle working the rather rickety elevator that carried the hay to the top of the last rick. In the dusk, the final load was safely stacked, and all the

The River Wensum from Carron Bridge, Norwich. Watercolour by Thomas Lound (Norwich School)

helping neighbours crowded into the great kitchen for a glorious tuck-in, under the noble salted hams hanging from the rafters.

On the first warm days of July, this is the picture, idealised maybe by the long passage of time, that comes vividly back to me. So for our visit to the countryside this month, I am bound to turn to a part of Britain where they harvest the crops on a grand scale and where the inhabitants can claim that they have agriculture rooted in their very souls; where industry is not, and is never likely to be, their main preoccupation – East Anglia. This most easterly section of Britain has always been a place apart, a country that keeps itself to itself. There are moments when East Anglia seems to be an independent kingdom on its own. The roots of this independence go far back into history. This is solidly Anglo-Saxon territory. True, the Celtic

Iceni were here before them, and that fiery virago, Boudicca (she was Boadicea when I was at school) led the great revolt against the Romans; but the Romans departed at last and the Saxons came flooding over the seas from the continent in their dark boats to row up the winding estuaries and make this the land of the North Folk – Norfolk – and the South Folk – Suffolk. The East Saxons settled below them in Essex. Historically, East Anglia is just Norfolk and Suffolk with Ely – the Isle of Eels – added. Today, all the big counties are swept together in this one convenient label of East Anglia.

Those early Anglo-Saxon invaders left a splendid memorial to themselves, buried under a cluster of grassy mounds at Sutton Hoo, near the estuary of the River Deben. Archaeologists started to excavate them just before the last war. They drew a blank on the first few mounds, but under the largest one they hit the jackpot. They uncovered the remains of a great rowing-boat, 87 ft long. In the centre lay a rich treasure; silverware from Byzantium, Merovigian coins, strange standards, helmets and most impressive of all, jewellery of gold wrought with rare skill into complex patterns and decorated with precious stones. This was the burial place of a powerful 7th-century king of the old East Anglian dynasty of the Wulfingas. A ray of vivid barbarian light suddenly reached us from the darkest part of the Dark Ages. Here lay a ruler who had inherited from the Iceni and the Romans the long task of reclaiming the marshes and cutting back the forest.

It was going to take 1,300 years before there emerged the East Anglia we know today. Until the advent of the railways, it remained somewhat cut off from the rest of England. The great roads that radiated out of London all went to strategic points in Scotland, Wales or the West Country. The road to Norwich seemed a dead end, leading nowhere. The eastern borders of East Anglia, in those early years, were not exactly easy to cross. They were formed by the deep inlet of the Wash and continued down through the waterlogged Fens. A series of vast forests spread up from the Thames and the only easy track into East Anglia followed the line of

the chalk marked by the ancient Icknield Way. When Queen Elizabeth came to visit Norfolk on one of those celebrated progresses, with which she wooed her people so successfully, she rode through forest almost to the borders of Suffolk. The nobility and gentry may not have enjoyed the progress as much as the common folk, for they had to fork out considerable sums to make the occasion a worthy one. But all seemed worthwhile once the Queen came among them, for she had matchless tact and the art of saying the right word in the right place, so that she won loyalty with ease. As she well knew, to subjects 'no music is so sweet as the affability of their prince'.

When she reached the borders of Suffolk she was met by the sheriff and his escort, all richly clad since, for weeks before, the gentry had been busy buying up all the velvet and silks in the county. In front were 200 young gentlemen in white velvet. Then followed 300 men 'of the graver sort' in black velvet and gold chains and 1,500 servants, 'all bravely mounted'. Not to be outdone, the sheriff of Norfolk came to his border with 2,500 horsemen, all 'in a most gallant manner assembled'. Her entry into Norwich was marked by a wave of loyal emotion, and a supreme instance of her tact. The schoolmaster became nervous as he prepared his Latin speech of welcome. She smiled and said, 'Be not afraid,' and after he had stumbled through it, declared, 'It is the best that ever I heard; you shall have my hand.' And then – supreme flattery – she sent back a messenger to ask his name after she had moved on. No wonder her people cherished the memory of every small incident of her journey to East Anglia. They remembered how, on leaving the city, she had declared, 'I have laid up in my breast such good will, as I shall never forget Norwich.' As she passed the gates, she turned 'and did shake her riding rod' and, with tears in her eyes, said, 'Farewell, Norwich.'

After Elizabeth, precious few of England's sovereigns evinced special affection for East Anglia. They made their short visits there in the course of duty, but when it came to the matter of building a country house for themselves, an informal retreat from the sometimes oppressive

splendours of the royal palaces, they looked elsewhere. Charles II slipped down to Newmarket for the racing, but James II, Anne and Dutch William were not exactly drawn to the area. The Hanoverians firmly made East Anglia unfashionable. Neither of the first two Georges ever made an official visit to the home of their trusted Prime Minister, Sir Robert Walpole, and yet he was a Norfolk man who built a great house at Houghton and filled it with a glorious collection of paintings, which his spendthrift son sold off to Catherine the Great of Russia. Here Walpole, after parliamentary sessions ended, came down in the Summer for what were nick-named the 'Norfolk Congresses'. All the leading statesmen of the day stayed at Houghton and mingled with Walpole's tenants and place-men while consuming enormous meals, quaffing gargantuan quantities of wine and settling affairs of state between potations. No wonder that Walpole's accounts show that he bought four hogsheads of

An evening view of Ramsholt on the River Deben estuary in Suffolk

Château Margaux at a time and a hogshead of Château Lafite every three months. Connoisseurs of today can only turn green with envy!

George III remained faithful to Windsor and Kew, while George IV is forever associated with the raffish splendours of Brighton, and Victoria and Albert sought seclusion in Balmoral and isolation on the Isle of Wight. East Anglia's turn came at last with Edward VII, but curiously enough it was the Prince Consort who made the actual purchase of a Norfolk home for his son, then Prince of Wales. Perhaps he was worried by the somewhat worldly turn his son's career was taking, and looked for somewhere for him, which would be healthy and far from temptation. The Prince Consort was offered Walpole's old mansion at Houghton, but felt it was too grandiose for his purpose. Some of these great Norfolk houses are indeed spectacularly grand. Holkham, with its magnificent domed entrance hall, is William Kent's masterpiece, surrounded by grounds showing 'Capability' Brown's genius at its best. The Prince Consort needed something more modest. His choice fell on Sandringham, a quiet country house tucked away at the top of the county beyond King's Lynn and not so far from the Wash. Then the Prince Consort suddenly died. What was to become of Sandringham? Fortunately, the Prince of Wales married the charming Princess Alexandra of Denmark and needed a place where he could relax with his young bride, and, one suspects, as far as possible from his formidable widowed mother. At Sandringham he could enjoy excellent shooting, and invite his personal friends to his own version of a 'Norfolk Congress'. Sandringham had started on its long career as the most relaxing and informal of the royal houses. By tradition, the Royal Family always spends Christmas there. George v and George vi both died there. In the richly decorated parish church, a brass cross is inset on the floor of the chancel. Here the royal coffins rest before being taken to Windsor but no-one ever walks on the cross and the choir divides when passing it. The big plantations, farmlands and parks stretch for a

Above: Trainers exercising strings of racehorses at Newmarket, the centre of horse-racing in Britain and the site of the National Stud

Right: The rare avocet, with its unusual up-turned bill, which nests on the salt marshes of eastern Britain in late Spring

Opposite: A salt marsh and creek near Blakeney on the Norfolk coast

considerable distance around Sandringham, and make certain of a very welcome privacy for its royal owners.

When you come to Sandringham, you feel that you are very near the limits of exclusive East Anglia. Beyond it lies the low coastline bending like a bow from King's Lynn, facing towards the Wash, to Cromer which looks uncompromisingly out towards the North Sea. I say uncompromisingly because from the North Sea come those bitter winds that try your courage and endurance in mid-winter. 'Bracing', they call them in East Anglia! I once walked along the low chalk cliffs at Hunstanton with a friend who had come straight from the less demanding, soothing winter climate of Torquay. 'This,' he gasped when the wind hit him, 'is like having sandpaper drawn down your face!' But this northern section of the coast amply makes up for its winter roughness in high Summer, and above all in July. This is one of the driest parts of Britain with an average rainfall almost half of that on the west coast. The sun shines down on the dunes, the long sandspits and the secluded shallow creeks alive with summer yachts. This marshland coast between Holme-next-the-Sea and Weybourne is part of the area designated as one of Outstanding Natural Beauty and geographers claim that it is the finest example of its type in Europe. Above all, it teems with bird life. On Scolt Head Island the colonies of the graceful, fork-tailed Common and Sandwich terns rise, screaming and wheeling to dive-bomb any intruder. The Arctic tern is about. He does not breed further south than the Farne Islands on Britain's east coast. A pity, since the Arctic tern is the country's long-distance champion in the bird world. Every year, after breeding, he leaves Britain to travel an incredible 10,000 miles to the icy waters of Antarctica.

However, the East Anglian coast has its own rarities to offer. Further south, in Suffolk, the rare avocets with their remarkable curved-up bills still come in the late Spring to breed on the salt marshes and sandy flats – or rather on one or two carefully unpublicised sandy flats. I have a particular affection for the avocets since I once visited a colony of them, and the young birds – little balls of

fluff on tiny stilts – trotted trustingly towards me over the sands as if I were one of their hard-working parents, back with a beakful of food.

The East Anglian coast does not consist entirely of sands, flats, marshes and wide estuaries winding deep into the gently rolling land. Surprisingly in what is popularly supposed to be generally flat countryside, you come across a long line of cliffs near Cromer. Perhaps cliff is too grand a word for these steep, crumbling, yellowish-brown slides of soft earth. A Cornishman would look at them with superior scorn. But they are steep enough for careless people to fall over them and crumbling enough to betray their strange origin. They are, in fact, formed from the moraines left behind by the retreating glaciers at the end of the last Ice Age. The ice not only ground the Norfolk chalk but carried loam, gravel and boulder clay. The sea is attacking these cliffs vigorously and drives the detritus southwards to help build up strange spits of sand and shingle, like the remarkable Orford Ness in Suffolk. The most easterly point of England, Lowestoft Ness, is also composed of this tide-swept material. I walked out to it some time ago, but, as far as I could see, the actual most easterly point of English ground was a long sewer outfall. I had rather hoped to find some symbolic monument on the spot, for I like to see these evocative places commemorated. The most westerly point of England, Land's End, rather overdoes it, with its hotel, souvenir shops and gentlemen offering to photograph you with the Longships Lighthouse in the background. Scotland has managed it better. John o'Groats has its hotel, named, apparently, from a Dutchman, John de Groot, who came over in the 15th Century to run the Orkney ferry; but the hotel is not on the actual northernmost point. This is some miles away at Dunnet Head. To reach it you have to walk past the 'last house in Scotland', a white-washed cottage with a roof of Caithness flagstones. You can pick up the European cowrie shell, called locally 'Groatie Buckies', on the beach, and walk out on to the headland and look across to Orkney and Stroma Island, in the middle of the Pentland Firth. If you have ever had to bucket your way through the Pentland Firth at speed in a destroyer on a winter's day with the tide racing in full flood, you can easily understand how the Firth got its reputation of being the roughest stretch of coastal water around the shores of Britain. All highly satisfactory and romantic! Lowestoft Ness hardly qualifies for this league. Yet the coast builds up and wears away so rapidly in East Anglia that Lowestoft Ness may appear quite different in a hundred years from now. For there is an intriguing paradox about this part of the country. Norfolk and Suffolk seem the quintessence of unchanging agricultural England, as you drive through them. Here stand the Great Houses, of which the most extraordinary is surely Ickworth House in the village of Horringer in Suffolk. It has an impressive domed rotunda as its centrepiece, and a park filled with noble oaks and wide-spreading cedars, laid out, it is hardly necessary to say, by 'Capability' Brown. It now belongs to the National Trust and the visitor can wander through the state rooms and be surprised by the fine paintings by Gainsborough and Hogarth and the superb collection of silver. His surprise will be all the greater when he learns that the house was planned and nearly completed by a bishop. An 18th-century bishop, of course, the Bishop of Derry who conveniently also happened to be the wealthy 4th Earl of Bristol. In East Anglia, where feudal attitudes died hard, no-one raised an eyebrow at a High Churchman living in this splendour.

There are plenty of unchanged villages too, with names like Great and Little Snoring; or like Finchingfield in Essex, with its village pond intact and surrounded by half-timbered houses, and Kersey in Suffolk, with a water-splash in the centre of the village, and again the timbered houses with jutting eaves, that allow Kersey to compete with Finchingfield for the title of the Most Photographed Village in England. Kersey was famous for its cloth right up to Shakespeare's day. The whole of this area on the borders of Suffolk and Essex had a prosperous woollen industry in the 15th Century, which has left a remarkable legacy in the great 'wool' churches that seem twice as large as they need be for the little towns and villages they

The main street of Kersey in Suffolk, with its half-timbered, pastel-coloured houses and the watersplash across the road where cars have to give way to ducks

dominate. But what other industry has left behind such a legacy of faith linked with beauty as we find in the superb churches at Lavenham or Long Melford? All around stretch the rich farmlands, yellow with the ripening corn in July. There are even some splendid windmills left at Saxted Green and Cley-next-the-Sea.

You look at all these testimonies to the unchanging nature of East Anglia and – here comes the paradox – the whole structure rests on a foundation of the most recently formed and potentially the most changeable rocks in Britain. The chalk in the western section slopes steadily down to the east and has been overlaid with marine gravels and shelly sands called 'Crag' laid down just prior to the great Ice Age. When the ice melted back it also smeared the country with boulder clay

or left moraines like the Cromer ridge. Then the returning tide flooded up the low-lying river valleys. Change still continues. Geologists tell us that Britain is slowly tilting to the east as the western half of these islands slowly rises. The high tide has, on occasions, broken in over the low-lying dunes on parts of the Norfolk coast, as it did in 1953 near Stiffkey. There is no need to be alarmed, however. The sinking is taking place at what I might call 'geologists' speed'. To them, an inch in a thousand years is fast, and any rock a million years' old is recent!

The most recently formed part of East Anglia is also one of its greatest tourist attractions, the Norfolk Broads. Behind Yarmouth the low-lying country is dotted with shallow lakes connected by winding waterways. The lakes are fringed with waving reeds and the dry land emerges almost imperceptibly between the Broads. The birds of the marshlands find a home here and even the rare spoonbill has been seen on Hickling Broad in July. The coarse fishing is naturally good and I have vivid memories of days spent on Hickling Broad when I was unwise enough to let myself be persuaded by a keen fisherman to do a radio commentary on the catching of a pike. The pike, he maintained, was as sporting a fish as the salmon. What he did not explain, however, was that the best time to go fishing for pike was not July, as I had assumed, but mid-winter. We rowed up and down the Broad in a wind that came like a cutting knife across that deserted mere, direct from the North Sea which is only a few miles away from Hickling. Hour after freezing hour we stuck to it as our fisherman stood in the boat, and trailed out the live bait, with his line stretching far astern. Then suddenly the rod bent, a great swirl in the water – a strike! There followed the long struggle to hold the fish away from the safety of the reeds and, at last, the reeling-in and the big fish, with his ferocious jaws, safely brought on board. No, not a record but surely justifying the toasting afterwards in hot punch in the welcoming inn on the staithe, our happy landing place after that freezing winter day.

But for most visitors, ice and freezing wind is not the memory they take back from the Broads, but rather of gently sailing down long reed-lined channels in the drowsy heat of July or August, the

Right: A view thought to be of Dedham by Gainsborough

Opposite: The Norfolk Broads: boating on the River Thurne. In Summer the Broads are covered with boats of every kind

Below: Cutting osiers for basket-making

sound of small birds piping among the rushes, days of leisurely relaxed bliss 'away from it all'. Not completely away, I'm afraid, these days, since in high Summer the waterways are crowded with pleasure boats. There remains, however, the strange charm of sails moving through the meadows, which seem, to an onlooker beyond the reeds, as if the boats are sailing on dry land.

The Broads are indeed slowly returning to dry land and many of the waterways can only be kept open by dredging. This silting is all the more inevitable because the Broads may not be, as was once thought, produced by the sand spit near Yarmouth slowly extending across a wide bay, thus facilitating the deposit of material carried down by the rivers Bure, Yare and Waveney flowing into it. According to this theory, the deeper parts of the bay thus being filled remained as Broads. The bay has undoubtedly silted up in comparatively recent times, for there are mediaeval records of herring being caught as far inland as Norwich. But geologists have always had difficulty in explaining why so many of the Broads were by-passed by the rivers and some were only connected with them when the area was developed for tourism. A new theory now holds the stage: the Broads are the result of peat-cutting on a big scale in the Middle Ages. Whatever their origin, they remain a place of delight, and I return again to the pleasure of seeing the sails moving amongst the meadows. They take me straight to those paintings by Old Crome, who delighted in the East Anglian scene and made a masterpiece out of the wherries on the River Yare and I wonder, again, why East Anglia has produced so many of our greatest landscape painters.

Painting has always been the premier East Anglian art. In our own time, music might claim precedence with Benjamin Britten, who was born in Lowestoft and, besides his splendid compositions, left East Anglia in his debt for organising the now world-famous Aldeburgh Festival. He also paid pious tribute to East Anglian poetry by using the Rev George Crabbe's poem, 'The Borough', as the basis for the libretto of his opera, 'Peter Grimes'. Crabbe was also an Aldeburgh man, but

A pumping-mill in the marshes near Walberswick on the Suffolk coast

although his verse can have the astringent power of those East Anglian winter winds, he is hardly the man I would back against Tennyson from his Lincolnshire Wolds, Wordsworth from dramatic Cumberland or Coleridge in his soft West Country. East Anglians, I sometimes feel, are a little too practical for poetry. They can produce great statesmen, soldiers and sailors – above all, sailors, for Nelson himself was a Norfolk man, born at Burnham Thorpe. Even if East Anglia does not possess the great natural harbours of Devon and Cornwall, there were always the long estuaries of Suffolk and Essex, where the great-sailed wherries moved with ponderous dignity, carrying half the trade of the counties before the railways clipped their wings and the road hauliers finally laid them up for ever. But not before the painters had had time to immortalise them.

How remarkable was this great outburst of landscape paintings in East Anglia in the late 18th and early 19th Centuries! The Cromes, father and son, were at work in Norwich, with John Sell

Cotman giving depth and form to water-colour, but Suffolk produced the two greatest painters, Gainsborough and Constable. Gainsborough was the pioneer. He was born in the little town of Sudbury, but although he set up as a portrait painter at Ipswich, and later on at Bath and London – and became a highly successful one, too – landscape was his real love. He even introduced it into his portraits. He gave Mr and Mrs Andrews full value for money when he painted them in the grounds of their country house, but he set them against a background of harvest time in Suffolk, with the stooks of yellow corn making a lovely pattern under the tranquil summer sky. This picture was far more than a portrait commission. It was a celebration of the splendour of the East Anglian landscape at its unspoilt best.

Constable was born at East Bergholt, and it was a painting by Gainsborough owned by his rich uncle, that fired him with the determination to turn to his own countryside for his inspiration. England, and above all his own part of the Suffolk–Essex border along the River Stour, was the driving force behind his masterpieces. Unlike Turner, Constable never went abroad. His powerful personal vision was fixed on his own homeland. As he drove with a friend towards the valley of the Stour, Constable looked out of the coach window and declared with fervour, 'It was this part of the country that made me a painter.' To this day, it has stayed the 'Constable Country'. There can be few painters whose subjects have remained so unchanged. You can still visit Flatford Mill, where Constable lived as a boy, and constantly painted. You can stand on the very spot where he created the 'Leaping Horse' or the 'Hay Wain'. Dedham Church remains as he depicted it. I look at those brilliant first sketches for the 'Leaping Horse', so full of vitality and exciting rhythm, and realize that Constable, and indeed all the other landscape painters of this remarkable generation, had taken up their brushes and set up their easels at a fortunate time – perhaps the only time when their work would be appreciated and paid for by their patrons. The enclosures were almost over, the new hedges were growing, and the rich landowners were beginning to see the results of their work in a countryside that had ceased to be shaggy with forests or wide open with the out of date three-field system. The railways had not yet appeared to start their work of expanding our industrial towns. For a brief golden moment the land of England stood happily unspoilt in the warm confidence of July. The gentry wanted pictures of it and were prepared to pay. The painters were delighted to supply the need. They were, in fact, recording the first success of what historians have called the Agrarian Revolution. This went side by side with the Industrial Revolution and East Anglia was in the forefront when it came to agriculture.

I once stood with a farmer friend in front of a Constable painting. He looked at it carefully and spotted some cattle in the background. 'Poor fellow, this Constable of yours,' he said, 'he wouldn't get much for beasts like that at Norfolk cattle market next week.' Constable might have made the same comment, if he had looked at the rare images Hogarth made of cattle in 1740. For, in truth, there have now been two agricultural revolutions in our history and East Anglia is the best place to study them both.

The first one occurred in the 18th Century. The open three-field system disappeared with the enclosures, but there was no point in enclosing unless you also adopted worthwhile new techniques. North Norfolk was the scene of the experiments which led to what became known as the new Norfolk Husbandry. This area was poor land, if farmed by the old methods. Two rabbits, they say, fought here for each blade of grass. All this changed dramatically once the new system got into its stride. The secret of success lay in the use of root-crops, especially turnips. The cultivation of roots allowed sheep to be run over the light, sandy soils and so prepared them for a cereal crop, particularly barley. Clover and exotic grasses were also introduced, and, dramatically, the yield almost doubled. There were great protagonists for the new husbandry: Lord Townsend, nick-named 'Turnip' Townsend, and later on, Coke of Holkham, who entertained lavishly and achieved European fame. Perhaps we shouldn't give all the praise to Norfolk and East Anglia. The germ of the new techniques

came from Holland, with the turnip, and as far back as the late 17th Century, Colonel Walpole, Sir Robert's father, was planting turnips and marling. There were pioneers outside Norfolk as well. Jethro Tull, once a law student who took up farming for the sake of his health, invented the drill that allowed for even planting depths and regular seeding. All these people, from Tull to Townsend and Coke, had an almost missionary fervour in preaching their new agriculture gospel; and like missionaries they occasionally had to sacrifice themselves to the Cause! Robert Bakewell in Leicester won fame by his skill in selective breeding and dramatically improved cattle and sheep. Like Coke in Norfolk he also kept open house, with his sister, to visitors from all over the world. Unfortunately he was not as rich as Coke of Holkham and eventually went bankrupt – a martyr to the new husbandry. Others made fortunes by

adopting his methods. In fact, the structure of British agriculture was firmly laid for the next 200 years.

Of course there were changes, vast changes, long after Coke entertained the world in the lavish surrounding of Holkham and his grateful tenants contributed £4,000 to raise a 120-ft high column to his memory in the grounds graced by 'Capability' Brown. All through the 19th Century new techniques and machines were constantly being introduced. Take, for example, that vital moment in the agricultural year – harvesting the grain crop. Until the 18th-century agricultural revolution, the sickle was the favourite instrument for cutting the corn. It had remained unchanged in shape from those far-off days of the first Neolithic farmers. The blade may have altered from flint to iron and on to steel, but the method of using it would have been the same for Ruth in Old Testament times as for

Wordsworth's Solitary Reaper in the Highlands, singing at her work and 'o'er her sickle bending'. You can see the peasants, clutching their handfuls of stalks and cutting them with a gentle sawing movement, in those vivid sketches of country life in the Middle Ages, carefully drawn by the old monks in the famous Luttrell Psalter. An overseer with a large stick stands by, which makes me doubt some of the pictures of peasant happiness in mediaeval days drawn by certain 19th-century romantics. But although the sickle was gentle and did not lose much grain, its speed was against it. A man – or a woman (for the sickle was used by gangs of women harvesters in Scotland or the North of England) – could only cut a quarter of an acre a day with it.

The man with a scythe did better. A good worker could cut an acre a day, and he came to his own in the hay harvest or in mowing the lawns of the gentry. A good scythe man was an artist at his job. When I look back to my holidays on the farm in the 1920s I remember how I was permitted to watch him clearing the outer edge around the corn to allow the reaper and binder space to work. He was a model of how to expend long conserved energy with grace. I can still see the glitter of the wide sweep of the blade and hear the gentle swish of the falling stalks.

It was the reaper and binder that ended the glory of the scythe. The American McCormick exhibited his machines at the Great Exhibition of 1851, but was he the real inventor? Apparently a Scottish clergyman, the Rev Patrick Bell, had made a practical model in the 1820s and some specimens were exported to the United States. There, labour was difficult to obtain as the pioneers spread out to conquer the prairies. In Britain, you could still hire cheap labour until the 1870s. So the Americans got

the credit. Slowly and inevitably, however, the machines multiplied in Britain. Other inventions also came to aid the farmers and in particular the steam-driven threshers. Steam power, curiously enough, proved difficult to apply wholeheartedly to the farm. The steam engine would puff along the lanes during the winter months, and a team of workers would tackle the ricks gathered with such labour during the warmth of August and September. You could hear the smoking monster snorting over its work for miles through the still, frosty air. But steam engines could not drive the plough. They could pull ploughs backwards and forwards by cable, but you needed big acreage and big money for that sort of exercise to pay. All through the ups and downs of farming after the first industrial revolution – through the prosperous 'High Farming' of the 1850s and its savage decline in the 1880s when cheap American wheat poured in, on to the partial recovery in the 1900s and the miserable uncertainties of the 1920s and 30s, one factor stayed unchanged, one steady, faithful source of power remained the farmer's unfailing friend – the old, patient, ever willing farm-horse.

He was a source of awe and joy to me when I used to watch the grand parade at our agricultural show. What power and pride those splendid stallions exuded as they were led around the ring, with their manes and tails carefully plaited with bright ribbons and the prize rosettes fluttering on their brow-bands. It was hard to tell which breed looked most noble. There was the Cleveland Bay with a white star on his forehead; the Shire Horse, claimed to be the descendant of the Great Horse on which the armoured knights rode to battle; the powerful Percheron from northern France; the Clydesdale, with those strong sturdy white legs, their fluffed-out hair beautifully combed for the show; and the splendid Suffolk Punch, East Anglia's pride, with unfeathered legs and a glorious chestnut coat. Alas, they are nearly all gone from our farms and fields. A.E. Housman would have got a dusty answer today if he had asked his celebrated question:

'Is my team ploughing,
That I was used to drive
And hear the harness jingle
When I was man alive?'

The horse-team no longer comes up over the brow of the hill, with the white gulls following after the plough. The harness – from the horse-collars to the handsome brasses – have gone to decorate the bars of country hotels, smartened up by the brewers. The horse was the most notable victim of the second agricultural revolution, the surprising change that has crept over the face of the British countryside since the war, almost unnoticed by the average townsman.

The change was already being prepared before the last World War. The number of tractors was

steadily growing in East Anglia, although they were slower to appear on the small farms of hilly western Britain. Today the second agricultural revolution is in full swing. Fantastic new machinery has appeared to send the reapers and binders of my youth rusting in the corners of the fields or in the least used part of the farmyard. 200 years ago, Arthur Young became the first Agricultural Correspondent and a great propagandist for the new Norfolk Husbandry. How he would have rubbed his eyes with astonishment at the sight of a big modern combine harvester moving through the vast, new fields of East Anglia, driven by one man, and clearing two acres in an hour. And how he would have approved of the yield! New fertilizers have been injected into

the soil; new pesticides have destroyed weeds and insects that the old-style farmer never dreamt could be controlled. The very shape of the farm is changing before our eyes. The clucking poultry have left the care of the farmer's wife for the battery hen-houses. The new silage towers rise like minarets above the farm buildings. Hedges are being bulldozed and field-gates widened to allow the big machines to move freely across the land. As for the dairy farm – the churns and the very dairy itself have long since disappeared. The churns are in museums or have been sold as antiques. The brucellosis-free cows, each yielding 1,000 gallons per lactation, walk into milking-parlours as spotless as laboratories. They are milked by machinery, and away goes their product in big

Modern agriculture near Prickwillow on the plains of
Cambridgeshire

tankers to be dealt with by the Milk Marketing
Board. Modern science has been applied to modern
farming with spectacular results. With a tenth of
their old work force British farmers now produce
over half the food needed by this crowded country.
It is a remarkable achievement. British agriculture
can claim to be the most efficient in the world.

Critics of the new agricultural methods are not
wanting. Are we not brutally raping the inherited
fertility of our soil for immediate profit? What will
be the ultimate effect on plants and animals of many
of the chemicals we now use so confidently? If we
remove too many of our hedges, are we in danger
of creating a British dust bowl? These, and a score
of other vital questions, are constantly being
debated by the leaders of the agricultural world.
There are signs that more hedges may be spared in
the future and no further government grants will
be given for clearing them. Even the faithful old

horse is being looked at more favourably as the cost
of petrol and oil fuel soars. Enthusiastic societies
have made certain that the breeds will never die
out. Perhaps the sturdy Suffolk Punch is waiting in
the wings to come to the rescue when he is needed.

I pin my faith on the average British farmer,
whose father and his father before him, worked and
tended his land with such care for the soil. All
through the ups and downs of the industry, he has
never lost his respect for the fertility placed there by
the hard labour of his predecessors. He will keep
faith with the land. That faith is summed up by the
proud reply given by an Essex farmer, Tom Mann
of Virley Hall overlooking Salcott Creek, to that
great lover of East Anglia, James Wentworth Day.
Just before the last war Tom was offered a loan to
'modernise' his farm. He refused. 'No,' he said,
'there's too much of other people's money buried
in this heavy three-horse land. I'm here to get it out
by sweat, not by loan.'

The new methods may have reduced the sweat,
but they surely haven't altered the spirit of the
British farmer.

July with the Poets

The haze of noon wanned silver-grey
The soundless mansion of the sun:
The air made visible in his ray,
Like molten glass from furnace run,
Quivered o'er heat-baked turf and stone
And the flower of the gorse burned on –
Burned softly as gold of a child's fair hair
Along each spiky spray, and shed
Almond-like incense in the air
Whereon our senses fed.

WALTER DE LA MARE

Summer has spread a cool, green tent
    Upon the bare poles of this tree;
Where 'tis a joy to sit all day,
    And hear the small birds' melody;
To see the sheep stand bolt upright,
    Nibbling at grass almost their height.

And much I marvel now how men
    Can waste their fleeting days in greed;
That one man should desire more gold
    Than twenty men should truly need;
For is not this green tone more sweet
    Than any chamber of the great?

W. H. DAVIES

The poetry of earth is never dead;
When all the birds a faint with the hot sun,
And hide in cooling trees, a voice will run
From hedge to hedge about the new-mown mead;
That is the Grasshopper's – he takes the lead
In summer luxury, – he has never done
With his delights; for when tired out with fun
He rests at ease beneath some pleasant weed.
The poetry of earth is ceasing never:

On a lone winter evening, when the frost
Has wrought a silence, from the stove there shrills
The Cricket's song, in warmth increasing ever,
And seems to one in drowsiness half lost,
The Grasshopper's among some grassy hills.

JOHN KEATS

August

August is the lucky month, the month of sunshine when the successful corn harvest should begin and the farmer starts to see the first results of his labours. It was named by the Romans in honour of the godlike Emperor Augustus. In modern Britain we should rededicate it to the God of Holidays. For this is the time of year when most of industrial Britain plans to leave work, and the town-dwellers race, like hordes of lemmings, towards the nearest sea. But holidays have also been a feature of country life from earliest times. The Church was careful to take over a number of the old pagan holidays, for no peasant, however sturdy, could be expected to perform the back-breaking work of old-style agriculture without some hope of regular relief. Before the first threshing machines were invented, for example, threshing was one of the toughest jobs of the farming year. It was winter work. The corn was laid out on a specially smoothed area of a big barn, and the workers attacked it with flails – poles with a stick attached by a leather hinge. The broken chaff flew in the air, as Coleridge described in 'Kubla Khan':

'Huge fragments vaulted like rebounding hail,
Or chaffy grain beneath the thresher's flail.'

No wonder that threshing was one of the first agricultural operations to be mechanised. By the time threshing was over, the worker was more than ready for a day's holiday.

And until the 19th Century, a day was the accepted length of a holiday. The days were scattered throughout the calendar, and although the Puritans frowned on many of them and preached the gospel of continuous hard work, country folk clung obstinately and rightly to their precious breaks in the steady rhythm of their hard-working year. Some of the curious local holidays have survived into our own time, although their purpose and origin have long since been forgotten.

On Shrove Tuesday at Ashbourne in Derbyshire a wild football game between the Up'ards and the Down'ards monopolises the town. If there are any rules, none of the hundreds of participants bothers to observe them. At Olney, in Buckinghamshire, the women run the annual pancake race which ends at the parish church, where the winner is kissed by the ringer of the Pancake Bell. The Harvest Festivals which now universally take place at churches all over Britain are a comparatively modern innovation. The Rev Stephen Hawker, the

Dartmoor ponies living wild on the moor. They are rounded up every Autumn when many of them are sold

vicar of Morwenstow in Cornwall, felt that country folk ought to give thanks after a successful harvest for the Lord's gift of the fruits of the earth. The idea proved popular and, after all, there is no reason why new festivals should not be created if they fulfil a need. The Church had no hesitation in starting a St Valentine's Day for the exchange of lovers' vows. Poor St Valentine was an Italian bishop who was martyred on February 14th, AD 269, and would have been horrified that later generations annexed his name to give a spurious sanctity to the old licentious feast of the Roman Lupercalia which fell in mid-February. If the Church had not been broad-minded on this occasion, I'd have missed the charming traditional valentine verse noted down in the notebook of the squire in the 18th Century at Llangennith in Gower:

'Streams of pleasure, rivers of wine,
Plantations of tea and a young girl to mind.'

As the 19th Century brought an ever-increasing prosperity, the time and scale of the holiday widened too. When the railways spread through the land, they brought more remote places within the holiday orbit. The Londoner who in 1820 had thought of a trip to Margate as the height of holiday adventure found the Cornish coast within his reach by 1900. 70 years on, and the motor car has allowed the holiday-maker to move westwards in a flood. Tourist statistics put the West Country at the top of the holiday league and thus we must dedicate August to the delectable counties of Somerset, Devon and Cornwall, while admitting that if you visit them during this month you will find that a great number of people have had the same idea. No matter. The charm of the West Country survives the crowds.

This long sea-girt peninsula running far out to the west between the ever-widening English Channel to the south and the Bristol Channel to the north, to break down dramatically into the Atlantic with the Isles of Scilly, has always felt itself to be somewhat apart from the rest of England, something special in its own right. The concert party tenor, during the years between the wars in the seaside pavilions of Weston-super-Mare or Torquay, could always be relied on to bring down the house with ballads which announced that he 'belonged to Somerset, where the cider apples grow'. Or else he appeared as an old gaffer, in a smock and with rosy cheeks, to persuade us, in a surprisingly youthful voice (as far as I can remember the words):

> 'Oi be nigh on ninety-seven,
> Born an' bred in dear old Devon,
> And folks may be as old as Oi
> In other parts of England. . . .'

But, of course, they hadn't had the advantage of being born in Devon, and of being brought up on the correct West Country diet:

> 'For I thank the Lord that I was bred
> (pause for a resounding chord)
> On Devonshire cream and zider!'

Devonshire 'zider' is not so much in evidence these days – that product has now almost been monopolised in the west by Somerset. But the cream is still there, as you would expect in such an intensive dairying county; and the best cream should be clotted, with a yellow crust thick enough to hold a spoon upright. One succulent mouthful of Devonshire cream will convince you that the West Country is rich agricultural land. You must not expect to find the enormous farms of the Midlands or East Anglia with their flattened hedges and heavily mechanised corn output. The West Country, with the exception of the extensive reclaimed fens along the Brue and the Parrett in Somerset, is a land of ups and downs, of winding lanes, high hedgerows and patterned green fields – a land for dairying or skilful mixed farming. It is also a land of remarkable geological variety and, in this matter of geological variety, Somerset comes first of the three western counties.

In the north there is actually a small coalfield. In the centre lie the mysterious Mendip Hills, where the limestone is riddled with caves and swallow-holes and the spectacular Cheddar Gorge makes a deep crack in the surface of the hills guarded by cliffs 300 ft high. The Quantocks are constructed of Devonian slaty rocks and rise to over 1,000 ft. You can still walk the paths that Wordsworth and Coleridge knew, as they tramped the Quantocks in 1797, planning their poetic bombshells of the 'Lyrical Ballads' and the 'Rime of the Ancient Mariner'. The highest point in the county comes on the fine moorlands of Exmoor where Dunkery Beacon reaches 1,705 ft, with glorious views northwards over the wide Bristol Channel to the mountains of South Wales. How opinions change over the years about the attractions of the wilder parts of Britain. Back in the 17th Century old William Camden, the antiquary, took a look at Exmoor, shuddered and called it a 'damp, barren forest'. Forest, of course was the term used in the Middle Ages to describe a hunting area, usually reserved for the king. It need not ever have been covered by trees. From the summit of Dunkery Beacon the whole northern skyline across the Bristol Channel is formed by another great royal forest, the Forest Fawr, which once stretched from the Brecknock Beacons to the Carmarthenshire

Vans. This is the most splendid mountain country in South Wales, with great 'cwms' (mountain hollows), guarded by high cliffs of Old Red Sandstone, but never in history was it covered by trees. Exmoor was also a treeless wilderness and was once more extensive than it is today. But early in the 19th Century great parts of it were enclosed by John Knight, a midland ironmaster. You can still sense the atmosphere of those royal hunting days, however, if you can spot some of the red deer, which have descended unbroken from the herds that roamed here in prehistoric days. There are still over 500 of them and they stay for most of the time in the deep, wooded valleys. In Spring they come out on to the more open moorland, attracted by the fresh new grass on the higher ground. They may have to share these wild pastures with the famous sturdy Exmoor ponies, which are also, it is claimed, descendants of the primitive ponies of the eastern European type. Deer and ponies add excitement to the wide expanses of the moor, which breaks down to the sea in a magnificent plunge of cliffs.

The red deer of Exmoor

The tourist driving down the motorway, intent on reaching his caravan park in Devon or Cornwall, will not see much of these special glories of Somerset, but even he cannot fail to notice one particularly attractive feature of the Somerset countryside. Peeping up over the hedgerows come the tall towers of the village churches. And what splendid towers they are, crowned with delicately traceried parapets, with elegant pinnacles at the four corners! There are memorable towers at Blagdon, Staple Fitzpaine and Bishops Lydeard, but my own favourite – mainly, I admit, because of its intriguing name which seems to take us far back in ecclesiastical history – is Huish Episcopi, on the outskirts of Langport. They are nearly all 15th-century towers, built when the wool trade was flourishing in Somerset and rich weavers and wool merchants naturally felt it right and proper to give their surplus wealth to beautify their village church. That noble tower of Huish Episcopi reminds me of one aspect of the Church we tend to overlook. It would never have been built if the church hadn't represented something

of vital importance to the whole rural community. We may admire our great cathedrals, lament the ruins of our ancient abbeys and shake our heads over the proud prelates and bishops of the Middle Ages and the 18th Century, but the real heart of the Church – the place from which it drew its strength and the cash which it needed for its organisation – was the countryside and the country parish.

There was no single part of England and Wales, however remote, which was not eventually placed under the care of a parson and his attendant officers, from churchwarden to sexton. Of course the parson varied in character and quality all through the centuries. At one end of the scale you might get the snug cleric pictured by Colin Ellis:

'In Queen Victoria's early days
When Grandpapa was Vicar,
The Squire was worldly in his ways,
And far too fond of liquor.
My grandsire laboured to exhort
This influential sinner
And to and fro they passed the port
On Sundays after dinner.'

At the other end stood Chaucer's poor parson:

'Christës love and his Apostles twelve
He taught, but first he followed it himself.'

In between lies a whole fascinating gamut of varied types. I pictured the poet Herrick penning his love verses between sermons in his Devon vicarage, Gilbert White, the naturalist, watching the swallows skim over his lawn at Selborne, sturdy Charles Kingsley writing his novels in praise of 'muscular Christianity' – there is no end to the variety of the scene in the country parsonage. But the most important thing about the country parson was, after all, the mere fact that he was there. His church was the largest and most impressive building that the majority of his flock would see until the advent of the railway. His voice was the most educated and authoritative that they heard every Sunday. He had had the most experience of the outside world. As often as not, he was the only hope of some kind of justice against the squire or the remote, ill-understood system of the law. He may have neglected his duties, gone hunting or even drunk too much – no matter, to his churchyard all country folk had to come in the end.

These country churchyards are always moving places to me with their headstones under the ancient yew trees, but the headstones were a comparatively recent innovation. Until the 18th Century, and even later, the poor would be laid to rest with no inscription, and a law which was not repealed until 1814 ordained that they should always be wrapped in a woollen shroud, presumably to help the wool trade. The south side of the churchyard was the popular resting place, since the shadow of the church was cast to the north and all country folk knew that the Devil lurked in that shadow. Epitaphs only came into their own with the 18th Century and the earlier they are, the franker and therefore the better they are. There is a touching one from the 17th Century in the church at Baltonborough in Somerset in memory of William Martin and his wife:

> 'Would you know whom this tombe covers,
> 'Tis the nonpareil of lovers?
> It's a sweet william, sweeter far,
> Than the flowers that so stil'd are,
> And Elizabeth his wife
> Both expecting a beautifying life.'

In contrast I translated a delightfully candid one from a West Wales churchyard:

> 'Deep in this grave lies Lazy Dai,
> Waiting the Last Great Trump on high.
> If he's fond of his grave as he was of his bed,
> He'll be the Last Man Up when the Roll Call's
>   said!'

Over Lazy Dai's headstone stand the guardian yews, which are so impressive a feature of our churchyards, especially in the West Country. All sorts of reasons are given for their presence, but it seems likely that they were planted with government encouragement to safeguard the supply of wood for the great, all-conquering weapon of England and Wales in the Middle Ages, the long bow. The yew is poisonous to cattle so it was safer to plant the trees within the protection of the churchyard wall. Yews live for a remarkable span of years – from 1,000 to 2,000, say the experts – so that some of the trees we see in the West Country churchyards could have been planted at the time of

Opposite left : The ruined tower of St Michael's church on Glastonbury Tor

Opposite right : The Holy Thorn in Glastonbury Abbey grounds, believed to be a cutting from the tree that grew from the staff of Joseph of Arimathea

Below : Sunset over the Mendip Hills in Somerset

Crécy or Poitiers. The church, standing in its churchyard, is the oldest part of any village – the repository of its history, its strongest link with the past.

There was another link between the parson and his flock which might not have been greatly appreciated. They had to support him with the tithe, in theory one tenth of the annual increase in livestock. If the parish belonged to a monastery or was assigned for the revenues of a cathedral, great tithe barns were built, where the product of the tithe could be collected. Noble structures they are,

with their great wooden beams and oak pillars. We admire them now, but to many parishes they represented an unfair tax levied on the hard-working farmer. In his opera 'King Arthur', Henry Purcell set the words of John Dryden to a rollicking tune that summed up the anti-tithe feeling:

'We've cheated the parson, we'll cheat him again,
For why should the blockhead have one in ten?'

The tithe position became even more difficult with the spread of Dissent, and the church authorities were glad to change and eventually abandon it. They heaved a sigh of relief when the Tithe Commutation Act of 1936 put the whole business on a commonsense money basis. Those tall church towers of Somerset and the churches they adorn have now to be supported in another way and in a harsher financial climate.

There is one church tower in Somerset which seems to rise clear of all mundane considerations and to belong to another, more mysterious world. It crowns the 520-ft high Glastonbury Tor which lifts dramatically from the fens of the River Brue in the romantically named Isle of Avalon. The church of St Michael was long ago destroyed by a landslip and the tower stands in lonely splendour in the centre of a countryside drenched in legend. Near at hand is Weary-all Hill where, so legend maintains, St Joseph of Arimathea came in AD 60 to bring Christianity to Britain. He stuck his pilgrim staff into the ground, and miraculously it burst into flower. The cuttings from the original staff still flourish. The one in the grounds of the ruined but still majestic Glastonbury Abbey has become famed as the Holy Thorn (*Cretaegus monogyna praecox*) which always flowers around Christmas-tide. The Thorn has acquired a powerful and unshakeable hold on popular imagination. In the 18th Century Bristol traders did a flourishing trade in it as good luck tokens for sailors, and Sir Charles Sedley, the rakish Restoration poet, used it to pay a charming compliment to his ageing but still beautiful mistress, who

'Blooms in the winter of her days
Like Glastonbury Thorn.'

In vain carping critics cast doubt on the whole story and even suggest that the Chalice Well, at the foot of the Tor, may not be the place where the Holy Grail was hidden. The very spirit of the place – to many people who come here as if on a pilgrimage – seems to support the legends.

The Tor, they suggest, possesses some interior mystical power. They look at the Ordnance Survey maps and the aerial surveys, and out of the pattern of the hedges, roads and river lines trace the signs of the Zodiac, spread in a 10-mile radius around this magical mount. Furthermore, they claim that similar Zodiacs on an equally gigantic scale can be traced as far apart as Kingston-on-Thames, Nuthampstead in Hertfordshire and Pumpsaint in North Wales. The Zodiac enthusiasts took their inspiration originally from a volume published in the 1920s by a Hertfordshire man Alfred Watkins. In 'The Old Straight Track' he maintains that it is possible to plot straight lines across the map aligning sites of ancient importance. These sites might be marked by a church which had replaced some pagan shrine or by clumps of trees, a notch in the hills, a mark stone, and, of course, the remains of the sites themselves like cromlechs or barrows. The industrious searcher, claimed Watkins, could track these 'leys' for miles across the landscape. Who established the leys and for what purpose? Ah, there lay the mystery! The men of old, these sages of pre-history, possessed knowledge and skills we never guessed at, say Watkins's later disciples, and they have proceeded to criss-cross the whole of the British Isles with ley lines, all reported and analysed in their magazine, 'The Ley Hunter'. The professional archaeologists may tear their hair in fury and classify the whole business as utterly unscientific. No matter; the ley hunters go happily on, for the landscape of Britain is a fascinating palimpsest, in which the marks made by the earliest inhabitants show vague and blurred beneath the impress of hundreds of subsequent generations. Who can be absolutely certain of the meaning of those most ancient remains of our distant past? The ley protagonists claim that a ley runs directly westwards from Glastonbury, passing – among other places – through Brentor on Dartmoor, on to the strange holed stone of Men-an-Tol near Morvah in Cornwall, to end at St Michael's Mount. We take the easier and less controversial way westward by sweeping down the motorway out of Somerset into Devon.

Devon is a large county and looks both north and south, with one foot, as it were, in the Bristol Channel and another in the English Channel. Mentally, I have always divided it, like Gaul, into three parts: the coastline, Dartmoor, and what I call deep Devon, the country that lies apart from the tourist-crammed roads, and cultivates the rich earth that seems to delight in lying at all sorts of angles. The coastlines first, for there are two of them. The northern coast of Devonshire is one of the most splendid and least publicised in Britain. There are wide, sandy beaches but its glory lies in the tremendous cliffs formed from the Carboniferous shales and sandstones, intensely crushed and folded. The sea has cut into the softer rocks and left isolated stacks. The rocks are dark but the cliffs are bright with flowers and rich vegetation. I pick Hartland point as the climax of the cliff splendour, and the plunging rocks are alive with coastal waterfalls like Wargery Water, a few hundred yards south of Hartland Quay. For good measure you have England's most picturesque coast village not so far away – Clovelly, where the charming houses seem to cascade over the cliff. The narrow cobbled main street drops nearly 300 ft in steps down to the inn by the little harbour. No cars, naturally, but plenty of tourists, especially in August.

The same can be said of Devon's south coast. Much of it has paid the penalty of popularity in a plethora of caravan sites, car parks, hotels and boarding houses, but so much remains. There are great cliffs carved out of the ancient Precambrian rock at Bolt Head, but to me the charm of South Devon lies in the numerous estuaries that wind far inland amongst the fertile farms, in the famous brick-red earth. These are valleys, drowned when the land gradually sank or the sea-level rose at the end of the Ice Age, and the high tide turns them into still lakes that mirror the deep woods around them. They are great places for the yachtsman and

it's no wonder that dynamic 'Jackie' Fisher fixed on Dartmouth for the great new college he built when he was ruthlessly driving through his reconstruction of the Royal Navy before the First World War. For all these waterways, especially the vast estuaries around Plymouth on the very western edge of the county, are rich in memories of the old Elizabethan 'sea dogs'. Drake himself bought Buckland Abbey, some miles inland near the valley of Tavy, with the loot he gathered during his famous voyage around the world.

South Devon claims to have the mildest climate in Britain especially in the area they call the South Hams that lies behind the coastline from Dartmouth to Plymouth. 'Ham' in Old English means an enclosed and sheltered place, and the valleys of the Hams are certainly snugly tucked away and sheltered from the Atlantic winds. Sub-tropical plants grow easily here and John Leland thought it was the most fruitful part of all Devonshire.

The rock here, apart from the hard ancient Precambrian of Bolt Head and Prawle Point, is Devonian, part of the system that lies between the Carboniferous and the Silurian beds. The great pioneer geologists, Sedgwick and Murchison, worked in South Devon in the limestones which crop out at various points between Plymouth and

Ladram Bay near Sidmouth with Great Picket Rock, a typical example of the isolated rock columns off the South Devon coast

Above: Cheddar Gorge in the Mendip Hills, which has spectacular caves under its limestone cliffs with some very beautiful formations of stalactites and stalagmites

Below: The upper reaches of the River Dart below Hockington Tor on Dartmoor

Torquay and gave them the name Devonian in 1839. Curiously enough, however, the vivid red rock that the public usually associates with Devonshire does not belong to the actual Devonian system but to the more recent New Red Sandstone of the Permian. When the early holiday-makers saw it splendidly exposed on the cliffs at places like Sidmouth, and admired the lush pattern of red fields it created along the valley of the Exe, they naturally supposed the New Red to be the characteristic hall-mark of Devon. Gerard Manley Hopkins, walking down to the farming country from a holiday tour of Dartmoor saw, with a poet's eye, the 'soft maroon or rosy-cocoa-dust-coloured handkerchiefs of ploughed fields'. But we can follow these maroon-coloured fields up along the Exe valley into that deep country of dairy farms, stock-breeding and sunken lanes that lies between the wilds of Exmoor and Dartmoor and forms the heart of Devonshire.

In the northern section the botanist can rejoice in the tall, unusual Pyrenean lily which has escaped from the gardens to grow wild in the woods, and the trout streams come pleasantly down from the moors. They may not have the charm of some of the other more famous Devonshire rivers like the Dart or the Teign, but the Taw and the Torridge, flowing north to the Bristol Channel, have their devoted fans among fishermen, and it was a Devon stream, after all, which harboured the most famous of the animals in modern fiction – Henry Williamson's Tarka the Otter. The otter is probably the most attractive of all our native wild animals. The badger runs him close but the poor badger has recently become suspect to the Men from the Ministry as a possible carrier of disease to farm animals and, in certain areas of the West Country, they have set about exterminating him, or at least drastically reducing his numbers. Frankly, I do not wish them success. I get a thrill out of sometimes seeing one caught in my car headlights as he goes lolloping along the side of the road, like an old English sheep-dog with a white band down the middle of his head. 'Brock' still flourishes outside this prohibited zone of the west. Authority has dealt more kindly with Tarka, and he has now

The South Devon coast at Sidmouth, where there are some particularly fine cliff walks

become a protected species. There has been an alarming drop in his numbers, not just due to otter-hunting but to river pollution and the disturbance of his habitat. I have only once seen an otter swimming in a West Country river and count myself very lucky to have done so. All I saw was the tip of his nose and the wake left by his head as he disappeared into the fast-running stream. A friend of mine was more fortunate. He was driving along the road through the tall waving reeds of the Penrice marshes near Oxwich in the Gower peninsula. He stopped to enjoy the quiet of the evening when, to his delight, he saw two otters, one large and the other smaller, slip quickly across the road. He had hardly time to take a breath when two more appeared and shot across the road into the reeds. Then, to his delight, another pair crossed in front of him. Other pairs followed and he had counted 24 otters before the noise of a distant car

ended the procession. He was about to rush back to his car to record a most conclusive proof of the survival of the otter in Gower, when he noticed that a drain ran under the road, sloping down to the further marsh. The water poured through it, making a delightfully slippery slide. He had been watching, not 24 otters, but just one mother otter happily playing sliding games with her offspring – down through the drain and then back across the road for another slide!

The playful otter has now been offered a better chance of survival. The Devon otter hounds now hunt the mink – a useful job, for these small but powerful predators have become a nuisance. They were first reported on the River Teign, where they had escaped from a fur farm. They have since spread into other English and Welsh rivers, as has that other undesirable fur-farm escapee, the South American coypu. Coypus have become a serious pest in the Norfolk Broads. Other deliberate introductions to Britain have been more accept-able. Several types of small deer have escaped from gentlemen's parks, especially from Woburn where

A badger searching for insects and slugs under a beech hedge

the Duke of Bedford was keenly interested in exotic animals in the 1890s. From Woburn came the charming little Chinese water deer and the muntjak or barking deer with his humped back. They have both spread through the woods of southern England. The most extraordinary newcomers to Britain's fauna, however, are the Tasmanian wallabies which established themselves in the Peak District above Leek, after 1939. There are other colonies in Ashdown Forest and in Sussex. The Peak wallabies may have suffered severely in the great freeze-up of 1979, but one little foreigner safely slept through this cruel winter – the edible dormouse. Our native dormice seem to have become rarer and maybe Lord Rothschild thought of improving the native breed when he imported these European delicacies, but they are still confined to a small district around Tring and Aylesbury. The Romans used to eat them with relish after they had been specially fattened on walnuts; but then, the Roman gourmets ate some very peculiar things indeed. I certainly would not have the heart to eat these rather endearing and harmless small balls of fur. I hope they list them for protection. And I also rejoice that our native otter is now safe. May his numbers increase, especially in those rivers that flow down through woods and over tumbled rocks from Devon's great central fastness of Dartmoor.

Sooner or later, everyone who comes to

Devonshire turns to Dartmoor, for no piece of the wilder part of the English countryside has received such continuous publicity. Long before I saw it I felt that I knew its innermost spirit, for Sir Arthur Conan Doyle had sent my boyhood detective hero, Sherlock Holmes, to it, together with his stolid friend Dr Watson, to solve the blood-curdling mystery of the dreaded 'Hound of the Baskervilles'. Conan Doyle made certain that all Dartmoor's scenic stock-in-trade was liberally scattered through his pages – the strange shapes of the granite tors that outcrop all over the moorland, the sudden mists that swirl around them, the grim Princetown Prison with its convicts on the southern outskirts, the stone huts of the earliest Bronze Age inhabitants – and, to crown it all, the villain came to a satisfactorily sticky end by being sucked down in one of the numerous impassable morasses that Conan Doyle convinced me were scattered over Dartmoor. He regarded it as the 'last unconquered wilderness in southern Britain', and in spite of the encroachments of Army firing ranges, forestry, new reservoirs and the deluge of tourism, the heart of the moor remains inviolate to this day. Geologically, Dartmoor is a great boss of igneous rocks that welled up from below after the Carboniferous rocks were formed. These have now been worn away and the granite has been left to the mercy of the weather. This coarse-grained crystalline rock wears into strange shapes like Bowerman's Nose behind Manaton, where John Galsworthy used to live. There are about 170 rock outcrops in all, though not all the tors are equally impressive. The highest is Vixen Tor where the rocks rise to 93 ft on the northern side, and the largest area is covered by Sheep's Tor. Only two main roads cross the moor proper so to see the best of it you must walk, properly shod and carrying a compass with you, for the wilder parts of the moor are no place for the casual, inexperienced hiker. The annual Ten Tors circuit, which takes place every Whitsun, is a stern test of map-reading and endurance, and it is well to remember that at High Willhays and Yes Tor, the moor is over 2,000 ft. But the walker's reward comes when he reaches the remarkable Bronze Age hutments and enclosure of Grimspound, or follows the strange stone avenue over the moor at Kes Tor, or crosses the ancient clapper bridge at Teign Head, made out of single slabs of granite and used by the mediaeval pack-horses. And he may be lucky enough to be there for the annual Wild West excitement of the round-up of the Dartmoor ponies.

Dartmoor gives rise to a whole host of southward-flowing streams, all with rocky and splendidly wooded valleys, but strangely enough, the most famous of all West Country streams, the Tamar, is not among them. It marks the boundary between Devon and Cornwall, and takes a most extraordinary course for it rises not so many miles behind Hartland Point in the north, very near the source of the River Torridge. The Torridge makes a wide, sickle-like sweep and falls into the Bristol Channel, but the Tamar flows sternly south, right across the peninsula, to enter the sea through the maze of beautifully wooded estuaries that lies behind Plymouth. Brunel's great railway bridge, and now the modern road bridge, leap over it at Saltash, but the Tamar is still, emotionally, a genuine boundary – a deep moat separating Cornwall from the rest of England, as it has done all through history.

True, Cornwall became firmly linked politically to the Anglo-Saxon when the little Celtic prince-doms were finally conquered by King Athelstan in AD 930, but the Cornish have never felt themselves to be completely absorbed into the English scene, even when the county became in 1337 a part of the Prince of Wales's inheritance of the Duchy of Cornwall. For a long time most of the inhabitants spoke the old Celtic language, and the celebrated Dolly Pentreath, claimed to be the last native speaker of Cornish, died as recently as 1745. Today the members of the Gorsedd of Bards of 'Cernew' lead a group who hope to revive the old Cornish tongue. The place-names of many of the towns and villages bear witness to their unmistakeable Celtic origin – Poldhu, Landewednack, Trewellard, Perranporth, Mevagissey. But there is now a plentiful sprinkle of names with an undoubted Anglo-Saxon tinge set among the Celtic ones, so perhaps we ought to regard the modern

The otter, one of Britain's endangered species but now on the protected list

Cornishman as taking his character from both sides of the Tamar. Celtic, English, or a racial mix-up? No matter; the Cornishman is independent and takes his own view of the world.

He has to, for he could easily be overwhelmed by the world once the August rush to the sea gathers full momentum. The coast is Cornwall's fortune and it is hardly necessary to list its attractions – they are far too well known. The cliffs are magnificent and so are the coves in between them. There are fishing villages galore, fierce headlands, sandy beaches alive with thundering surf. The North Cornish coast, which takes the full force of the Atlantic wind, is the rougher with the finest cliff scenery. The south shore, facing the wide English Channel, has its cliffs as well, but the climate is softer and lends an almost Mediterranean charm to the long, sea-drowned valleys that wind inland from Falmouth, Helford and Fowey. The whole world seems to come to the Cornish coast, but if you want to understand Cornwall fully in all its moods and to appreciate how it has been moulded by its strange, complex history, you have to move inland away from that seductive coastline.

Left: A ruined stone engine-house and chimney stack of a tin-mine on the Cornish coast

Opposite: Pordenack Point on Land's End with the Longships lighthouse in the distance

Below: The Cheese Ring stone on Bodmin Moor

Inland Cornwall has never had much praise lavished on it. Guide books tend to dismiss it as 'uninteresting' or bestow on it those most depreciatory words in the guide-book writers' vocabulary: 'There is little here to attract the tourist.' But that formidably omniscient polymath, Professor Nikolas Pevsner, pronounced that 'Cornwall possesses little of the highest aesthetic quality though much that is lovable and much that is moving'. As usual, he was right. The highest point of Cornwall, Brown Willy on Bodmin Moor, although composed of the same dark, volcanic granite, does not possess the grandeur and sweep of Dartmoor. Around its edges lies the extraordinary landscape of vast, glittering, white pyramids cast up from the china clay pits. China clay, or kaolin, is formed by a rare process of decay in granite and the Cornish pyramids are the result of a full century's digging, which has made the streams around St Austell flow milk-white to the sea. But the real hallmark of inland Cornwall, the sight you hardly ever escape from throughout the county, is the abandoned tin-mine, with its tall chimney and ruined engine-house, gaunt against the skyline. The ruins may not be 'lovable' but they certainly meet Professor Pevsner's classification as 'moving',

for they represent a long, ancient and honourable tradition of winning wealth from the hard rocks, that goes back into the mists of history.

The Phoenicians came to Cornwall to barter for their tin and these astute traders set up their market for dealing with the natives on the safety of the islet of Ictis, which is, undoubtedly, the modern St Michael's Mount, near Penzance. The Romans exploited the tin-mines, and all through the Middle Ages and beyond the Cornish tin-mines flourished, strictly controlled by the Stannary Courts. The great modern period of tin-mining began when the Industrial Revolution gave new power to the old mining technique. It was then that the stone-built engine-houses sprouted all over the Cornish landscape. The Cornish tin-miner, with his ingenious beam-engine, was the innovator in the mining business, and 'Cousin Jacks', as the Cornish miners were nick-named, travelled the world. But in the 1880s the glory had begun to fade. Cheaper sources of tin had been found elsewhere in Malaya and sadly the miners left their hard-won galleries underground, their pit-shafts filled with water and their engine-houses turned into picturesque ruins – the 'slighted' forgotten castle towers of industry. Perhaps the soaring price of world tin might revive interest in these once-profitable eldorados.

But the tin-miner has left his indelible mark, not only upon the scenery, but upon the social life of the county. When John Wesley made his memorable missionary journeys through the land in the torpid mid-18th Century, the Cornish tin-miners were among the most eager converts. You can see the remarkable Gwennap Pit, a deep hollow formed by a collapsed mine, in which Wesley took refuge from a gale in 1702 and preached to his rapt congregation safe from the wild winds. It was remodelled as a green amphitheatre in 1806, and commemorative services are still held there. In Somerset I looked at the splendid church towers and remembered how the country parson had, over the long centuries, made himself one of the essential elements of village life. In Cornwall, I pass the humbler later-built chapels and remember that they, too, have played a vital part in the way country folk have lived.

Yet Cornwall can show far, far older buildings than churches or chapels, inspired by the presence of the vital metal, tin, in the dark rocks. All through the country you come across the dolmens, tombs and standing stones left by the old megalithic builders who, perhaps 4,000 years ago, followed the lure of the metal from peninsula to peninsula along the coast of western Europe until they came at last to this rocky peninsula jutting out into the waste Atlantic sea. Cornwall is one of the richest counties in Britain in megalithic remains. I think of those strange stones called the Hurlers near St Cleer, and the magnificent neolithic tomb of the Trethery Quoit. And strangest of all, the Men-an-Tol – the stone with a hole in it. Anxious mothers, until recent times, passed their children through the hole to cure them of rickets.

So ancient beliefs still lived on here in the far west, even when overlain by centuries of Christianity and then by the scepticism of the Age of Reason. We are right to be distrustful, however, about some other popular legends that the tourists delight in when they come to Cornwall. Tintagel is a magnificent site with the scanty remains of a noble castle boldly perched on a narrow ledge above the ever-restless sea. 'Black cliffs and caves and storm and wind,' noted Tennyson with splendid brevity, when he came here in search of local colour for his Arthurian epic, 'The Idylls of the King'. But I'm afraid that all the romantic tales about Tintagel as the birthplace of Arthur – and how he was washed ashore on the ninth wave into the hands of Merlin the Magician – and the rest of the stories, came originally from the fertile imagination of the Welshman, Geoffrey of Monmouth, later embroidered by the writers of the French Arthurian romances and given a final polish by Sir Thomas Malory.

And what of the land of Lyonesse, where King Arthur fought his last fatal battle:

'A land of old upheaven from the abyss
By fire to sink into the abyss again:
Where fragments of forgotten people dwelt . . .'?

Could this be in the area of the sea beyond Land's End, and are the Isles of Scilly the last broken granite fragments of the lost land of Lyonesse? Again, the experts shake their heads. The Silonian granite is undoubtedly closely related to the granite of Devon and Cornwall but it welled up from below millions of years ago, far out of the range of human memory. Yet the Isles of Scilly make a splendid finale to the western peninsula of Britain. They are a strange, romantic, enchanting scatter of islets, where the daffodils grow early in the tiny fields and which break down at last into the deadly rings of the Western Rocks, on which a whole British fleet under Sir Cloudesley Shovel came disastrously to shipwreck in 1707. Recently, in a comparatively still August sea, I sailed carefully amongst them, these rocks with strange evocative Celtic names – Hellweathers, Crebinnicks, Crim, Gorregan, Malledgan, Crebawethan, Inisvrank, Minmanueth. At last, we saw the tall stone tower of the Bishops lighthouse rise boldly out of the sea, crowned by the new helicopter platform as if by a top hat.

I was 300 miles from central London. Westward there was no further land, no single speck of rock, until the equally savage coast of Newfoundland far away on the other side of the sundering wastes of the Atlantic ocean.

August with the Poets

When Westwall Downs I gan to tread
Where cleanly winds the green did sweep,
Methought a landskip there was spread,
Here a bush and there a sheep:
    The pleated wrinkles of the face
    Of wave-swollen earth lend such grace,
    As shadowings in imag'ry
    Which both deceive and please the eye. . .

Here and there two hilly crests
Amid them hug a pleasant green,
And these are like two swelling breasts
That close a tender fall between.
    Here would I sleep, or read, or pray
    From early morn to flight of day.
    But, hark! a sheep-bell calls me up,
    Like Oxford college bells, to sup.
                  WILLIAM STRODE

Too quick despairer, wherefore wilt thou go?
  Soon will the high Midsummer pomps come on,
  Soon will the musk carnations break and swell,
    Soon shall we have gold-dusted snapdragon,
    Sweet-William with its homely cottage-smell,
      And stocks in fragrant blow;
  Roses that down the alleys shine afar,
    And open, jasmine-muffled lattices,
    And groups under the dreaming garden-trees,
  And the full moon, and the white evening star.
                  MATTHEW ARNOLD

August for the people and their favourite islands.
Daily the steamers sidle up to meet
The effusive welcome of the pier, and soon
The luxuriant life of the steep stone valleys,
The shallow oval faces of the city
Begot in passion or good natured habit,
Are caught by waiting coaches, or laid bare
Beside the undiscriminating sea.

Lulled by the light they live their dream of freedom;
May climb the old road twisting to the moors,
Play leapfrog, enter cafés, wear
The tigerish blazer and the dove-like shoe.
The yachts upon the little lake are theirs,
The gulls ask for them, and to them the band
Makes its tremendous statements; they control
The complicated apparatus of amusement.
                  W. H. AUDEN

September

September is the harvest month, the farmer's time of fulfilment, when ripeness is all. Our name for this most mellow of months is neither accurate nor descriptive. As usual we borrowed it from the Romans. They used it to mark the seventh month of their calendar, whereas it is the ninth month of ours. The Welsh did better when they called September 'Mis Medi' – the reaping month. To the Anglo-Saxons it was 'gerst-monath' – barley month. No matter what you call it, September in Britain is the most pleasant of months, if our capricious British climate allows it. For when we speak of September as the harvest month we have to put in a qualification. A fine Summer in southern Britain may see everything 'safely gathered in' by the end of August. A damp Summer means that southern England may have to join the north, Wales and Scotland in a September harvest. But no matter when the harvest occurs, September seems to me a month of purring satisfaction. The farmer doesn't sit back, however, and beam smugly over the land. He has to get ready for the October ploughing, or for burning off the stubble of the short-stalked wheat.

In the past, before the days of the combine-harvester, the artificial drier, the tractor and all the mechanical aids to farming, the successful completion of the harvest was the occasion of ripe, rural rejoicing. The last load was brought in with appropriate ceremony, and until comparatively recent times the last sheaf was made into a corn dolly. There are plenty of countrymen who remember the art – for art it is – of weaving these fascinating figures out of straw and each part of the country had its own design. In the south-west they called it the Neck; in Staffordshire and Hereford it was the Mare; in Wales the Hag; and up in the north and Scotland they talked about Harvest Queens and Kirn Maidens. It was secretly unlucky to scythe down the last sheaf; the reapers threw their sickles at it, and then carefully plaited the stalks, complete with the fully ripened ears of corn, into elaborately beautiful patterns. In some places they believed that the Devil took refuge in the last stalks of corn. Some archaeologists trace the patterns as far back as the female fertility goddess of the Near East in the early days of neolithic farming 7,000 or 8,000 years ago. She had to be placated by human sacrifice, and indeed many of the corn dollies have a suggestion of the female form. When the first neolithic farmers came to Britain around 3000 BC they must have brought this custom with them, and so the simple and charming corn dolly,

A doe in a wood of fir trees

like so many other British rural customs, links us unexpectedly with our remote past. Today corn dollies have achieved a new popularity as decorations. You see them in country pubs reconstructed in Brewer's Rustic style. They are sold in country craft shops where many of them are made from artificial straw! They are part of the classes in Women's Institutes. The corn dolly, in fact, has left the cornfields to become part of our housefurniture. And very handsome it looks there!

The corn dolly is a symbol of September and I have to decide to which part of Britain I should award it. Where does September best bring out the full character of the landscape? The plain truth is that all parts of Britain look their best in this kindly, most human month. But I will pick two parts of these islands where I have made September journeys in recent years – places where I saw the harvest finally gathered in, where the fields were still bathed in warm sunshine, and where as the month ended I felt the first hint of the changing colours of autumn, bringing what the 18th-century

Making corn dollies. It is supposed to be lucky to hang up the dollies made with ripe corn with the sap still in the stem

poets would describe as 'a pleasing melancholy' to the scene.

So it was on my first September journey, made a few years ago, through the rich Vale of York and the adjacent Vale of Pickering which lies sandwiched between the East Yorkshire Moors and the Yorkshire Wolds. I had gone to look at the harvest for this is the most northerly extensive part of England where wheat is a main crop. The mean annual temperature reaches 60°F (15.6°C). The great river of this fertile plain is the Yorkshire Ouse which has probably enlarged itself by river-capture on a big scale. It has cut back from the Humber estuary to trap all the streams flowing eastwards from the Pennines. The River Derwent, which formed the Vale of Pickering, has an even more extraordinary history. It originally flowed eastwards into the North Sea near Filey, but the great glaciers that filled the North Sea in the Ice Ages

dammed the waters back to form a huge lake which eventually overflowed westward to cut through the Hambledon Hills at the Kirkham Gorge and discharged its waters into the Ouse. This is the most extensive glacial river diversion in England.

But as I travelled I kept noticing the structure of the cottages and how different they were architecturally from those in the south. They might have walls of red brick in the heart of the Vale of York, or of pleasant grey stone when you came through the Hambledon Hills or went on up into the edge of the East Yorkshire Moors, but thatch was distinctly uncommon and there was no sign of the timber-framed cottage you get along the Welsh border or the tile-hung cottages of Sussex and Surrey. For until the mid-Victorian period – when the invention of the Hoffman Kiln in 1858 made mass-production of bricks profitable and railways were at hand to distribute them to all parts of the country – cottages had perforce to be built from local materials, which therefore dictated local styles. Britain can thus show a vast range of cottage styles. In the west, in the areas which were once well-wooded, you can still see cottages with cruck-construction, that is, built of two curving tree trunks fixed at the top to make a gable, and with bays in between. In parts of the south, in Dorset, Devon and Wiltshire, you could have cottages built of cob – unbaked earth, with a mixture of mud, straw and small stones, topped by a thatched roof shaped in scallops to allow room for the upper windows. The further north or west you go, the more stone appears – rough stone walls roofed with slate when available. The most primitive form of all survived in the Hebrides in the 'black houses', with no windows or chimney but with just a square of rough walls roofed with heather thatch which was weighted down against the wind with great stones.

Throughout their early history, country cottages were usually pretty primitive affairs. In the 18th Century progressive landlords sought to improve them, and occasionally a great landowner might remove a whole village and rebuild it on a new site – usually to improve the view from his newly built Great House. The classic example is Milton Abbas in Dorset, where Lord Dorchester created a backdrop of charming thatched-roofed small houses, each with its trim lawn before it and all of them a vast, if high-handed, improvement on the hovels they replaced. Lord Dorchester's super-cottages were exceptional. The average cottage was nothing like so pleasant a place to live in. Those pretty Victorian water-colours of thatched cottages with roses round the door may have given a false impression of the realities of rural life. When I was a small boy I remember my uncle showing me with pride a picture he had just bought: 'a genuine Birket Foster'. Birket Foster was a much admired late-Victorian artist whose elaborately worked water-colours are now coming back into fashion. This example of his work showed a dear old lady sewing in her garden, with a beautifully kept thatched cottage behind her and, around her, apple trees laden with fruit. The sun poured down through the orchard boughs and I thought it was the most beautiful picture I had ever seen. A modern economic historian would soon have damped my enthusiasm with a series of stern questions.

How was that dear old lady's cottage lit? By candlelight, probably, for she didn't have an old-age pension and couldn't afford oil. Did she have fresh water from the tap? No, her daughter had to bring it to her from the village well which was of doubtful purity, carrying the buckets slung from a heavy wooden yoke around her neck (another delightful subject, however, for a new Birket Foster). Did the cottage have an indoor lavatory? No, again. The 'ty bach' or 'little house', as it is tactfully called in Wales, wasn't in Birket Foster's picture. It was tucked away at the bottom of the garden (a long walk on a drenching wet evening) under an old apple tree which had the disconcerting habit of dropping over-ripe fruit suddenly on the roof. No wonder country labourers hopped quickly into the new cottages built by rural councils as soon as they had the chance. In their place have come the weekenders and the commuters, when the stretch of country is within driving distance of a station with fast rail services to the city. Country life is changing before our eyes. Will Ambridge be Ambridge in 20 years' time?

Yet, as it disappears from living memory, I cannot help feeling that the life lived in those old country cottages was not all misery under leaking thatched roofs. I remember the rosy-cheeked old men I met in my childhood, who seemed to have a quiet contentment in everything they did, and the old ladies who could tell me stories of the days when they may have had to curtsey to the squire when they met him but they also had freedom to run, play, or collect the blackberries in September in car-free lanes. And that Birket Foster cottage garden must always have been a very special place. It started, of course, for purely practical reasons. The Enclosure Acts sometimes provided for small plots of land to be offered in compensation for the loss of commoners' rights, and a farmer always needed to supplement his wages with all the food he could grow for himself. To begin with he stocked his garden not with the roses, pinks, sweet williams and hollyhocks of the Victorian painters, but with cabbages, beans, turnips, leeks and, later on, with potatoes. This American import had a great and eventually disastrous success in Ireland, but the English labourer was suspicious of it at first and only welcomed it into his garden in mid-Victorian days. What flowers there were drifted in from the wilds or were of practical value. One of the most beautiful of cottage-garden flowers is the Madonna Lily (*Lilium candidum*); one old writer gives a perfect description of it as 'an herbe with a white flower; and though the leaves of the flower be white, yet within shineth the likeness of gold'. This beauty was only there, however, because it was 'an herbe'. You could make a soothing, healing ointment out of the bulb. Yet, unintentionally perhaps, the cottage garden became a refuge for many plants that were becoming rarer as agriculture became more scientific and intensive, and the labourer's wife had always appreciated them for the pure pleasure they gave.

It was the new cottagers, the middle-class refugees from the spreading towns, who really created the modern 'cottage garden'. Their prophetess was that remarkable old lady, Gertrude Jekyll, who died in 1935 at the ripe old age of 92. She was a passionate advocate of naturally massed

Left: A summer cricket match at Hambledon, where the game developed into its modern form in the 18th Century

Opposite: The New Forest, which was made into a royal hunting forest in the 11th Century by William the Conqueror from his court at Winchester

grouping of flowers and of the planting of older types that had gone out of fashion in the formal gardens around the great Victorian houses. She was ably abetted by William Robinson, who was in charge of the Royal Botanical Society's herbaceous collection. Together they transformed the appearance of the English garden. At Sissinghurst Castle in Kent you can see the result of this new approach to garden-making which was inspired by the humble cottage garden. Here the writer Victoria Sackville-West and her husband Sir Harold Nicholson created one of the finest gardens in England. There is an Elizabethan-style section, but the great glory of Sissinghurst is the heaped profusion of the plants; or, as Victoria Sackville-West herself explained, 'a kind of haphazard luxuriance, which of course comes neither by hap nor hazard at all.' As I walked through the enclosures, or 'separate rooms' into which the

garden is divided, each one planted with a different theme, I thought of the debt the countryside of Britain owes to the enterprise of individuals. Our island is packed with curious delights that you may discover by luck as you wander through it, but few of these pleasures have been created by order of the state, fewer still by a vote of a rural district council.

Sometimes these individuals have been, shall we say, slightly eccentric like the rich landowners who decorated their parks with 'follies'. There was a great vogue for these at the turn of the 18th Century under the influence of the Romantic Movement. Grottos, Chinese temples, Druidic groves, hermits' cells popped up all over the place. I remember with affection the grotto at Hanbury Park near Pontypool, which had a roof shaped like a giant sea-shell and was supported inside by the trunks of living trees, and Paxton's Tower overlooking the valley of the Towy and Dyer's

The Folly at Hadlow, one of the extravagances built by 18th-and 19th-century noblemen to improve the view from their country seats

Grongar Hill, put up in honour of Nelson. Paxton's Tower was easily beaten by the soaring Keppel's Pillar at Wentworth Woodhouse in Yorkshire, which commemorates the victory of the British Fleet of Ushant. Nearby is the Needle's Eye, a tall stone pyramid pierced by a narrow arch. The Marquis of Rockingham built it, so they say, as a challenge to a famous whip who boasted that he could drive a coach and horses through a needle. All follies seem to have stories about them and one of the princes of the folly business was 'Mad Jack' Fuller of Brightling in Suffolk. He had a whole collection of them on his estate, from a Needle's Eye to a Rotunda and an Observatory, but his finest folly was the Sugar Loaf at Dallington. He had boasted at a dinner party that he could see the top of the church spire from his dining-room window and his guest had proved him wrong. He had the top of the spire reproduced on the skyline at Wood's Corner and won his bet at the next dinner party. 'No-one,' he boasted, 'could tell one from t'other.' Hermit cells were also popular. At Tong in Shropshire George Durant, who had also constructed such delights as a gazebo called the Pulpit and an Egyptian Aviary, succeeded in getting a retired gentleman to live happily in his hermit's cave. Other would-be owners of hermits were not so lucky and successful applicants for the job (the advertisement usually specified that good food would be sent down daily from the Big House) seem to have had a nasty propensity for taking to liquor. It was probably safer to erect a Druids' Circle. The one at Stout Hall in Gower is still there as a perpetual puzzle to the innocent visitor interested in archaeology. I confess I feel a bond of sympathy with the folly builders. After all they were only doing what we all long to do if only we had their money – giving their wildest dreams reality.

I feel the same about those other enthusiasts who are now re-establishing the cultivation of the vine in Britain. They, too, are giving reality to a dream, but in their case, the word 'folly' no longer applies although there were plenty of people who shook their heads when the pioneers planted their first vineyards, and talked of the folly of trying to grow grapes north of Paris or Champagne. Yet wines have been produced in Britain since Roman days, and continued to be produced after the Romans left. The Venerable Bede in his Ecclesiastical History (circa 734) stated that 'Britain also produces wine in some places'. And who would doubt the Venerable Bede? With the Norman Conquest, wine-making became general in southern Britain, especially in the monasteries. Domesday Book lists 38 established vineyards and they flourished until the change of climate in the mid-14th Century, when it became easier to import wine from those parts of Bordeaux which, after all, had been under English rule for 300 years. When

Henry VIII dissolved the monasteries he broke a tradition which then went back for 1,000 years.

We have no idea of the quality of the wine made by the monks. I have a feeling that a lot of it was drunk as a penance, and in any case it was better to drink sour wine than much of the water from mediaeval wells. Wine-making, however, remained under an obscure cloud until the Marquis of Bute made his great attempt to revive it in South Wales in the 19th Century. The Marquis was one of the richest men in Britain and he spared no expense in establishing his vineyards at Castell Coch and at Swanbridge in the Vale of Glamorgan. Castell Coch, the red castle, is a site that demands a vineyard. The castle, restored by William Burges with high pointed turrets and set among the woods and limestone rocks at the point where the Taff breaks out on the plain, has a suggestion of a Rhine

The Wootton Vines at North Wootton near Shepton Mallet, a successful commercial vineyard, re-establishing the tradition of English viticulture. The acreage under vines in Britain is now as much as it was in the Middle Ages

fortress about it. The Castell Coch wine went on the market and received rather a cool welcome from 'Punch'. 'This wine needs five men to drink a glass; one to drink it and four to hold him down.' This was very unfair for the wine turned out to be a very acceptable hock-type affair, and I still cherish a label from a bottle, beautifully designed by Walter Crane. Unfortunately, it did not survive a succession of bad years and the beginning of the First World War. 'Welsh weather,' said one old vigneron to me, 'is basically tee-total.'

The new pioneers after the Second World War began on a smaller scale and met all the obvious difficulties of English weather. But they have had

the benefit of more resistant varieties from research stations in France and Germany, and by the early 60s the breakthrough had occurred. It is no disrespect to the pioneers to say that the leader of the breakthrough was Sir Guy Salisbury-Jones who planted his vineyard at Hambledon in Hampshire in 1952, and was the first to place his vines on the market. Others followed including Lt-Col and Mrs Gore-Browne at Beaulieu in Hampshire, which was then the biggest vineyard in Britain, planted on a site which may have been originally planted with vines by the Cistercians of Beaulieu Abbey in the 13th Century. Today there are vineyards throughout southern Britain, and one has been planted in Yorkshire very near the latitude beyond which the vines will not ripen. This bold venture must be the most northerly vineyard in Europe.

I asked one of the new vignerons if British viticulture presented special problems. 'No,' he said, 'we are attacked by the powdery mildew (*unicula nicator*) a little more vigorously than they are in France, but we deal with it as they do with sulphur dusting. And perhaps we shouldn't complain, because this is a fungus from America that we passed on to France after it had first appeared in Margate in 1845.' Then he gave a deep sigh. 'If only we could train our birds to hate grapes.' Apparently British birds regard them as a rare treat. Blackbirds – and those rats of the air, the starlings – find them irresistible. In France they don't have birds in the vineyards on our scale. There is no cover for them, and the local huntsmen shoot at and eat everything that flies. It was a Frenchman who once told me why Vaughan Williams's violin fantasy, 'The Lark Ascending', could never have a success in France. 'We don't want to see a lark ascending. We want to see him flutter down to settle on a piece of buttered toast for Alouette-sur-Canapé.' You can net your vineyard in, but that becomes expensive when you cover more than an acre; or you can do as Lt-Col and Mrs

Right: Lulworth Cove from the west side, a beautiful stretch of coastline with its cliffs of Purbeck limestone

Opposite: 'The Gleaning Field' by Samuel Palmer, the well known English landscape painter of the 19th Century

Gore-Browne did and remember the Duke of Wellington's celebrated advice to Queen Victoria. She asked him how they could get rid of the sparrows in the Crystal Palace before opening day. 'Sparrow-hawks, ma'am,' grunted the Duke, 'sparrow-hawks!' The Gore-Brownes successfully reared a flock of sparrow-hawks, which did the trick.

But as I contemplate one of Sir Guy's tall bottles and pour out the bright, clear wine with appreciation, I remember, hurriedly, that the name Hambledon can mean something other than wine. This was the village that became one of the birthplaces of cricket, and now it is almost a place of pilgrimage to all lovers of the national game of England. The place has retained its Georgian charm and is surrounded by wooded downlands – as English a place as you could wish to see. On Broadhalfpenny Down the gallant Hambledon men, between 1750 and 1787, developed the game into the forerunner of the cricket we know today,

and then handed on the task to the M.C.C. Outside the Bat and Ball Inn stands a memorial to them, but perhaps their real memorial is in the cricket played every Saturday on the village greens of southern England. The last time I drove from Hambledon westward through the Hampshire lanes in the warm September sun, every village that I passed seemed to be out watching its local team. Village cricket – 'a ballet-dance in blanco-ed boots' as one poet called it – seems to sum up the whole essence of English village life. The setting, on a warm summer evening, has a seductive charm – the discreet ripple of applause around the field after a good stroke, the clink of glasses from the wide open windows of the local inn, the vicar on his way to join the bell-ringers and stopping to see the blacksmith make the winning stroke with a blind swipe to leg. It is time standing still, in the pleasantest possible way!

And it is here, on the village green, that I start my second September journey, for ahead of me lies a part of southern England which is at its best in this month. Side by side with the Vales of York and Pickering I award it my special Corn Dolly for September. My journey starts at that remarkable stretch of secret country, the New Forest. I entered it from the Southampton side and from this end the forest seems to grow and thicken around you as you drive. Unlike so many other areas marked Forest on the map of Britain, the New Forest does have trees – plenty of them in great variety, from the pines planted by the Forestry Commission to the birches, the beech-groves and stands of ancestral oaks. There are open glades here and there, and even stretches of heathery heath, with ponds and little villages in clearings among the woods. The deer are coy and stay hidden in the deep undergrowth but the New Forest ponies are only too evident and are a danger on the roads through the woods. The Forest is administered once again by the ancient Verderers' Court which meets at Lyndhurst and the 'commoners' rights are firmly protected by the Agisters who ride through the woodlands in green jackets and hunting caps. If you drive through the Forest it is well to remember that, by order of the Verderers' Court, animals have priority. New Forest villages are delightful but the prize must surely go to Swan Green with its thatched Tudor cottages around the green, and the deepest parts of the Forest within easy reach.

But over the Forest broods an ancient memory, that of the stern, ruthlessly efficient Norman, William the Conqueror. He it was who declared the whole area a royal hunting preserve. Legends have gathered thickly around the creation of the Forest, and talk darkly of 22 Saxon villages being flattened to make room for the deer, for, says the Anglo-Saxon Chronicle, the King 'loved the tall deer as their father'. He certainly extended the Forest but he did not create it. Edward the Confessor, who was also hunting-mad, as indeed were all rulers in those days, delighted in the New Forest as much as William did. As for those 22 villages, they just weren't there to be removed. Still, the forest laws were extremely strict and savage, and it was William's son, the red-faced William Rufus, who finally paid for all the injustice done in the creation

of the forest. A stone near Minstead marks the traditional spot where William Rufus was accidentally killed by an arrow shot by Sir Walter Tirel. But was it an accident? William's brother Henry was suspiciously quick in leaving the forest and getting himself crowned king at Winchester within three days of Tirel's arrow missing the flying deer and piercing Rufus's breast. This is the speediest coronation in the history of England. Recently Dr Margaret Mead came forward with a startling theory. Rufus, she claimed, was an adherent of the Old Religion, for Dr Mead maintains that with the advent of Christianity to Britain, the old pagan cults went 'underground' and continued in a debased form which eventually became centred around the witches' 'covens'. Rufus was aware that by the tenets of the Old Religion a king must submit to a ritual death for fertility reasons. 'Do thou justice according to the things thou hast heard,' Rufus is supposed to have said to Tirel, whereupon Tirel shot the arrow that killed him.

Dr Mead's assertions set the official historians into an uproar. With tremendous quotations from William of Malmesbury, Oderic Vitalis, Archbishop Suger and John of Salisbury they claim to have shot her thesis down as surely as Tirel's arrow shot Rufus. But the general public is not concerned with critical niceties. Here, apparently, is one of those intriguing mysteries – like Richard III's murder of the Princes in the Tower – which add zest to the history of Britain. Dr Mead's theory, I'm sure, will still go marching on, and it certainly adds a sense of foreboding to the deeper groves of the New Forest. Avoiding the deadly arrows of the historians, I drove out of the Forest along the lovely wooded reaches of the Beaulieu river to the old ship-building yards of Bucklers Hard. Here you are in clearer, more cheerful history. Using great oaks from the New Forest, the shipwrights built some of the ships that sailed in Nelson's fleets. Bucklers Hard, so quiet and peaceful today, was once alive with the hammering that produced the floating Wooden Walls of old England. 4,000 men worked here and amongst the ships launched was the 'Agamemnon', which was Nelson's favourite ship – not the 'Victory'! You will feel close to our

maritime history if you can sail down the Beaulieu River in the falling tide and come out on to the busy waters of the Solent, alive with yachts, with grey sleek naval vessels from Portsmouth and great liners going up to Southampton – the one port in Britain blessed with double tides caused by the rising water moving in succession around both sides of the Isle of Wight.

The Isle of Wight is a curiously self-contained world of its own. The Romans called it Vectis, and it rather kept itself to itself throughout most of its history. It had a fright in 1588 when the Armada sailed up the Channel and its admiral, the Duke of Medina Sidonia, contemplated seizing the island as a base, only to be pushed away from it by the bull-dog determination of the English fleet under Lord Howard and after the expenditure of a 'terrible value of great shot'. Thereafter the Isle carefully stayed out of history, and happily varied agriculture and fishing with a little smuggling. It was the Victorians who 'discovered' the Isle of Wight and set their seal of approval on it with their villas,

A view of Ventnor on the Isle of Wight near St Boniface Down, the highest point on the island

seaside resorts, cast-iron piers and monuments on the downs. It supplied genuine 'pretty' scenery in contradistinction to the 'picturesque' grandeur demanded by earlier generations. Everything was on a pleasantly manageable scale. They could collect the multi-coloured sandstones on the crumbling cliffs at Alum Bay and put them in layers in the bottles that decorated their mantelpieces. They could ride on their hired donkeys on the sands at Shanklin and admire the wooded 'chine' and the undoubtedly 'pretty' thatched cottages of the Old Village. They could take picnic excursions out to the clean, white chalk spires of the Needles that guard the western entrance to the Solent, whose waters effectively protected the diamond-shaped island from vulgar invasion by cheap excursionists from London. The Isle of Wight, up to the turn of the century, prided itself on being rather exclusive.

Queen Victoria and Prince Albert themselves selected it as a place of domestic retreat away from the formalities of Windsor and Buckingham Palace, and Osborne House is a wonderful mausoleum of Victorian taste and feeling. I felt I was back 100 years as I looked at the Dunbar Room with its Indian decorations, the dark Antler Room filled with hunting trophies, the terrace with its memorials to favourite dogs where the Queen and the Prince used to take breakfast in high Summer to the sound of the bagpipes. The royal nightingale, Lord Tennyson, could not bear to be absent from such a Victorian scene, and settled on the island for the last period of his life. His home at Farringford is now a hotel. Well, this may symbolise the later development of the island, for the old exclusive feel of the Isle of Wight collapses in high Summer when the tourists descend. But by mid-September the tide of 'overers', as the islanders call them, ebbs rapidly and in the mellow sun the island resumes its Tennysonian charm.

I wish I could say the same thing for the long line of coast that lies immediately westwards from the Isle of Wight. Bournemouth has flung out its tentacles of villas, hotels, boarding houses, and desirable homes for happy retirement ever further among the pines, and it takes the waters of Poole Harbour to make a dyke against the development spread. At Swanage Bay we are back into a genuine old-style coastline again. The Jurassic strength is back to the sea and the chalk adds its usual splendid offering of steep cliffs, isolated stacks and dramatic natural arches. 20 miles of these white delights will

send you rejoicing past Lulworth Cove and Durdle Door on into Weymouth Bay. I always salute Weymouth Bay as the birthplace of that remarkable monument to mock-modesty, the bathing machine. I am old enough to remember our family using one on the South Sands in Tenby and I can still recollect the curious damp seaweedy smell of the interior and the problem of wriggling out of your clothes in the perpetual semi-twilight. The inventor was Ralph Allen, who was also the first to use it in 1763 actually to bathe in the sea – 'a treatment so strange and extreme that it savoured of madness'. But I cherish the picture of George III at Weymouth emerging from his bathing machine in 1789 while the whole population cheered and the band played 'God Save the King'.

Beyond Weymouth, and the great breakwaters of the naval base, rises the dark whaleback of the Isle of Portland and here, for the moment, we lose the chalk. Portland is the last appearance in the south of that remarkable bed of oolitic limestone that underlies the chalk and spreads up in a great bow through southern England, on through the Cotswolds into Northamptonshire and beyond, bringing with it, wherever it appears, one of the finest building stones in Britain. At Portland it has been worked for centuries. Inigo Jones and later Sir Christopher Wren appreciated its qualities and as a result the place is strangely austere, pitted by deep quarries and ending in the headland of Portland Bill. 'Many caverned, bald, wrinkled of face', Thomas Hardy called it, and in addition Portland is not really an island but is joined to the

Right: The Saxon ruins of Corfe Castle in Dorset which was besieged by the Roundheads in 1645–6; subsequently many of the stones were used for local building

Opposite: The foreshore at Lyme Regis looking towards Golden Cap, the highest cliff on the south coast of England

mainland by Chesil Beach, one of the most extraordinary phenomena on the whole coastline not only of Britain but of Europe. The beach is composed entirely of shingle – 'chesil' is the old English word for shingle – and it runs for over 18 miles from near Bridport where it lies against the land to the isle of Portland where it has opened out to allow a long thin lake to form behind it called the Fleet. The pebbles are carefully graded from west to east. At the Bridport end they are the size of a pea and they increase steadily to reach the size of a man's fist at the Portland end. The old smugglers claimed that they could tell exactly where they were on a dark night by picking up a handful, and the fishermen could tell by the sound of the sea on the pebbles. The origin of the beach is still a matter of dispute among geologists. Some maintain that the stones come mainly from the west, others that Portland island is the main source of supply. The mystery still remains. What is certain, however, as I know from practical experience, is that the beach is damnably tiresome to walk on. Winter storms can crash right over it, as they did with disastrous results to Chesil village in 1979.

Chesil Beach leads us on, westward, to the end of the chalk and to the Jurassic cliffs around Lyme Regis. This charming little port is guarded by the ancient pier of the Cobb on which the ill-fated Duke of Monmouth landed and where Miss Jane Austen took leisurely walks on her holidays. But I look along the cliffs and think of a woman, far more humbly born, who yet made a remarkable contribution to our knowledge of the rocks out of which Britain has been forged. I see the sturdy figure of Mary Anning, in her poke bonnet and basket in hand, on her way along the beach to chip at the rock and reveal, to an astonished world at the very beginning of the 19th Century, strange animals never before suspected by men. Mary was a poor carpenter's daughter and after the death of her father took to prospecting the rocks for fossils to sell to tourists. But she soon became far more than a mere souvenir collector. She developed a remarkable technique of excavation and a flair for discovery that brought her the respect of the scientific world. The early geologists, Buckland, Sedgwick and Murchison, came to study her methods as she uncovered such remarkable fossils from 100 million years ago as the terrifying reptile, Ichthyosaurus, the strange swimming Plesiosaurus and most extraordinary of all, the flying reptile Pterodactylus. As I looked along the Cobb in the September sun, I wondered if Miss Austen and Mary Anning ever met, or if the young ladies in 'Persuasion', who came to Lyme Regis, like most of Miss Austen's heroines in search of a suitable husband, had any inkling of the monsters locked up in the rocks on the seashore!

At Lyme Regis I was on the very westernmost boundary of Dorset. Beyond lay the red earth and the high red cliffs of Devon. As the September sun cast its long shadows before me, I turned back towards the east, on through Dorchester to my hotel in the lush Vale of Blackmoor, Tess of the d'Urbervilles' valley of the Great Dairies and one of the homes of that delicious Dorsetshire cheese Blue Vinny, made from hand-skimmed milk and veined like Stilton. My resting place was chosen for its gastronomic reputation, and I planned to eat my Blue Vinny with the crisp rolls they call Dorset knobs and wash it down – why not – with a Hambledon 1975. I stopped to ask my way, and I savoured another vintage as the friendly farmer gave me directions. He had a rich Dorsetshire accent, the sort of accent that William Dewey and the rest of Thomas Hardy's countrymen possessed when they lived 'far from the madding crowd'. I fear the passing of the local accents. They are one of the pleasures of travel through the countryside of Britain. The full dialect vocabulary has gone from many parts of the country. I wonder if some Durham miners still use that remarkable dialect they christened Pitmatic, or if the Devonian 'burr' still survives in all its glory. Accents take us back to very early times, when the Anglo-Saxons settled in small tribal units. The variation in sound is immensely subtle. Nothing irritates someone who is familiar with his own country accent more than to hear it imitated by an actor, however competent. No wonder the poor actor has to fall back on the rural jargon known on the boards as 'Mummerzet'.

My friend's accent was the genuine thing, but it was not Thomas Hardy I thought of as he spoke. Instead, I remembered an old Dorset clergyman whom Hardy was proud to acknowledge as his master. William Barnes was himself born in Dorset and loved every detail of the Blackmoor Vale. He was a master of many languages, an archaeologist and a scholar, but above all he loved the soft sound of Dorsetshire speech on the lips of Dorset folk. He composed the verse that kept running through my mind at the end of my September journey, and which seemed to crystallise the goodness of this most happy months in the countryside:

'When leaves that leätely wer a-springen
   Now do feäde -ithin the tops,
An-painted birds do hush their zingen
   Up upon the timber's tops;
An-brown-leav'd fruit's a-turnen red,
In cloudless zunsheen, overhead,
   Wi-fruit vor me, the apple tree
Do leän down low in Linden Lea.'

September with the Poets

What wondrous life is this I lead!
Ripe apples drop about my head;
The luscious clusters of the vine
Upon my mouth do crush their wine;
The nectarine and curious peach
Into my hands themselves do reach;
Stumbling on melons, as I pass,
Ensnared with flowers, I fall on grass.

ANDREW MARVELL

My room's a square and candle-lighted boat,
In the surrounding depths of night afloat,
My windows are the portholes, and the seas
The sound of rain in the dark apple-trees.

Sea monster-like beneath, an old horse blows
A snort of darkness from his sleeping nose,
Below, among drowned daisies. Far off, hark!
Far off one owl amidst the waves of dark.

FRANCES CORNFORD

Next him, September marchéd eke on foot;
Yet was he heavy laden with the spoil
Of harvest's riches, which he made his boot,
And him enriched with bounty of the soil;
In his one hand, as fit for harvests' toil,
He held a knife-hook; and in th' other hand
A pair of weights, with which he did assoil
Both more and less, where it in doubt did stand,
And equal gave to each as justice duly scanned.

EDMUND SPENSER

Sweet Cupid, ripen her desire,
Thy joyful harvest may begin;
If age approach a little nigher,
'Twill be too late to get it in.

Cold winter storms lay standing corn,
Which once too ripe will never rise,
And lovers wish themselves unborn,
When all their joys lie in their eyes.

Then, sweet, let us embrace and kiss,
Shall beauty shale upon the ground?
If age bereave us of this blisse,
Then shall no more such sport be found.

WILLIAM CORKINE

October

This can be a richly rewarding month in Britain. As the days pass, the autumn tints begin to show on the leaves. Amongst the beech woods in the Chilterns or in the Sussex Weald, the trees flame with colours that rival the Fall in North America. Smoke drifts from the fields where the farmers are burning the stubble. The last of the summer migrant birds chatter for a moment as they gather on the telegraph wires and then are away to the sunshine of Africa. In their place come the fugitives from the advancing cold in the distant Arctic wastes. You can watch the Bewick's swans arriving from far-off Siberia with a thunderous wing-beat as they settle in the Lower Severn valley at Slimbridge for the Winter.

But Winter is still many, many weeks away. There is still a kindness in the air over the lowlands of Britain. October days can take on the warmth of August, when the North Atlantic anti-cyclone spreads temporarily into the north-east to give us a blissful 'Indian Summer'. The term is a 19th-century importation from the USA, where, apparently, the Indians used these late, unexpected spells of fine weather to store their corn and prepare for the cold days ahead. I am all for returning to the old term of St Luke's Summer, for St Luke's Day is October 18th.

These warm days of St Luke can be a true saint's gift in the lowlands of Britain. They can be even more satisfying in the mountains, and especially in those areas where these mountains take on their wildest form – Snowdonia, the Lake District and the Highlands of Scotland. Over most of the high ground of Britain, the mountains have a rounded outline. They may have craggy outcrops on them as in Dartmoor, or lines of low cliffs as in the limestone hills of Derbyshire. But they rarely rise into the jagged peaks most people associate with the great mountain ranges like the Alps or the Rockies. Yet foreign travellers rub their eyes with

surprise when they see the wild hollow of Cwm Dyli under the stern precipices of Snowdon, or the savage outline of the Cuillins rising from the shore of Loch Coruisk. These are genuine mountains, complete with great rock-faces, dangerous slides of scree, lost tarns and savage, lonely plateaux where the careless or inexperienced climber can die and frequently does. There are no glaciers in Britain,

Francis Towne's watercolour of Keswick Lake

although the summit of Ben Nevis at 4,406 ft is not many feet below the level at which permanent snow will lie in that latitude; and in most years there are always some small, unmelted snow-beds hidden in the deeper gullies all through the Summer. Yet, as far as geological time goes, it is only yesterday since the great glaciers flowed down from the Nant Francon valley in North Wales or out from the great hollows under Scafell in Cumbria to join the glaciers of Scotland to form an ice-sheet rivalling those of Antarctica, filling the whole Irish Sea with ice to a depth of thousands of feet.

When the mists roll amongst the corries of An Teallach in the Western Highlands, and part to show the savage pinnacles of Corrag Bhuidhe rising from the shores of Toll an Lochan, the traveller, making his way upwards through the scattered moraines and past the bare, scraped surface of the rocks, feels that the glaciers are still hanging above him amongst the mysterious summits ahead. The height of these British peaks is low compared with many of the world's great mountain ranges. Snowdon is only 3,560 ft and Scafell Pike, the highest mountain in England, is a mere 3,210 ft. They look smaller still on the latest editions of the Ordnance Survey where the mountain heights are now given in metres. Somehow the splendid rock-peak of Tryfan in North Wales seems to be slightly deflated when it is marked as under 1,000 metres instead of its old, confident 3,010 ft. In my old-fashioned mind a mountain seemed to have achieved something and to be invested with a special quality when it had risen up to that magical 3,000-ft level!

But it is not the mere height that matters. Form and boldness count far more. Besides, our most savage mountains are generally placed near the sea or rise, almost from sea-level, out of deep-cut valleys. They make every inch count. The mists and clouds that float amongst them from time to time simply add to their stature. When they are buried in snow they demand the respect accorded by climbers to the peaks of the Alps. In fact, they always commanded respect, and even fear, from the people who first travelled amongst them. Today the crowds flock to them. In high Summer endless strings of hikers labour up the slopes of Helvellyn or tramp the Llanberis track to the crowded summit of Snowdon. But by October the crowds will have gone home. The woods in Borrowdale are golden with the autumn leaves. You can have the summit of Lliwedd to yourself. The winter snows have not yet made Buchaille Etive, the 'shepherd' that guards Glencoe, an Alpine expe-

dition. It's the best time to see again the wild places of Britain as they were 200 years ago.

I have chosen the date of 200 years deliberately, for it was about this time that the mountains began to change character in the eyes of the beholder. All through the preceding centuries the wilder parts of Britain had been regarded as places best avoided by sensible men. To the English, Snowdon was a stronghold held by the intransigent Welsh, a pile of worthless stones inhabited by rebels. Cumbria and its savage rocks was a 'horrid wilderness' to Bishop Burnet in the late 17th Century. Dr Johnson and his bear-leader Boswell felt that their tour of the Scottish Highlands in 1773 was a bold adventure – as indeed it was for the period. Less than 30 years before, the Highlands had been in full rebellion for 'Bonnie Prince Charlie' against the English crown. As for the scenery, had not Dr Johnson himself written in his poem, 'London':

> 'For who would leave, unbrib'd, Hibernia's land
> Or change the rocks of Scotland for the Strand?'

Yet leave London he did, in his sixty-first year, and gallantly rode and tramped and sailed through the wildest and most inhospitable scenery. 'This uniformity of Barrenness' was his description to Boswell of the mountains of Skye; and although he relished the sturdy independence of the Highlanders, he did not altogether approve of their happy propensity for dodging useful work whenever they could, and for living up to the old Highland verse:

> 'Ah, wad the peats would cut themselves
> The fish leap to the shore,
> So thou and I might lie abed
> And love for evermore!'

Even ten years after Johnson's journey, however, his attitude to mountains began to seem old-fashioned. Change was in the air, and the Romantic Movement had begun. Rousseau had invented the Noble Savage, and untouched Nature was the source of all goodness. It was not long before Wordsworth was busy applying Rousseau's principles to the mountains of his native Lake District.

Climbing in Nant Gwynant in Snowdonia

If ever a man put his own stamp on a landscape, it was Wordsworth. Even today, I cannot think of Lakeland without seeing that 'unfinished sheep-fold, Beside the boisterous brook of Greenhead Ghyll', or picturing the daffodils on the shores of Ullswater, 'fluttering and dancing in the breeze'. Inevitably, as Wordsworth forecast they would, 'they flash upon that inward eye, which is the bliss of solitude'.

Wordsworth and his fellow Lakeland poets, and the generation of Keats, Byron and Shelley that followed them, had made the mountains of Britain fashionable, and a new breed of travellers was inspired to make the still slightly uncomfortable journeys to the Lakes and Wales. Dr Syntax and his like set off in search of the Picturesque. The Napoleonic Wars closed the continent, and the romantic-minded visitors had to make do with the local mountains. They rushed into print and hardly a year passed without one or two 'Tours through the Beauties of Cambria' coming from the press. Meanwhile, the greatest publicist of all had appeared in Scotland. Wordsworth may have made the Lakes famous throughout Britain. Sir Walter

Scott made the Highlands of Scotland famous throughout Europe and eventually the civilized world.

So the High Places of Britain, from being the most shunned and desolate sections of the country, became the pride of the nation. All through the 19th Century their popularity increased. The advent of the railways made the pilgrimage to the hills easier for the increasingly prosperous middle class. Queen Victoria set her seal of approval on the mountain world when she settled at Balmoral with Prince Albert, and published the journals of her life in the Highlands, full of ecstatic underlining of her emotions as she travelled through the hills with her beloved Albert. Soon there wasn't a house in the land that didn't possess an engraving of a noble stag, 'The Monarch of the Glen', painted by the Queen's favourite Sir Edwin Landseer.

In the 1880s a new phase began in the appreciation – or should we now say the exploitation –

of the mountains. The first rock-climbers appeared on the scene in what was then the county of Cumberland. Mountaineering had already become a growing sport in the Alps, mainly pioneered by wealthy Englishmen who had the leisure and the money to hire the sturdy Swiss peasants as guides. John Ruskin, the great art critic who had been one of the most eloquent popularisers of the moral values of mountain scenery, thundered his disapproval from his home at Coniston in the Lake District. 'The Alps themselves, which your own poets used to love so reverently, you look upon as soaped poles in a bear-garden, which you set yourselves to climb and slide down again with "shrieks of delight".' He was even more indignant when the climbers appeared not in the distant Alps but on crags which were in sight of his own home. Moreover, these new exploiters of the hills were distinctly middle-class – dons, civil servants, public-school masters. Later on, local men took to the crags. On the Lakeland mountains, two of the most daring of the new race of climbers were actually local photographers, the Brothers Abraham of Keswick. Surely the end of an era had been reached!

Actually it was the beginning of another wave of ever-increasing popularity for the wild mountains. Today rock-climbing and mountaineering have become big business – and completely class-less. The leader of the 'new wave' in the 1950s was a working-class lad from Manchester, Joe Brown, and the present-day climbers have adopted new techniques which have enabled them to tackle ever-increasing difficulties. When I first went rock-climbing in the late 1920s our equipment was still that of the early pioneers, and we looked with awe on the great unconquered precipice of Clogwyn du'r Arddu, the Black Cliff on the dark, north-eastern side of Snowdon. The rocks plunged savagely down hundreds of feet to the icy tarn at their feet. This was surely the ultimate challenge, the point beyond which no climber dared go. We quoted with approval the words of the Climbers' Club guide-book, which declared that 'no breach was possible or even desirable' along the length of that forbidding rock-wall, although there might be

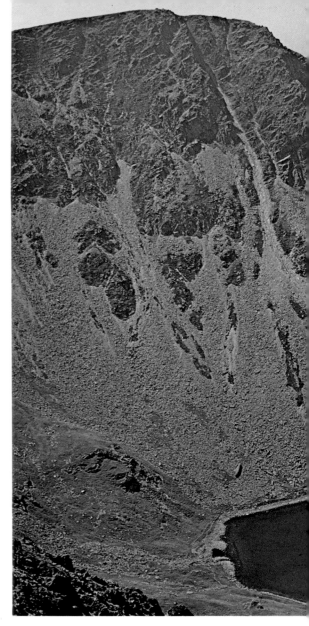

'the faintest of faint hopes for a human fly' at the far end. The Black Cliff of my youth has become 'Cloggy' to the young climbers of today, who have gaily festooned it with many hair-raising routes.

I sometimes look at the photographs of the old pioneers, clad in their thick tweeds, Norfolk jackets and knickerbockers and carrying coils of climbing rope strong enough to moor a battleship, and wonder what they would make of their modern counterparts, complete with clinking karabiners and slings and wearing crash-helmets on their heads, queuing up to take their turn on some 'Hard Severe' in Llanberis Pass and watched through

Right: The east face of Tryfan (3,010 ft) in Snowdonia, looking over Cwm Tryfan

Left: Llyn y Gader and Cyfrwy on Cader Idris in North Wales

binoculars by tourists in the cars on the road. As they wedge their pitons into the rock, I can hear the voice of an old president of the Alpine Club, who, when asked what he thought about the new techniques of rock-climbing, exploded: 'The hand that could drive a piton into English rock could shoot a fox.' But you can recapture the atmosphere of the old days of 100 years ago (when the sport of rock-climbing was young) by going up to the old inn at Wastdale Head in the Lakes, from which the Brothers Abraham and the brilliant Welshman O.G. Jones – 'the only, original Jones' as he described himself – set out, with their hobnailed boots, to make the first routes up the great crag of Scafell or the Napes ridges on Great Gable. Or you can visit Pen-y-Gwryd in North Wales, under the shadow of Snowdon. Here they will open for you the famous Locked Book, where men like Archer Thompson recorded their exploration on the 800-ft face of Lliwedd; and as proof of the long continuity of the history of rock-climbing in Wales, you can see, in the same inn, mementoes of the first ascent of Mount Everest and Kanchenjunga. The members of these successful expeditions did their final training on the cliffs of Snowdonia.

But in October, not only the climbers but the

majority of the tourists have gone and you can see the true character of each of our three wild regions. And how markedly they differ from one another. Snowdonia, first – and that area may be taken to include the whole stretch of wild mountain country now included in the National Park, and extending from the mural precipices of Cader Idris to the rugged cliffs of Penmaenmawr, where the 3,000-ft Carneddau make their final plunge into the sea. The very names of these hills indicate that under all the surface changes wrought by tourism, this land has remained stubbornly Welsh. The Welsh language is still spoken in the valleys. The old Celtic legends still cling around the cliffs. On the rocky crag that rises above Llyn Dinas, in the Vale of Gwynant, stood the hall of Uther Pendragon, and over it, so the legend claims, the Red Dragon fought the Black Dragon of the Saxons and by its victory became the national emblem of Wales. The summit of Cader Idris is the rocky chair of the giant Idris and whoever dares to spend the night of the New Year in it will wake next morning either a madman or a poet.

But while the legends give a picturesque glamour to the hills, the men who live in their shadow have to get down to the hard, practical business of earning a living out of what is pretty poor country from the agricultural point of view. Sheep farming, inevitably, has to be the answer. These hardy animals are everywhere on the bare hillsides. In some parts, you can still come across the mountain goats that were once the feature everyone associated with Wild Wales. I remember meeting with one herd in the Rhinogs, which are perhaps the roughest walking country in southern Britain, where Nature has hacked and slashed at the earth's surface with a gigantic knife and the heather grows to enormous heights in the cracks. Heather is the Welsh hill-farmers' least favourite plant. It marks the worst soil. Does not the old Welsh saying point out clearly the character of this ankle-breaking plant, which always looks at its best from a distance:

'Aur dan y rhedyn
Arian dan yr Eithyn
Newyn dan y grug.'

Gold under the bracken, silver under the gorse, famine under the heather.

My goats on the Rhinogs made light work of leaping over the heather. They were led by a magnificent bearded patriarch of a billy goat who looked as if he was the direct descendant of goats that came here as the ice retreated. An illusion, since the 'wild' goats of Wales came from the domestic flocks once kept on the hills.

The hill cattle are always the Welsh Blacks, tough, hardy and once the sole owners of the hills before they were replaced by sheep in the 19th Century. For generations they were the only source of ready money in the country. The drovers collected them and drove the vast bellowing herds to the markets in London and the Midlands. Archbishop John Williams, in the time of the Civil Wars, compared them to the Spanish treasure fleet: 'that Spanish Fleet of North Wales which brings hither that little gold and silver we have.'

In the 1800s another source of money-making came to Snowdonia as the slate quarries were developed. The Silurian and Ordovician rocks of the National Park once curved in a great arch over the central core of ancient Cambrian rocks of the Rhinogs that geologists call the Harlech Dome. But, during the almost unimaginable period of 400 million years, these Silurian and Ordovician rock-beds have been twisted, torn, sheered and laced with igneous rocks welling up from below in periods of volcanic action. In some areas the pressure on the beds was so intense that the shales and mudstones were transformed into slates – and slates of remarkable quality. In North Wales they claim that these slates are the finest in the world. They certainly came on the market at exactly the right time. The great industrial towns of Lancashire and Yorkshire were rapidly expanding, and the slates of North Wales were perfectly suited for roofing thousands of Coronation Streets.

Huge excavations were carved on the hillsides at the entrance to the Llanberis and Nant Francon passes. The Dinorwic Quarry at Llanberis is probably the biggest man-made hole in the surface of Britain, and, although very little slate is now being produced, the abandoned quarries are a

notable feature of the mountain landscape. Somehow or other, they have acquired a strange impressive beauty in decay, with their vast terraces climbing thousands of feet up the mountains, and the deserted inclines built out of the rubble like the fortress walls of a modern Mycene. From the quarries the light railways took the slates down to the sea, and some have remained to become one of the country's greatest tourist attractions – the Great Little Trains of Wales. The Festiniog railway twists itself into the mountains in a series of astonishing curves, and through the waving banner of steam from the panting engine, you look up to the beetling crags of the Mochwyns. Snowdon itself is climbed by a rack railway, the only one in Britain.

Railways and quarries! Does this mean that the

Wild ponies grazing on Drum mountain near Aber in North Wales

wilds of Snowdonia have been tamed and domesticated? Far from it. These things are visible from the roads in the valleys. Once you step out on to the hills you are back in the consoling wilderness.

The same thing is even more true of the Lake District. Here there has always been less big-scale industry than in Snowdonia. Quarrying and mining were never so important as agriculture. Industry stayed down on the coast in the coalfield around Workington. The rugged heart of Lakeland remained inviolate; and rugged it is indeed! The core of the whole district is the knot of mountains

Opposite: Burnthwaite farm at Wasdale Head, in the heart of the Lake District

around the highest point in England – Scafell Pike (3,210 ft). Here stand most of the crags made famous by the early climbers: the dark, forbidding precipice of Scafell, the high dome of Great Gable, and the cathedral-like Pillar Rock. Standing on these bold summits, you notice one remarkable thing about the geography of Lakeland – all the valleys seem to radiate out of this hub of central summits like the spokes of a wheel. This central core of Cumbria consists of hard, ancient, contorted rocks which were originally buried under more recent formations. In the last period of mountain building, the Tertiary, this whole complex of ancient and more recent rocks was arched into a dome, with the rivers naturally running out from the centre, 'like the spokes of an umbrella'. The recent rocks naturally got worn away first, but the rivers formed on them went on cutting down their valleys on the same line when they reached the older rocks below. The whole area is the delight of geographers who point to it as the supreme example of 'superimposed drainage'!

In the valleys, which were deepened and U-shaped by the ice, the lakes formed as the ice melted; and what enchanting lakes they are, every one with its own character! The biggest, Windermere, winds out from the higher hills towards the lowlands, and carries its quota of small, wooded islands; the deepest, Wastwater, is set in more savage surroundings with the rocks of the Screes sending down their cascades of rough boulders to the lake shore. Ullswater holds both types of charm – Wastwater's wildness at its head, the grace of Windermere at its foot. It also has Wordsworth's daffodils, still there as he described them 'continuous as the stars, that shine and

Left: Derwentwater near Keswick in Cumbria

Above: Wastwater in Wasdale in the western Lake District, with Great Gable in the background

twinkle on the milky way'. But every lake has its own supporters. Ruskin thought that the view from Friar's Crag over Derwentwater towards the head of Borrowdale was supreme. Wordsworth himself selected gentle Grasmere when he came to settle back in his native country with his sister Dorothy. The tourists, as a result, swarm to Dove Cottage as the supreme shrine of Lakeland.

But, after all, it is not the tourists who make Lakeland. They pour in throughout Summer; they applaud the Guides' Race as the competitors run up and down the crags with amazing speed, they admire the Falls of Lodore, even when not full of water, because Southey wrote a poem about them.

But by October the main hordes have gone, most of the hotels close for the Winter, and the real, age-old life of Lakeland pursues its immemorial course. The shepherds bring down their sheep from the higher fells and you can hear some of them still counting their ewes in numbers that take their origin from the original Brythonic inhabitants: 'Yan, tan, tethera, pethera, pimp,' and so on up to 'bumfit' (15) and 'figget' (20). The name of the fells – Scawfell, Honister, Whinlatter – show their conquest by the Vikings and their subsequent absorption, with some difficulty, into the rest of England. The Lakeland farmer carries on his work, still with that sturdy independence that Wordsworth so much admired. And the lovers of the unique beauty of this Cumbrian treasure-house of mountain rarities, continue their fierce defence of the Lakeland National Park against all those who would despoil it for their personal gain. Long may they continue to do so.

We look northward now, 200 miles, to the last of our three wild mountain fastnesses of Britain, the Highlands of Scotland. Here we enter a landscape on an altogether bigger scale from Snowdonia or Lakeland. In some respects it can claim to be the last untamed wilderness in western Europe. There have been developments in recent years that have driven some aspects of modern living deep into areas where they were unknown and unimagined when I first climbed in the Highlands 50 years ago. Who could then have pictured oil platforms being assembled in lonely Loch Caron or that a giant

sports centre at Aviemore would be the centre for ski-lifts into the heart of the Cairngorms? If you contemplated developments on this scale in Snowdonia for example, you would disrupt the delicate balance of the landscape. The Highlands can take them in their stride and still retain huge areas of bare, rocky loneliness. The golden eagles still sail majestically in the lonely glens of the Monadhliath and the red deer gather in the high corries in Summer. The Last Wilderness is still basically intact and not completely tamed.

How menacing it once seemed to the guardians of Stirling Castle as they stood on their battlements and looked away to the north and saw, rising above the fertile lowlands, the outlines of the hills forming the celebrated 'Highland Line'. Out from those fastnesses, until tamed by the guns of

Left: Herdwick sheep on the fells of the Lakeland mountains. The grey wool from their fleeces is very hard-wearing and virtually waterproof

Above: 'A host of golden daffodils' in Dora's Field on the slopes above Rydal Water. Wordsworth bought this field in 1826 and it was given to the nation by his grandson in 1935

Culloden and bound by the military roads of General Wade, the clansmen issued through the mountain passes at regular intervals to alter the course of Scottish history and loot the lucrative farmlands. By the time Sir Walter Scott threw his romantic glamour over the Highlands their character had already been profoundly changed. The clan system had been broken up. The chiefs no longer felt that patriarchal concern for their clansmen, which was the core of the old clan loyalty. They were beginning those sadly dramatic 'clearances' which drove out the crofters and brought in sheep in the place of men. Later even the sheep were replaced in the heart of the Highlands by the red deer. The rich Victorians and Edwardians came hunting, shooting and fishing to the Highlands in increasing numbers. Had not the

Prince Consort dressed himself in a tartan kilt and gone deer-stalking with his faithful ghillies? Deer-stalking is no sport for weaklings. It involves long crawls through damp heather in high rocky corries before you get in your shot – and miss as often as not! But there is no more thrilling sight on the mountains of Britain than a great stag, with full antlers, moving over the skyline with his herd of hind; and when October comes, the hills are full of the sound of 'the roaring' – the time when the stags are locked in fierce combat over the hinds and the wild places of Scotland seem very wild indeed.

I once met an old ghillie who was swinging with the steady pace of a born hillman, up that hidden valley behind Ben Nevis where the great waterfall of Steall fills the whole glen with continual thunder. 'I'm away for Corrie Mousca,' he said, and

Above: Deer in the wild country above Kingussie, in the Scottish Highlands

Right: The Cairngorms which lie between the Spey and Dee valleys, and have recently become an expanding tourist area in both Summer and Winter

waved towards the Mamore Forest. 'This is a great day for the hills.' 'Are the stags roaring around here yet?' 'Aye, they'll be up in the high corries as far as they can get. They'll be roaring all night. The stag is a mad animal – he loses his brains once the roaring is on him. It's fighting for him all day and night and he's skin and bone at the end of it. He becomes stupid with it all. Why, he'd walk past you now without noticing you.' And away went our friend, as fast as any stag, into the upper corrie.

The red stag is King of the Hills, but there have been attempts to introduce other animals including the reindeer. The tourists at Aviemore are taken out to gaze at the only herd in Scotland, but I confess that, compared to the red deer, the reindeer seem singularly domesticated creatures.

The birds of the Highlands remain, however, as untamed as the deer. The ptarmigan turns almost completely white in Winter and stays on the highest tops. I have never seen one below 2,500 ft – it's the true bird of the summits. Lower down, the

Left: Salmon leaping up-river to spawn. The Scottish Highlands contain some of the finest and most famous salmon rivers in the world

Below: The golden eagle, which builds its eyries up to 2,000 ft high on the crags of the Scottish mountains

capercaillie breeds in the forests and sometimes ventures out on to the moorlands; a big, ponderous bird it makes a resounding clatter when you disturb it amongst the fir trees. But for me – apart from the supreme delight of seeing the golden eagle soaring effortlessly against a clear blue winter sky – the bird I associate most with the hills of Scotland is the grouse. Disturb him in the deep heather and he startles you with the sudden whirring of his wings, and his squawks of protest as he skims away across the grey rocks. These birds are part of the rare pleasure you can only get in the Highlands.

With so much to see, how can a visitor master the whole? It's impossible to 'know' the Highlands unless you give a lifetime to them, and – may I add – learn a little Gaelic. It is the Celts who have named the mountains and the glens, and although the language is rather under stress today, great efforts are being made to ensure its survival. Gaelic has a soft, caressive sound, but its orthography can be puzzling to a stranger. As George Abraham plaintively remarked: 'When we are told that Beinn-mheadh-onaidh is pronounced Ben Venue, the difficulties of the language are apparent.' As a Welshman I suspect they are more apparent than real. At any rate, the names of the hills, when pronounced by a native, sound appropriate as well as romantic. Sir Walter Scott was well aware of the help he got from Gaelic names when 'selling' the Highlands. 'The Lady of the Lake' is littered with references to the 'grey pass where birches wave, On Beala-na-bo' or 'the spell-bound steps on Ben Venue'. It was the 'Lady of the Lake' that sent the romantically minded travellers to the Trossachs, and made this area of rocky peaks and lakes the Highlands' first lucrative tourist centre. The Trossachs are delightful but not exactly the wildest of Scotland's hill country. They are the nearest to Glasgow, however, and that makes the difference.

I was last there when a bus discharged a collection of tourists on the shore of Loch Katrine. They were 'doing the Trossachs', and obviously some had also been doing themselves well on another famous product of the Highlands. The guide assembled his charges and pointed to the view. 'Ye'll all remember Sir Walter Scott's famous lines, "the stag at eve had drunk his fill".' Then he fixed a stern eye on one particular whisky-enlivened gentleman. 'And it seems he was nae the only one tae do so!' How romance can get diluted down through the years.

You will be in no danger of such a disillusioning experience if you penetrate deeper into the Highlands – and if you walk or climb. Ben Nevis, the highest of all the great hills, should be the first peak you ascend, not only because it is the highest

Loch Maree, in the remote north-western Highlands of Scotland

but because, in spite of its fame, it retains surprising secrets. Seen from the shores of Loch Linnhe it can disappoint as a mountain form. 'That great lump' was how one disappointed writer described it, but once you penetrate into the recesses of the Allt a'Mhuilinn (pronounced Voolin) you see before you one of the grandest rock-faces in the whole of Scotland. Under snow, it has an Alpine splendour. The old travellers found climbing the Ben, even by the easy way on the Fort William side, a hard task. John Keats described the ascent as 'almost like a fly climbing up a wainscoat'. The descent seemed even worse: 'I have said nothing yet of our getting in among the loose stones, large and small, sometimes on two, sometimes three, sometimes four legs, sometimes two and a stick ... so that we kept on ringing the changes on foot, hand, stick, jump, boggle, stumble, foot, hand, foot (very gingerly), stick again, and then again a game at all fours.' But the poet did it! I wonder what he would have said to my friend Mrs Jane Glass, who is just turned 30 and the mother of three sons and who holds the women's record for the climb to the summit from Fort William and then back – two hours, five minutes! Times have changed in the mountain world.

I have never tried record-breaking on mountains, above all in Glencoe. I climb slowly, savouring every moment of the experience. I remember reaching the summit of Bidean nau Bian, which sends down its rocky spurs to dominate the famous pass of Glencoe. It was a perfect Summer's evening and the land was bathed in that translucent golden glow that you only get in Summer in the western Highlands. The whole mountain world seemed before us – from Ben Lomond, past Nevis and around to the bold outliers of the Grampians. The lonely moor of Rannoch stretched away to the east, sparkling with its little lochans. It was then that I fully realized the scale of the Highlands – and their rich diversity. No other mountain group in Britain holds such contrasts. Away to the south, in the Firth of Clyde, lay the Isle of Arran with its strange peaks of rounded granite above Glen Sannox; far beyond Ben Nevis to the west over the horizon was Skye with the ridge of the Cuillins, rock-climbers' ground if ever there was one! You cannot traverse that awesome ridge without rope and proper boots. The Cuillins and their pinnacles are Gothic in feeling. The Cairngorms, in the very centre of the mountain mass, have a solid Roman grandeur. These bare, rock-strewn plateaux are all near or over the 4,000-ft mark, and form the biggest area of high ground in Britain. The highest point – and the second highest summit in Britain – is Ben Macdhui (4,296 ft). Even to tramp the pass through the central part of the Cairngorms, the Lairig Ghru, is a mountaineering challenge.

The Great Glen divides the Highlands into two. This faulted valley runs from Inverness to Fort William, and is so close to sea-level that it can hold not only deep and dark Loch Ness and its now world-famous 'monster', but the water of the Caledonian Canal as well. In a curious way, it is possible to sail through the Highlands.

In some respects, the country that lies north and west of the Great Glen can be counted the true glory of the Highlands. Nowhere in Britain can you find such mountain forms, linked with the deep sea-lochs that cut far into the land. I can give a roll-call of great hills and find it hard to say which is the most remarkable. Is it Liathach (3,456 ft), with its five-mile long, steep wall of rose-coloured sandstone, standing over Glen Torridon? Or its extraordinary neighbour, Beinn Eighe, whose white quartzite screes make parts of it look under permanent snow, and where Coire Mhic Fhearchair lays claim to be the grandest mountain hollow in all Scotland. Further north is the strange, bare landscape of Sutherland, where the dark, scraped rocks look as if the ice had only just melted from them. Out of this lonely, forbidding, treeless world of ancient rock leap strange, sharp mountains that stand apart from each other amongst myriads of small lakes – Stack Polly, with its pinnacle ridge like a hedgehog's back, Suilven on its pedestal of gneiss, and the last of the peaks of mainland Scotland, the 2,950-ft conical Foinaven in the Reay County. Beyond it you have to tramp many a bleak lonely mile to the most north-westerly point of the mainland, Cape Wrath. Here is a place which lives up to its name in mid-winter, but on a rare October day – if the firing-range is quiet – it can seem almost benign in its isolation.

Dr Johnson had teased Boswell. 'Your country,' said the sage, 'consists of two things – stone and water. There is indeed a little earth above the stones in some places but very little, and the stone is always appearing. It is like a man in rags; the naked skin is still peeping out.' At the end of a journey across the 'naked skin' of Britain – through Snowdonia, Cumbria and the Highlands – I rejoice in the 'skin and bones' of these islands. Where would the lush lowland landscape be without the contrast of our Wild Places?

October with the Poets

The trees are in their autumn beauty,
The woodland paths are dry,
Under the October twilight the water
Mirrors a still sky;
Upon the brimming water among the stones
Are nine and fifty swans.

The nineteenth Autumn has come upon me
Since I first made my count;
I saw, before I had well finished,
All suddenly mount
And scatter wheeling in great broken rings
Upon their clamorous wings.

I have looked upon those brilliant creatures,
And now my heart is sore.
All's changed since I, hearing at twilight,
The first time on this shore,
The bell-beat of their wings above my head,
Trod with a lighter tread.

W. B. YEATS

A springful of larks in a rolling
Cloud and the roadside bushes brimming with whistling
Blackbirds and the sun of October
            Summery
            on the hill's shoulder,
Here were fond climates and sweet singers
    suddenly
Come in the morning where I wandered and listened
            To the rain wringing
            Wind blow cold
    In the wood faraway under me.

DYLAN THOMAS

In this short span
    between my finger tips on the smooth edge
    and these tense feet cramped to the crystal ledge
I hold the life of man.
Consciously I embrace
    arched from the mountain rock on which I stand
    to the firm limit of my lifted hand
    the front of time and space :-
        For what is there in all the world for me
        but what I know and see
    And what remains of all I see and know,
        if I let go?

GEOFFREY WINTHROP YOUNG

November

I have never yet decided if November is the last lingering farewell of still kindly Autumn or the harsh approach of advancing Winter. I remember sitting with an old Somerset countryman near Wedmore, looking out over those long levels and damp meadows that make the valley of the little river Brue a sort of foretaste of the Fens. 'November,' he said, emptying his glass of the rough but dangerously powerful cider they call 'scrumpy' in those parts, 'she's an edgy old month. Never know the way she's going to jump. Could go any way.' Indeed she could! In 1978, southern Britain had its mildest and driest November for over a hundred years. There were days when you thought you were back in September. The trees in the woods that bend over the waters of Llyn Gwynant in Snowdonia held their red leaves unshaken by the wind until the end of the month. Incredibly a serious drought was proclaimed in the West Country and Cornwall. But the average British November is surely inclined on the side of Winter. This is a month of increasing cold and gathering rain, with fog over the level country – the sort of weather in which I first saw the landscape I always associate with this double-edged month, the Fens.

The Fens are the lower portions of the basins of those rivers which flow into that strangest and most aptly named of the many indentations in the coastline of England, the Wash. In those far-off days when I went to my first school, we were taught the basic facts of British geography by chanting the names of the principal rivers around the coast, ending at the Wash. I can still remember our relief as we came past the Humber to the gloriously euphonic finale: 'The Witham, the Welland, the

The New Bedford River in Cambridgeshire, cut in 1651 by Vermuyden in one of the early attempts to drain the Fens

Nen and (cry of triumph!) the Great Ouse.' The very name, the Great Ouse, seems to sum up the way the Fens were originally formed by the slow, winding approach of the quietly moving rivers to the shallow waters of the Wash, dropping their silt as they crawled toward the sea.

In the distant past, when the ice retreated for the last time, the four rivers united as they flowed down the shallow valley now covered by the Wash and went out over the then dry North Sea to join with the ancestors of the Rhine and the Thames to form a vast Mississippi-like river flowing north. Then, as the ice-cap continued to retreat, the sea crept back over the land and formed the Wash. The tides of the Wash, in those early days, ebbed and flowed further inland than they do today, and so the Fen country is now formed of two clearly defined types of soil. Near the sea the soil is composed of the silts washed in by the tide. Further inland lie the silts brought down by the rivers and deposited when the four streams met the highest tides. It is this second type of silt that was the basis of the true Fenlands.

As the long centuries passed, this area became covered with brushwood, sedge-plants and water-loving trees which rotted down to form layers of underlying peat – a strange, rather forbidding landscape of sluggish streams and shallow lakes out of which rose islands of clay and gravel covered with thickets of willow and alder. Yet when early man arrived on the scene, he found this damp wilderness a hunter's and fisherman's paradise. His descendants, the true fenmen, lived a semi-aquatic life, fed by the swarms of duck and wild geese that flew over the waving reed-beds and by the endless supply of fish in the shallow waters. When the Christian faith spread through Britain, the hermits, and later the monks, found in the islets of the Fens a safe retreat from the outside world. The great abbeys of Crowland and Ely lifted their walls and towers above the watery waste.

Until the 17th Century this part of England remained totally separate from the rest of the country. The fenmen were a race apart, like the Marsh Arabs of Iraq today, content with their lot and marvellously adapted to the life in their strange surroundings. They built their houses and huts on the small patches of dry land scattered through the marshes. They had a plentiful supply of reeds for thatching, clay for brick-making and osiers for basket weaving. Peat gave them their fires, and they kept cattle wherever the land allowed it, herded by men on stilts. They sent eels to the London market, and everything that flew or swam went into their pot, including the heron and the bittern. There were drawbacks to this idyllic life, of course. The 'Marsh Fever' was the common lot of all fen-dwellers – rheumatism and swarms of gnats in high Summer. Opium pills against the ague were still being sold in Ely market at the beginning of this century. But to the true fenman, these inconveniences were a small price to pay for the rights he enjoyed under the vast open sky of the Fens. It is not without significance that the last man to hold out against the Norman invaders, Hereward the Wake, took refuge in the Fens. Even when the rest of England became heavily enmeshed in the tangles of the feudal system, the fenmen retained surprising freedoms which they were ready to defend fiercely against all comers. And as the 17th Century dawned, their determination was first put to the test, when the men of progress put forward the first scheme for draining the Fens. The story of the old fenmen's battle to retain the Fens as they had been since time immemorial – a battle which went on through most of the century and which they eventually lost – has been called the first fight of the Conservationists. The battle is still being fought today whenever a new giant scheme for a motorway, an airport or an oil terminal has to be pushed through in overcrowded Britain. The fenmen's fight has always had a special interest for me since I heard about it on my first visit to Cambridge in the 1920s. I had just read Professor Hammond's great book on the English Agricultural Labourer – social and economic history were very much 'in the air' when I was reading history at Oxford, as a reaction against the

The octagonal lantern of Ely Cathedral rising above the Fens. The lantern was built in the 14th Century when the original Norman tower collapsed

Opposite: Sunset over Horsey Mere in the Norfolk fenlands

Above: Packing bundles of reeds which are still used for thatching in many parts of the country

hundreds of years of history about wars and kings and religion. My progressive young tutor said to me, 'I see you are going across to the Other Place' (as Cambridge was then called in Oxford academic circles). 'Go down to the Fens. They are the real birthplace of the Labour Party.' That was, perhaps, a bit of airy Oxford persiflage, but there was a kernel of truth in it. The fenmen's fight had some surprisingly modern features, from strikes to strong-arm picketing. I dutifully got on my bicycle and pedalled out against the November wind along the road to Ely. I faced a real Fen blow, for the wind has its will in the Fens when Winter approaches, and as I pedalled against it, I began to appreciate to the full the extraordinary nature of the Fenland landscape.

I had been brought up in Wales in sight of the sea and the hills. Until I saw the Fens I could not conceive of a genuinely flat land – as flat as if it had been laid out with a spirit-level. There wasn't the slightest suggestion that this country would ever wrinkle its face. There are other flat areas in Britain, some of them of considerable extent. The lower Severn valley is technically flat, so is Romney Marsh and the York plain. But they are always broken by some slight undulation here and there, and on most days, the hills are in sight. But as I cycled out towards Ely I felt I had embarked on a long voyage over a vast soil-sea, and I greeted the towers of Ely Cathedral as if I had made a lucky landfall as darkness crept over the waters. Next day, I went deeper into the Fens and a second feature of the landscape impressed me profoundly. This is a land of straight lines. The long water-channels march undeviating to the distant horizon, and so do the roads. Chesterton may have sung that 'the rolling English drunkard made the rolling English road'. If so that drunkard had certainly signed the pledge by the time he came to reclaim the Fens. This is the widest stretch of purely artificial country in Britain. There are other patches of reclaimed land, of dykes and drainage ditches and great sea-walls, some of them in unexpected places. You will be surprised to find a piece of little Holland in Wales, of all areas. It lies along the north shore of the Severn Estuary, and stretches past Newport to Cardiff. The Wentlloog Levels are as flat as anything in the Fens, but they have nothing like the same extent. In Fenland it's the sheer scale that counts.

I reached the banks of what they call the Old Bedford River, a man-made channel that runs as straight as a die for 21 miles. In Britain the eye is not used to such uncompromising, ferocious straightness. This is a continental characteristic. You expect it on the prairies of North America or on the plains of northern Europe but not in England. You are not a bit surprised therefore to find that the Old Bedford River was built by a Dutchman, and it's the symbol of all that the fenmen's struggle was about. Their old life-style was all curves and leisure, while the improvers' plan was based on straight lines and efficiency. The clash was inevitable.

It began when James I ascended the throne of England. James was an extraordinary mixture of sense and stupidity. Not for nothing was he called 'the wisest fool in Christendom'. He was also anxious, after his impecunious Scottish upbringing, to lay his hands on any promising source of extra cash. It was not surprising, therefore, that when he was approached by the 4th Earl of Bedford and his Company of Adventurers with a scheme for draining the Fens, he agreed with enthusiasm to give them the concession. In all fairness to James it seemed the progressive as well as the profitable thing to do. Throughout Tudor and Stuart times the population of Britain had been increasing, and this meant increasing pressure on the land. Should 400,000 acres of potentially rich agricultural land be allowed to remain a trackless, damp bog? The promoters had only to look across the North Sea to Holland to see how wealth could be won by reclaiming land. They turned to Holland for help

and imported the brilliant, tough, resourceful and calculating Dutch engineer, Cornelius Vermuyden.

He was the first to undertake the reclamation of the Fens. Those hard, practical men, the Romans, had already gnawed away at the great marshland, and some traces of the sea-banks they built can be seen near Long Sutton; but Vermuyden, backed by the Earl of Bedford, was the first man to tackle the job in a big way. The system he adopted was to make straight cuts to shorten the course of the rivers, with minor drains feeding into the main cut in a herring-bone pattern. This would produce a faster run-off down to the sluices that guarded the outfalls to the sea. On the face of it, this arrangement seemed a good plan. Critics have since come forward to claim that it did violence to the natural flow of the rivers and to point out that what worked well in Holland, where you were reclaiming land from the sea, was not bound to be the best way to drain a bog based on peat. This is surely wisdom after the event. No-one in 17th-century Britain could match the Dutch in experience of big-scale land reclamation; and Vermuyden was a sort of Ferdinand de Lesseps of his time, with his unbounded enthusiasm for the project, his powers of organisation and his eloquent pen. All through the long years of the project that became his life's work and which met with every sort of opposition and difficulty, he never lost heart. He richly deserved the knighthood bestowed on him by the admiring Charles I.

The fenmen naturally saw him in a less attractive light. He was the foreigner who was planning to destroy the whole way of life they held so dear. These royal grants trampled on their ancient, acknowledged rights. Whole villages clubbed together to raise enough money to fight cases through the courts. They lobbied men of importance in East Anglia and London. They won Oliver Cromwell to their side and the future Lord Protector first came into prominence as the fenmen's champion. Denied in the courts, the fenmen were driven to take direct action. They boycotted Vermuyden's works and destroyed his depots. No fenman would put hand to spade to dig one of his ditches. Riots greeted the start of every

154

new drain and canal. The courtiers around Charles christened the rioters the Fenland Tigers. They chuckled at one unhappy traveller in the Fens who laughed at the beer the poor fenmen drank which reeked of dirty water from the muddy channels but which the fenmen 'reckon is highly convenient and necessary to avoid the devilish stinging of their humming gnats, which is all the town music they have'.

Vermuyden, however, pressed relentlessly on. Bit by bit dry land replaced the marsh over an ever-increasing acreage. The fenmen took new heart as the Civil Wars began. They joined Oliver Cromwell's Ironsides from the Isle of Ely in increasing numbers. Surely their cause was just the sort of cause that Parliament had taken up arms to support. Alas for the hopes of the humble and the righteous! No sooner had Parliament felt itself safely in power after the First Civil War than they passed the Act for the Draining of the Great Level of the Fens in 1645. Worse still, their first champion, Oliver Cromwell, now became an equally great champion for the schemes of Vermuyden. Scottish prisoners taken after his victory at Dunbar worked on the New Bedford Level cut parallel to the old one. Not for the first time did a politician forget his promises once he had got into power, and an admiring poet wrote complacently: 'I sing floods muzzled and the Ocean tamed', and talked of how:

> 'New hands shall learn to work, forget to
>   steal
> New legs shall go to church, new knees shall
>   kneel.'

The fenmen were not amused. They still struggled on, but by the time King Charles II was restored the heart had gone out of the fight. Slowly the Conservationists gave up the battle. New settlers moved in on to the reclaimed land, and today only a few patches of the original Fens remain. If you want to get an idea of what they looked like in the unreclaimed past, you must go to places like the Norfolk Broads or part of the shore of Lough Neagh in Northern Ireland. In Fenland itself Wicken Fen and the much smaller Holme and

A bittern with its young on its nest among the reed beds. Many species of water bird can be seen among the waterways and marshes of the Fens

Woodwalton Fens have become nature reserves. In Wicken you can still see the long water-channels wandering through the waving reed-beds. You can still hear the bittern boom, and spot the swallow-tailed butterfly amongst the sedge and the otter chasing the carp and the bream. Wicken Fen is the proverbial naturalist's paradise. They will tell you that, apart from the rare birds, 72 species of molluscs and 212 different kinds of spiders have been identified there. I'm glad to hear it, but I never look at Wicken without thinking that this strange, beautiful and uncontaminated place was the world the old fenmen first fought to preserve. Perhaps it is their best and only memorial.

Freiston Shore on the Wash in Lincolnshire where the dykes and sea walls are the only protection against the constant danger of flooding

The flat agricultural land of
the Fens near Ely

Left: The octagonal tower of St Botolph's church at Boston, the famous 'Boston Stump' on the River Witham. Until the Wash silted up Boston was a flourishing seaport

Opposite: A windmill on a drainage ditch in the Lincolnshire Fens. The east winds sweeping across the flat expanses of the Fens powered the pumps of hundreds of such windmills

Yet in an unexpected way, they had their revenge. What Vermuyden and his backers had not foreseen was that their cuts and channels would not just drain the peat areas of the Fens; they would also lower the water content of the peat itself. As the peat dried out, the ground level steadily sank. Vermuyden's channels became increasingly sluggish. The rate at which the peat can shrink has been demonstrated at Holme Fen. Sometime in the middle of the 19th Century an iron post was driven through the peat to the clay below. Then its top was level with the surface of the peat. Today the top of the post is 12 feet above the peat. You can see the same thing at Wicken, where the whole fen stands up clearly from the surrounding country. The shrinkage had gone so far in some parts of the reclaimed land that, by 1700, farms were being abandoned. For a time, the introduction of windmills saved the day, then large-scale reconstructions of the system were undertaken by the great Scottish engineer, Rennie. His work was based on what he called the catchwater principle. He relied on catching the water from the uplands before it got to the lowlands and leading it away by canals which follow the contour to the nearest outfall.

All very well, but it proved difficult to combine Rennie's system completely with Vermuyden's. Vermuyden needed plenty of water flowing through his cuts in order to stop them silting up. Rennie was busy robbing them of that very water. Today great electric pumps clear the area of its surplus water and vast tracts of the reclaimed lands lie well below sea level. There is no question but that the whole survival of the Fens needs eternal vigilance. Man has created this landscape. Man's ingenuity must preserve it.

It is now over 350 years since the first great reclamation scheme began. Can we cast up a balance sheet? On one side, we have lost a

romantic, strange, unique stretch of country. I was talking about the past the other day with someone who was concerned with the tourist industry. As we drove through the Black Fens – the land reclaimed on the peat – I was busy painting a vivid picture of the life once lived here by the old fenmen, and my colleague's imagination caught fire. 'What a loss – the greatest tourist attraction of the lot – a British Everglades! They'd be queuing in thousands to come.' Then I looked out again over the vast level countryside, stretching for miles without a hedge to interrupt acre after acre of waving corn or sugar-beet or potatoes. I forgot romance, for I was looking at what can claim to be the richest farmlands in Britain. We stopped and picked up some soil and let it run through our fingers. 'Black gold,' I thought. Deep alluvial soil with not a stone on it, full of fertility placed there by Nature, capable of giving double, even treble the yield you get in the less fortunate parts of these islands. An agricultural Klondyke! Vermuyden had justified himself.

Farming experts, however, sound a warning. It is possible even for a Klondyke to become exhausted. The peat continues to shrink, and the water levels rise. At Denver Sluice, where Vermuyden's 21-mile straight cut rejoined the Ouse, a vast complex of sluice gates and pumps dominates the landscape. The farmers themselves pay for this drainage effort, assessed at so much per acre. I think that they will still get their money's worth for many years to come.

In the meantime, the remarkable landscape of the Fens remains basically much as Vermuyden created it. His long artificial channels are still strangely impressive. The old and the new Bedford rivers run parallel with each other and the New Bedford River is 100 ft wide. In the Black Fens the countryside seems curiously deserted. For most of the time nothing moves in the fields – if indeed you can call them fields. To anyone coming fresh from the West Country, where the charm of the countryside is closely linked to the patterns of the hedgerows, these hedgeless, treeless acres seem to be directly imported from the steppes of Russia. Their deserted look comes from the fact that people have

to travel a long way to work them. The villages are perforce strung out along the banks of the drainage channels. Farming, too, is highly mechanised and the land has been collected into big units. The Fenland farmers are among the most progressive in Britain. They know they've got the country's richest soil. They are determined to make the most of it – while it is there!

With all this talk about water, floods and drainage, it seems a curious paradox that the Fens should be amongst the driest areas of Britain when it comes to rainfall and that, until comparatively recent times, a good supply of drinking water was also a problem. Yet this curious landscape of straight lines and treeless, level expanses possesses a strange beauty of its own. Over it hangs a sky that seems wider, more translucent, cleaner than any sky in the mountain and hill country. It is the special glory of the Fens.

And the area is not all treeless and angular. As you approach the Wash you leave the peaty soil of the Black Fens and come into the marine silts. Here there is a stronger growth of trees, the farms are dotted about the scene more generously than was possible on the true peat fens. This landscape extends around the north-east corner of the Wash into Lincolnshire, where to the east the flat land ends against the little hills and rolling downs of the Lincolnshire Wolds. Tennyson was born in this country and his early poetry echoes the duality of the two landscapes – rolling downs and level marshes. His brook chattered 'over stony ways, in little sharps and trebles' up in the kindly folds of the Wolds, while Mariana's sinister 'moated grange' was surely set in the lonely 'glooming flats' of the Lincolnshire marsh land.

Over all rises that tremendous sky-scraper of a church tower, Boston's famous 'Stump'. It towers twice as high when the November mists rise on the river, and the level countryside stretches away to the lonely sea-banks of the Wash. In this month, the Fenlands seem withdrawn, totally apart, wrapping themselves up to face the winter winds that will blow in from the North Sea, unchecked since they crossed the Ural Mountains over 2,000 miles away in the east.

November with the Poets

The rain set early in tonight,
The sullen wind was soon awake,
It tore the elm-tops down for spite,
And did its worst to vex the lake.

ROBERT BROWNING

Tonight the winds begin to rise
And roar from yonder dropping day;
The last red leaf is whirl'd away,
The rooks are blown about the skies;

The forest cracked, the waters curled,
The cattle huddled on the lea;
And wildly dashed on tower and tree
The sunbeam strikes along the world.

ALFRED LORD TENNYSON

The pale, descending year, yet pleasing still,
A gentler mood inspires; for now the leaf
Incessant rustles from the mournful grove,
Oft startling such as, studious, walk below,
And slowly circled through the weaving air.
But should a quicker breeze amid the boughs
Sob, o'er the sky the leafy deluge streams;
Till choked, and matted with the dreary shower,
The forest walks at every rising gale.
Roll wide the wither'd waste, and whistle bleak,
Fled is the blasted verdure of the field;
And shrunk into their beds, the flowery race
Their sunny robes resign. E'en what remained
Of stronger fruits falls from the naked tree;
And weeds, fields, gardens, orchards, all around
The desolated prospect thrills the soul.

JAMES THOMPSON

On a clear eve, when the November sky
Grew red with promise of the hoar-frost night,
These ancient men turned from the outside cold
With something like content that they, grown old,
Needed but little now to help the ease
Of those last days before the final peace.
The empty month for them left no regret
For sweet things gained and lost, and longed for
    yet
'Twixt spring-tide and this dying of the year . . .

WILLIAM MORRIS

December

December lies at the very heart of Winter and yet I cannot feel that it is the most tough and testing time of the year in Britain. In that curiously uncertain procession of rain, snow and sun which we call our weather, a comparatively mild December can sometimes surprise us. We traditionally expect a white Christmas but, as often as not, the snow doesn't oblige the makers of Christmas cards and carols. The work on the farms slows down. As the old country saying puts it, 'in December keep yourself warm and sleep'. But, of course, no farmer with livestock can ever act on that advice. Yet there is a sort of pause in the year as December runs its course. The Christmas festival makes an emotional finale to the 12 months, although the name December comes from the Latin 'decem' and reminds us that the Romans divided their year into ten sections.

I always think of December as linked with winter rain and, by a perverse association of ideas, with the Midland counties of England. I blame Hilaire Belloc for this, with his verse:

'When I am living in the Midlands
That are sodden and unkind.'

He must have written those lines on a particularly damp December day in Nuneaton! No, you cannot dismiss the whole of central England with those two adjectives. This is the very heart of the country. No-one can claim to understand England and how profoundly it differs from Scotland or Wales or Ireland, without taking a look at the Midlands. This is not officially tourist country except in one or two carefully selected spots such as Stratford or Warwick. Parts of it are irretrievably committed to industry, like the area around

The Hazelton Hunt preparing to move off after drawing a covert

164

Birmingham and Coventry and the ever-growing
cities of Nottingham and Leicester. There is mining
in Nottinghamshire, iron-ore extraction in great
open pits in Northamptonshire, and quarrying at
certain points all through the region. But there is
also a surprising amount of agricultural land and
'deep country' which has escaped industrial
development. Midlanders are not much given to
boosting their part of the world. No-one, as far as I
know, has written a rousing chorus to 'Rutland,
glorious Rutland' or saluted in verse the charms of
Eccleshall. You are not likely, indeed, to find
Midlanders spontaneously bursting into song in
pubs as they do in Wales. These solid citizens know
instinctively that they are the real backbone of the
country and see no reason to make a song about it.
And they don't mind at what time of year you come
to look at their country. It's as interesting in
December as it is in high Summer.

For me the southern limit of the Midlands is
marked by the belt of oolitic limestone that swings
north-east from the Cotswolds, getting steadily
lower as it goes on up through Northamptonshire
into Leicestershire and the old county of Rutland.
The stone retains the beauty and character it
showed in the Cotswolds, and the villages have the
same delightful honey-colour. The quarries at
Clipsham yielded the lovely light stone used to
repair the House of Commons after the war, and
the old and famous quarries in places like Barnack
and Ketton – some of which, alas, have been
worked out – supplied splendid stone to build great
churches, cathedrals and Cambridge colleges.
Cambridge, by the way, has had better luck than
Oxford when it comes to building-stone. Oxford
was tempted by the near proximity of the easily
worked Headington stone, which unfortunately
weathered fast. The 17th and 18th Centuries were
great building periods in both universities and new
college buildings went up in all directions. By the
time I went up to Oxford, over 50 years ago, some
of those buildings looked distinctly moth-eaten.

The celebrated statues of the Roman emperors
outside the Sheldonian Theatre were noseless and
earless. The weather had brought retribution to
those proud 18th-century masters and fellows of
colleges, rich in port and piety. Cambridge
colleges, out on the stoneless Fenlands, had to look
elsewhere for the stone they needed. They turned
to places like Ketton and were heartily glad that
they did. Cambridge had no need to undertake a
vast programme of face-lifting such as poor Oxford
found itself involved in through the recent years.

The Midland plain stretches away northward from the oolitic ridge. It is built of comparatively new rocks, much of it composed of New Red Sandstones, clays and gravels. Older rocks lie beneath it in places like Nottinghamshire, where pits have been sunk through it to reach the 'concealed coalfield'. Still more ancient volcanic rocks came up to the surface at the Lickey Hills near Birmingham or at Charnwood Forest. The plain is by no means a dead level one. There are big low-lying areas along the river valleys like those of the Trent and the Ouse, but near Nottingham you come across the curious rock called the Bunter Sandstone, which forms rolling hills that reach the 400-ft level. It can be as porous as the chalk, and assumes strange shapes, like the remarkable pillar called the Hemlock Stone near Bramcote a few miles beyond Nottingham. The Midlands thus hold surprises for those who are prepared to seek them. I recommend Cannock Chase for all who think the Midlands are 'sodden and unkind'.

Cannock Chase lies about six miles south of

Stafford and is a remarkable bit of country to find in the supposedly built-over industrialised Midlands; so surprising indeed, that the National Parks Commission had no hesitation in designating it as one of the Areas of Outstanding Natural Beauty. The rock is the dry sandy Bunter sandstone and this made it, according to old tradition, the last area to be tamed by man – if indeed it has been completely tamed – in the whole of the Midlands. Some areas have been planted with conifers, some remain open with gorse and bracken. In the Sherbrooke Valley, you can find rare plants like the fly-catching sundew and the even rarer long-leaved sundew. The fallow deer come down at dusk to the pond at Seven Springs, but for me the most interesting part of the Chase is Brockton Coppice. Not far away you get a great view over the North Midland plain, even as far as the distant Wrekin in Shropshire. But it is the trees that make Brockton Coppice memorable – great oaks of unguessed-at age. You

can look at their huge gnarled branches and feel that you are back in the original vast forest that covered most of the Midlands before the Romans came. Even in the early Middle Ages the records show that this stretch of country was thickly wooded as far as the present suburbs of Wolverhampton. Domesday Book noted it as a great hunting forest belonging to the king, and Edward I, in 1281 – at the moment when he was preparing to lead his army to the final conquest of Wales – found time to order that all the wolves in the Chase should be hunted down and killed. The great oaks of Brockton, or their direct ancestors, have seen all this history come and go.

These once vast Midland forests did not attract the Celts. They preferred the lighter unwooded soils. The Midlands are not the place to search for our pre-history. Even the Romans were glad just to drive their roads on the outskirts of the forests. It was the Anglo-Saxons, working their way up the

Above: The ancient Major Oak in Sherwood Forest near Edwinstowe, said to be the meeting place for Robin Hood and his men

Right: The Hemlock Stone near Bramcote in Nottinghamshire, a natural pillar of Bunter Sandstone

wide Midland river valleys, who began the task of taming the great tree-wilderness. They cleared the 'leys' or openings in the woods, so there are any amount of place-names ending in 'ley' in the Midlands. Yet no matter how vigorously they attacked the great oaks and the tangled undergrowth, the Anglo-Saxons could never give the death-blow to the forest. There just were not enough of them to do the job. Even at the time of the Norman Conquest, the total population of England could not have been above the two million mark. So all through the Middle Ages the forest remained, especially in the Midlands, the continual background to all aspects of life in the countryside. The rich and powerful hunted the deer in its leafy depths, the peasants collected their wood in it – their only method of heating. The iron-workers needed it for the charcoal used in smelting. And above all, the desperate, dispossessed men – of whom there were many in mediaeval society –

needed it as a last refuge from often ruthless authority. There is not an ancient forest area in Britain which does not have its authentic record of actual outlaw bands. The Midlands had them in plenty, and peerless amongst the outlaws – and ironically the one about whom all the records are dubious or non-existent – stands bold Robin Hood.

You can still see the remnants of Sherwood Forest, where Robin is supposed to have lived his romantic life with Maid Marion, Little John, Friar Tuck and the rest of the folk heroes. It is close to Nottingham and is, of course, a mere shadow of its former self, but still contains huge, noble oaks. Near Bilhaugh you can see the Major Oak which measures 30 ft around the trunk, and the Green Dale Oak when I last saw it was still vigorous and growing, although certain to be 800 years old and according to some experts could even be 1,500 years old. If so, it must be high up in the competition for being the oldest living thing in

Britain. At any rate this ancient tree would most certainly have given shelter to Robin and his Merry Men – if they ever existed!

As with so many of the charming stories we delighted in when we were first introduced to the history of Britain – from King Canute defying the tide to King Bruce of Scotland and his spider – the sober researchers have had a field day with Robin. He was never the dispossessed Earl of Huntingdon, they point out. There is no actual document connecting anyone of the name of Hood with outlaws in Sherwood. Your heart leaps up when you find that there was actually a Friar Tuck, or rather a Frère Tuk, a portly cleric originally named Richard Stafford, who left his monastery for life in the greenwood. Unfortunately this far from jovial figure, who specialised in kidnapping wealthy children and was still uncaptured and busy with his nefarious tricks in 1429, operated not in Sherwood but far away to the south in the Surrey Weald. As for Maid Marion, she first appeared in French romances as a lover of a French Robin and must have been imported into the ballads about the English Robin in the 15th Century. So what remains? Clearly, the strong desire of the poor and oppressed all through the ages to find a hero who defies their oppressor. The outlaws in the Sherwoods, the Cannock Chases, the Charnwood Forests may not have given to the poor but they certainly took from the rich. There could be deeper reasons still for the popularity of Robin and his Merry Men.

Learned anthropologists point out that there was a Teutonic wood-spirit called Hudekin, and this name is closely connected philologically with the name Hood. Robin-of-the-Wood could be of the same genre as Robin Goodfellow, a survival of our long-lost pagan past. Robin Hood isn't the only example of the Old Gods still being remembered right up to our own day. All over England, on certain days of the year, old dances are performed and old rituals observed. The church may have disapproved at first, but it was compelled to come to terms with strong local feeling; and so to this day, the inhabitants of the charming village of Abbots Bromley in Staffordshire, a cluster of black

and white houses around a cluster of pubs, turn out in early September to see the traditional Horn Dance. Six dancers carry reindeer horns, there are two musicians playing an accordian and triangle, and the other assorted dancers include a boy with a bow and arrow. Their dance must surely be based on some long-lost forest ritual. Was it originally performed to increase the fertility of the deer? Who can tell? But the clergy take care that, in between dances, the horns are stored in the church.

The forests may have long lost their old glory, but their ancient, mysterious power still seems to live on in our countryside, even though, by the 16th and 17th Centuries, their extent had been severely limited – with interesting consequences to the appearance of the land. The growth of the population, the felling of wood for charcoal for industry and the demands of the Royal Navy for oak, all played their part in causing the decline. The nobility looked on the process of forest denudation with mixed feelings. They profited by the growth in the acreage of agricultural land, especially after it was enclosed. But the dappled deer, the pride and joy of the chase, lost their hiding places. The kings might still be able to retain some royal forests at places like Windsor. The noblemen had to make do with their parks, where the deer were kept for ornament and not for hunting. As the 18th Century dawned, keen huntsmen sought a solution to the problem. If it wasn't possible to chase a deer across the landscape any more, they had to discover another animal to take his place. They found the ideal substitute in that wily predator, the champion survivor of the English countryside – the fox.

It was in the Midlands, and above all in Leicestershire, that fox-hunting acquired its social mystique and started to mould a whole countryside into its own image. A slight problem at first confronted the gallant huntsmen. While they were developing fox-hunting, they were also busy enclosing the open fields that gave them their finest gallops in Winter, for the hunting season opened after the crops had been safely gathered in. They had to find some means of making the new enclosing banks jumpable yet impassable to cattle. These banks were therefore planted with the quick-

growing hawthorn – the word 'haw' means hedge in Old English. This tough plant not only looked beautiful in late Spring when the may blossom covers the hedgerows with frothy white; the hawthorn could also be cut back and intertwined, to give something that a good hunter could easily clear at full gallop. 'Laying' a hedge properly developed into an important country craft, and a good hedger was in demand. It is essentially a winter job, and December is as good a month as any for it.

The hedger bends the tough boughs back at an angle and then weaves them around stakes of hazel, driven into the earthen bank at regular intervals. The top is crowned with tightly woven stems known as 'hethers'. The thorn has to be cut half-way through before it bends properly, and the expert hedgers know exactly how deep to cut without destroying too much of the bark and wood on which the growth of the hedge depends. A well laid hedge will last five or even ten years without too much attention.

The fox, which has been hunted in Britain for nearly 300 years but often escapes the hounds with its intelligence and cunning

The humble hedge is thus a comparative newcomer to the country scene, but where would Britain be – what would it look like – without the lovely green-quilted patterning the hedges bring to our landscape? They are also a natural wild life conservancy area, giving shelter to scores of small birds and mammals that make our countryside unique. Anyone who has had to march long distances over the hedgeless plains of Europe feels a strange emptiness around him. The skies are dumb and no small birds sing. The hedges are not there to give friendly nesting places for the birds, and shelter for the myriad insects they feed on.

It is different in Britain. If you walk along a hedge with the naturalist's eye, you will find a whole world of hopeful life hidden amongst the tangled and pleated branches. Blackbirds and chaffinches, wrens and hedgesparrows all make

their nests here, feeding on the insects and the berries which abound amongst the hawthorn. Butterflies are not natural hedge-lovers; only the brimstone's caterpillars feed here. But there are plenty of aphids to satisfy the ladybirds, and that most delightful of small animals, the hedgehog, really does live in hedges, when they seem safe and convenient – and he hibernates in them as well.

One hedge resident, the biggest of them all, is viewed with mixed feelings by the farmer – the rabbit. 'Watership Down' became a best-seller because the rabbit, somehow or other, looks cuddly and charming to any town-bred child. After all, no-one has ever written a publishing success with a brown rat as hero. But a farmer who sees his growing crops nibbled down and his hedge-banks tunnelled into by the ubiquitous rabbit is bound to take a more jaundiced view of *Oryctolagus cuniculus*. The rabbit is, after all, a foreign interloper, brought over in the 12th Century to supply fresh food for the Norman overlords through the long mediaeval Winter. For centuries it was regarded as a rarity, a dish for connoisseurs. Rabbits were bred in specially guarded warrens, and the name 'warren' survives in many parts of Britain. But as food production and distribution improved steadily from Tudor times, the rabbit became 'down-graded' in the hierarchy of the cuisine. It no longer paid to maintain the old-style warrens guarded by expensive warreners. The rabbits naturally moved out and the new enclosure hedges, and the earthen banks on which they were planted, gave them perfect cover. By the end of the last war, this over-prolific breeder had become one

Above: The traditional art of hedging, not yet completely replaced by the machine

Opposite: The herd of Père Davide's deer at Woburn. They came originally from China and are now extinct in the wild

of the principal loss-makers for British agriculture. As the old rhyme puts it

> 'The rabbit has a charming face;
> Its private life is a disgrace!'

Then, in the 1960s, came retribution. The unpleasant killing disease of myxomatosis broke out in Britain, or was it imported deliberately? In any case, the rabbit population was almost wiped out, and great was the rejoicing among the farmers on the fat acres of the Midlands, whatever might have been the lamentations of the small-holders and the professional rabbit-trappers further west. The rabbit has returned, but these 'myxo-free' animals have not yet become the pest they were. 'Give them time,' say the cynics. 'Give them time.'

It is one of the ironies of agricultural history that the rabbit is not a 'sporting' animal; otherwise the keen huntsman, deprived of his deer, might have turned to the rabbit as his substitute quarry and made a major contribution to the farmer's welfare. But this is a fantasy. This supine, furtive nibbler was only good enough for rough shooting or poaching. The fox, alone of the British mammals, could rival the deer when it came to the thrill of the chase and could outrival the deer in cunning and endurance. By the beginning of the 19th Century, he was the toast of the hunting squires all over England. The 'shires' – Leicestershire above all – led the way, and the little town of Melton Mowbray became the Mecca of fox-hunting. The whole countryside in this part of the world seems moulded to please the huntsman. Not only are the hedges 'pleated', but when the woods were being cut back and the enclosures in full spate, the fox-hunters realized that they were also depriving their quarry of cover in which to breed. So they planted clumps of trees, copses and spinneys, which now make beautiful patterns on the landscape. Hunting literature is full of the history of famous runs by the Quorn, the Belvoir or the Cottesmore, starting from spinneys well known to the hunting fraternity. They talk learnedly of Barkby Holt, of the 'Bellesdon Coplow' run by the Quorn in 1800, when Hugo Meynell was master; of the perils of the Whissendine Brook in the same detail as golfers devote to the Old Course at St Andrews. You talk about this exclusive world at your peril. They tell the story of the young newcomer who sought to make an impression by bragging of his Melton Mowbray acquaintances. Finally they asked him, 'Do you know Barkby Holt?' 'Of course,' he replied, 'I dined with him last week.'

A naïve story, but one which shows the social prestige held unchallenged by fox-hunting to our own day. It had become an integral part of the country scene. Oscar Wilde might sneer about 'the unspeakable in pursuit of the uneatable', but he was a rank outsider and country folk strongly supported their local packs. If you forget the fox, there is no pleasanter sight in rural Britain than a pack of hounds coming down a country lane, tails in the air, with the pink-coated huntsmen whipping them in

173

Above: The wild rabbit which is returning in increasing numbers to the countryside of Britain

Opposite: Belvoir Castle, the seat of the Dukes of Rutland. It was built by James Wyatt in the early 19th Century as a fake mediaeval castle on the site of several earlier buildings, the original castle dating from the 11th Century

Below: The hedgehog, which is very easily tamed and is often found in suburban gardens

and the master and the rest of the field clip-clopping behind. And then the sound of the horn in the clear air of a frosty December day, and away goes the baying pack with the well mounted riders clearing the fences or going timorously round by an opened gate, until the whole hunt disappears into the pattern of dark fields with perhaps a glimpse of the reddish-brown fox loping ahead ready to trick the hounds by running among a flock of sheep or even swimming the nearest water to drown his scent. But today, a strong body of opinion has grown up dedicated to taking the side of the fox. 'Ban Blood Sports' banners are flaunted at meets, false trails are laid to decoy the hounds and fierce letters of denunciation appear in the Press. Even the sacred shrine of the grave of John Peel himself has been desecrated. The protesters exclaim against the cruelty of it, the supporters claim they are usefully destroying vermin in a picturesque way. Who dares take sides without being overwhelmed by reproaches from huntsmen or demonstrators? But one keen rider to hounds remarked to me, as he ruefully contemplated the cost of a day out with the Quorn, 'What are the protesters making such a fuss about? Let them wait 20 years and there will be nobody left who can afford to hunt.'

The same might be said of the castles and noble mansions once inherited by the nobility and gentry who were the original patrons of fox-hunting; those Great Houses set in their wide parks which, even in their decay, are an essential part of the British landscape and give it a special distinction. Social change has played havoc with most of them and no-one nowadays will ever be in a position to set aside great acres of the countryside, enclose them, plant them and mould them to their heart's desire. No-one, not even a government department or the board of a state-owned industry, will dare do what the first Duke of Devonshire did at Chatsworth, on the edge of the Peak District where the Derwent prepares to break out on to the Midlands plain. He straightened out a long stretch of the river and removed a whole village, Edensor, out of sight of the house. His descendant, the sixth Duke, gave a free rein to Joseph Paxton, who went on to construct the Crystal Palace. Paxton created

vast cascades, ornamented waters and a fountain that throws a jet nearly 300 ft into the air. There were other dukes in the Midlands who were equally lavish in building; so much so that one area of Nottinghamshire is known as the Dukeries. At Clumber Park, the Duke of Newcastle enclosed 3,500 acres and engaged Sir Charles Barry, the architect of the Houses of Parliament, to build a huge mansion, with an artificial lake and a splendid avenue of limes three miles long. Nearby, at Welbeck Abbey, another great house arose in the 18th Century, which was nearly undermined by the fifth Duke of Portland in the 1850s. This extraordinary man was a recluse, with a morbid fear of being seen. He lived like a mole and put his library, ball-room, kitchen, even a mile-long approach way, all underground. Other noblemen, all over England, had no compunction, however, in displaying their love of landscape-gardening above ground. Would we be enjoying the rich country views in places like Stourhead in Wiltshire, Bolton Abbey in Yorkshire – and to return to the Midlands – Belvoir Castle (pronounced, I need hardly say, 'Beever') in Leicestershire, without the lavish and no doubt socially reprehensible expenditure of their noble occupants in the past? They chose to live for long periods on their country estates and took delight in improving them; in direct contrast to the French nobility, who fluttered like moths around the Sun King at Versailles and hardly dared to build their country houses further away than the

Île de France. The early Victorian songstress, Mrs Felicia Dorothea Hemens, could sing, with national approval, about

'The stately homes of England,
How beautiful they stand,
Amidst their tall ancestral trees
O'er all the pleasant land.'

These tall ancestral trees were more than 100 years old by the time Mrs Hemens, as one critic put it, 'strung her sympathetic lyre', and the face of the English landscape appeared very much the same as the best parts of it look today. Let us admit that many of its delights are entirely due to the cash and taste of the 18th-century aristocrats.

The parks around Tudor great houses still inherited some of the wildness of the forest. In their enormous 'preserves', it was still possible to go hunting the deer, as Queen Elizabeth did at Hatfield and hunting-mad James I at nearly every great house in south-east England. Their gardens were close to the house, and curiously wrought. Sir Francis Bacon, in that beautifully knotted prose of his, praised the great hedges, the alleys and twisting flower-beds of the Elizabethan garden.

'And because the breath of flowers is far sweeter in the air (where it comes and goes like the warbling of music) than in the hand, therefore nothing is more fit for that delight, than to know what be the flowers and plants that do best perfume the air.' Bacon goes on to give a long list of the plants that

Above : The mediaeval cross on Meriden's village green, claimed to mark the centre of England

Below : The church of SS Mary and Bartholomew at Hampton-in-Arden in Warwickshire. The village is thought to have been the original setting for Shakespeare's 'As You Like It'

scent the surrounding air 'most delightfully', including honeysuckles, 'so they be somewhat afar off'. But, naturally, not too far. Neither Elizabethan man or woman in formal dress was equipped for long walks in a wide park.

With Charles II the garden starts to enlarge itself, and the bolder gardeners were looking outward to see what they could do, not just with the grounds close around the house, but with the Great Park itself. Le Nôtre was busy creating the vast formal gardens at Versailles, which far surpassed in scale anything that the Elizabethans had planned. England did not hesitate to follow suit, as you can still see at Hampton Court. But this French formality was not altogether congenial to the English spirit. Even that most balanced and formal of poets, Alexander Pope, sounded a warning against over-elaboration. Avenues and statues by all means, he says in his beautifully turned couplets, but never forget to give Nature her chance – within the bounds of propriety of course.

'To build, to plant, whatever you intend,
To rear the column, or the Arch to bend,
To swell the Terrace, or to sink the Grot,
In all, let Nature never be forgot.
But treat the Goddess like a modest fair,
Not overdress, nor leave her wholly bare...'

As the 18th Century developed, a series of notable gardeners appeared who were prepared to follow Pope's precepts. Perhaps we should call them 'landscape artists', for their eyes were now fixed on far wider horizons than the tight-knit Elizabethan 'pleasaunces' or the grand but over-disciplined avenues of Hampton Court.

I think we must salute William Kent as the man who really pioneered the new style, this break away from the formality in gardening that had reigned supreme under the late Stuarts and Dutch William. At last, as the 18th Century developed, the great noblemen and their lesser satellites began to feel secure on their estates after the ups and downs of the turbulent 17th Century. The Hanoverians were safely on the throne and sturdy, common-sensible Sir Robert Walpole was managing politics and the economy. Trade boomed. Land, ever more scientifically farmed, was the solid basis of great wealth. And the noble families had most of the land. Why should they not enjoy it up to the hilt? The nation expected its great men to make a display, just as the Indians of the west coast of Canada expected their chiefs, from time to time, to squander all their accumulated wealth in one gigantic, glorious guzzle. In the 18th Century, our chiefs also set up their totem poles in the form of their great houses surrounded by superb parks.

One contemporary observed that the whole country seemed possessed by this building mania. Every man of substance seemed, as he put it, to be 'doing something in his place' and informs you that 'he is in mortar and heaving of earth, the modest terms for building and gardening. One large room, a serpentine river and a wood are become the absolute necessities of life, without which a gentleman of the smallest fortune thinks he makes no figure in his county.'

The scale of what some of the great men 'did in their place' staggers us today. Blenheim, Castle Howard, Woburn, Houghton, Petworth – the list can extend across Britain – all crammed with artistic loot from Italy or paintings by Gainsborough, Reynolds, Van Dyke or Rembrandt, all with their state rooms, vast bedrooms, servants' quarters and stables on a princely scale. Great entrance halls and vast flights of stairs impressed the visitor. When you walk through the corridors of Blenheim you are overwhelmed by the sheer length of them – 'the only place in Britain where you can get your hat blown off indoors'. Opulent, extravagant, these new rising palaces might be, but they were at least built and furnished with an elegance and taste which charms and delights us today. Palladio in Italy had set the tone and the classical style of a great man's country house, and William Kent transferred Palladio's inspiration to England.

These new-style houses clearly required a new-style setting. The country around them had to be landscaped to frame the classical colonnade, but landscaped according to Pope's precept: 'let Nature never be forgot.' Kent grouped his trees in 'a pleasing wildness'. Lakes were planned to mirror the white-columned façade; and Kent is credited

with inventing the 'ha-ha', the deep trench that separated the gardens immediately in front of the house from the park-lands beyond. Thus the deer could be seen from the state rooms, and the ornamental black and white spotted Jacob sheep were imported from the Mediterranean as natural lawn mowers. The pretty story that they swam ashore from the wrecked galleons of the Armada is without foundation. There were other great landscape planners besides Kent, including Bridgeman and the ubiquitous Lancelot Brown, nick-named 'Capability' from his habit of asserting that every park he was invited to plan was 'capable of improvement'.

Improved they certainly were. These parks around the great houses have now had nearly 200 years of life. The trees planted with such confident optimism by the 18th-century 'milords' have come to maturity. Ironically these landscapes created by the genius of Brown, Kent and their followers, are looking their best at the very moment when the whole world they represent has passed away. The great houses which the parks were created to frame, are becoming increasingly difficult to maintain. Their noble owners must perforce accept grants from government funds and open their castles to the public. Some have collapsed under the pressure of taxation and death duties. In the Dukeries, Clumber has been pulled down. Welbeck Abbey has become an Army training school. Tourists walk in the gardens and through the state rooms of Belvoir. Dutch elm disease attacks noble avenue after noble avenue.

Yet so much still remains; and above all, the parks. Arrogant, proud, spendthrift these dukes and noblemen may seem as they rode through their woods at Woburn, or arranged their elaborate picnics beside the lake at Blenheim, while their private orchestra dispensed the music of Handel from a barge floating on the still waters; but they left us a legacy of aristocratic country beauty which we must doubly value in these hurried, crowded democratic days. And so many of these great parks are in the Midlands, the heart of England.

But where, in geographical terms, is the exact heart, the central point of England? At school we

Above: Charocal burning in the ancient forests of England.
In the Middle Ages charcoal and wood were the only fuels
available

Right: Ambien Hill on Bosworth Field where Henry Tudor
defeated the last of the Plantagenets, Richard III, in one of the
most crucial battles in English history

used to puzzle ourselves by drawing lines on the map from the four deepest inlets on the coast – the Mersey, the Severn, the Thames and the Wash. We concluded that it was somewhere near Rugby, but our maps did not show the exact point in the estuaries at which the high tide ended. We did, however, elicit the interesting fact that there is no point in Great Britain which is more than 70 miles from salt water. Perhaps we should have picked the Dee or the Humber instead of the Mersey or the Wash. Some villages like Meriden, between Coventry and Hampton-in-Arden, have put up stones claiming that they have the magic spot on their village greens. At Lillington, near Leamington, they proudly show you the Midland Oak. I'd like to feel there is an officially appointed centre, but in its absence I propose that we pick somewhere where history was changed and the fate of England settled.

The Midlands can show two places which could claim that honour. The first lies near Market Bosworth, the little town which has given its name to the Battle of Bosworth Field. As usual, the exact spot where Henry VII defeated Richard III in 1485 and started the Tudor dynasty on its road to glory, is some miles away between the villages of Shenton and Sutton Cheney. But you can stand on the gentle rise that goes by the grandiose name of Ambien Hill and see King Dick's well, surrounded by its little wall. You remember, if you've looked up your history books first, that here Richard took his last drink before going into battle and heartened his men as he declared: 'I live a king; if I die, I die a king.' Die he did, die, fighting bravely. You look across to a second gentle rise – Crown Hill. Here, according to tradition, Sir Reginald Bray came with Richard's crown, which he had found in a thorn bush, and placed it on Henry's head. I am all for accepting these traditions, for folk-memory is tenacious. The Battle of Bosworth Field would have been the most vivid event ever to occur at Shenton or Sutton Cheney, until the drone of the German bombers sounded overhead on their way to Coventry.

I felt very close to the past, once again, as I went to see the second site in the Midlands where history was changed, Naseby – the decisive battle in the First Civil War, in the Summer of 1645. Perhaps this little village really should be the centre of England; 'the central boss of the Midlands,' John Buchan called it, 'the water-parting from which streams flowed to both the Atlantic and the North Sea.' And Buchan went on to point out that, from springs a few feet from Naseby village, the Avon runs to the Severn and the Nen to the Wash, while the Welland rose in a hollow behind King Charles's position on Dust Hill. 'It was fitting that the battle which was to decide the fate of England should be fought in the very heart of the English land.'

I had the countryside to myself as I walked on the battlefield on that crisp December day. The weather was in strange contrast to the warm summer day, bright after rain, on which the battle was fought. I came to the memorial which now marks the ridge on which the New Model Army was drawn up. Before me the ground sloped gently down to the very spot where the pikemen on both sides had met with a shattering crash. The land has now been enclosed for 200 years, but I could still walk to the grass-grown point where Cromwell's Ironsides made their devastating charge against the flank of Prince Rupert's Bluecoats, who fought and died where they stood. I looked over the hedges to Dust Hill. I saw the place where the unhappy King Charles, realizing that his army was collapsing, rode forward to lead his last reserves to the rescue. Lord Carnwath ran and seized the king's bridle, crying, 'Sir, will you go to your death?' The king, perforce, had to turn away, his reserves turned with him – and so did the history of England.

As I stood remembering that fateful day nearly 350 years ago, a tractor was working on Dust Hill, getting the earth ready for the plough. A horseman rode along the road, and a lorry passed carrying bales of hay for the cattle. All that history, from Bosworth Field to Naseby and the German bombers flying overhead through the night – yes, the Midlands had absorbed it all and just kept steadily at work. If this was the heart of England, then it was beating still – strong, firm, utterly dependable!

December with the Poets

A heavy frost last night,
The longest night of the year,
Makes the land at first light
Look spruced up for death,
Incurably white.

But the earth moving fast
Tips the shadow across
The field. It rolls past
Sheep who hold their ground
And into the hedge at last.

Nor far behind, a track
Of frost is following
That the sun cannot lick
Completely green in time,
Before night rolls back.

PATRICIA BEER

The time draws near the birth of Christ
    The moon is hid; the night is still,
    The Christmas bells from hill to hill
Answer each other in the mist.

Four voices of four hamlets round
    From far and near; on mead and moor,
    Swell out and fall, as if a door
Was shut between me and the sound.

ALFRED LORD TENNYSON

The cards that tumble through the door,
The footprints on the frozen ground
Of robins whistling in the snow,
The pleasant, sanctimonious sound
Of bells from tall St Mary's tower,
And carols in the empty street
Played by Salvation Army bands,
All that made childhood Christmas sweet –
To me, remembering Christmas Past,
These were the gifts the Magi brought
When, star-led through the bitter night,
The Manger and the Child they sought.
But, in their wisdom, they have left
One gift alone that we must find –
The gift most pleasing to that Child –
True peace and love amongst Mankind.

W. V. THOMAS

January

January is the tough testing time in the British calendar. Not for nothing is it named after the Roman god Janus, who was always depicted with two heads facing different ways. January can begin with deceptive mildness but sooner or later it turns savage and flings snow and ice at the helpless countryside. In 1979 January was a testing time indeed, and the snow lay for weeks on the hills, bringing to them a strange, unearthly beauty. High hills under snow, seen across dark, wintry lowlands, seem to belong to another world. Anyone who has had the vision of Snowdonia in winter from the low-flying island of Anglesey, or Arran under snow from the Ayrshire coast, will know that sudden shock of delighted surprise at the change wrought in a familiar landscape when it is redrawn in white under the cold, clear sun, bright in the pale blue sky that comes after heavy snowfalls. Then the clouds pile up again. The whirling flakes blot out the vision and you are drawn back, by two-faced January, into the harsh challenge of this harsh month.

My thoughts then turn to the hill-farmer who has to face this challenge in its toughest form. The narrow lanes to the farm-house will be skiddy with ice, and the farmer will be out checking on his sheep which, even if he has brought them down to comparatively lower ground, might be buried under deep drifts. Yet somehow they survive. After each snowfall I vow I will reconsider the title 'silly' that we apply so readily to these remarkable animals. Lowland sheep may be another matter. They can afford to be placid and obedient. The mountain variety has got to use intelligence to survive. Mountain sheep have to be agile as well. I remember one old Welsh hill-farmer saying to me

The west edge of Kinder Scout in the Derbyshire Peak District, looking towards Cluther Rocks and Kinder Low from the northern edge of Kinder Downfall

182

as he ruefully watched some of his flock clearing a high wall, 'Boy, these aren't sheep. They are antelopes in woolly pullovers.' And some instinct leads the old ewes to shelter in the safest spots on the snow-covered mountains. No-one has more experience of hard weather than the sheep-farmers up in the Yorkshire Dales. In fact, I regard not only the Dales but the whole range of the Pennines, starting in the Peak and ending nearly 200 miles north on the wild Northumberland moors, as the most winter-defying place in the whole country. The Pennines are the tough, unyielding backbone of England. They are now traversed by the longest footpath in England, which runs for a total of 250 miles, starting at Edale in Derbyshire, on over high moorlands, lonely bogs and up and down the steep valleys to come to a satisfying end on the grassy summits of the Cheviots on the Scottish border. If you succeed in walking the whole length of it, you will have not only marched through stern but splendid scenery; you will have gained an understanding of the difference in character between the people of southern England and the Men of the North.

You sense this difference immediately you enter the southern end of the Pennines in Derbyshire. As you drive up the valley of the Dove, you are in no doubt that you are leaving behind those fertile rolling plainlands of the south country. The hills close in and the Dove runs faster than the sleepy slow-moving Trent or any of the rivers of the Midlands. The Dove probably feels a special responsibility to look beautiful because it was the stream beloved of Isaac Walton, that most eloquent of fishermen, whose Compleat Angler has become the fisherman's secular Prayer Book. The trout you catch in the Dove must be the descendants of the fish so skilfully hooked by him over 300 years ago. In the narrowest part of the valley, Dove Dale itself, the bright rocks take on strange shapes christened with the usual variety of tourist-attracting names like the Twelve Apostles, the Lion's Head, the Lover's Leap and the Tissington Spires. You have left the lowlands far behind and you are among the remarkable formations, from isolated rocks, swallow holes and deep caverns,

peculiar to the mountain limestone country.

If you break out of the valley eastwards for a few miles you come to the village of Tissington itself – a collection of attractive stone-built houses around the village green, which is crowded on Ascension Day, when the whole countryside seems to arrive for the well-dressing ceremony. The local craftsmen design special panels depicting biblical subjects to beautify the five local wells which are then blessed by the clergy who go round in procession. Well-dressing takes place in other villages throughout Derbyshire where the wells are garlanded with flowers and complex patterns made from petals. Is this really a Christian custom, or does it go back into the mists of pre-history? About six miles directly north of Tissington, out in the open country between the deep dales characteristic of the limestone country – the 'White Peak' they call it – stands the remarkable stone circle of Arbor Low. It is at least 4,000 years old and reminds us that the Peak was one of those parts of Britain favoured, like the chalklands and the Cotswolds, by the earliest settlers. Did they leave some faint memories behind of their worship of a river god which survived in the well-dressing ceremonies? I would like to think so. The landscape of Britain owes a great deal of its charm to the ancient memories it holds, and this Peak country is rich in echoes from our distant past.

The Romans came here in search of lead, and lead mines and their remains lie everywhere in the Peak. One of the main veins has the picturesque name of the Great Rake. Daniel Defoe, that observant and enterprising traveller around Britain in the late 17th and early 18th Centuries has left a vivid description of a Derbyshire lead-miner coming out of one of the narrow cracks in the rock: 'the man was a most uncouth spectacle; he was clothed all in leather, had a cap of the same without brims . . . he was lean as a skeleton, pale as a dead corpse, his hair and beard a deep black, his flesh lank, and, as we thought, something of the colour of lead itself.' Before the industry fell on difficult days as foreign competition undercut prices, the area produced 10% of the country's lead requirements. The other great extractive industry of the

A herd of Wensleydale sheep under the watchful eye of the sheep-dog

Peak – and one which many people would wish to do without – is quarrying. The huge beds of mountain limestone are easily worked and have proved an irresistible attraction to industry. Some of these quarries are on a big scale and the white dust they create gives a strange, ghostly appearance to the silvered trees in the nearby woods. But so much of the 'White Peak' remains unspoilt that it has become a major tourist area. They crowd into Castleton to look at the marvels of the huge Peak Cavern and the grottos where the strange Blue John stone is found. Nearby is the miniature gorge of the Winnats Pass and the Speedwell Cavern that you approach by boat down the long channel cut by the old 18th-century lead-miners. All these delights are accessible by car, but to get to know the limestone country well you must walk. The best parts of the Manifold Valley, for example, are

walker's country and you have to climb to see Thor's Cave or the huge limestone face of Beeston Tor. Limestone cliffs are a feature of the 'White Peak', and one of the most spectacular of them, High Tor, is close to Matlock. The strangest must be Mam Tor, near Castleton, and technically this isn't a pure limestone cliff. The beds of shale and sandstone that lie under the 1,496-ft high summit are unstable and disintegrating to give the hill its picturesque name of the 'Shivering Mountain'.

It is quite safe, however, to stand on the ramparts of the Iron Age fort that crowns the summit. Here you look north over Edale into a different, sterner country. The bright limestone rock has disappeared and been replaced by the dark Yoredale Beds and the still darker Millstone Grits. These latter are not formations that yield to the weather like the limestone. They seem to defy it. The harder beds form lines of low cliffs like Axe Edge near Buxton or the Roaches above Sheffield, high enough to attract the rock-climbers. The gritstone rises to its climax on the highest part of the Peak, Kinder Scout and Bleaklow Hill. Bleak

indeed they are in January. Both are over 2,000 ft, and are the quintessence of the scenery of the 'Dark Peak' – heathery, boggy, criss-crossed by deep channels in the peat known as 'groughs' and with a rocky edge over which a stream tumbles to make the 100-ft high Kinder Downfall. In January the Downfall can freeze into a spectacular cascade of glittering icicles and you may be lucky enough to see the white hares which are a Kinder speciality. The curious thing about this lonely challenging country is its proximity on the map to the densely inhabited lowlands of industrial Lancashire. From the summit of Kinder, on a clear day, you can make out the suburbs of Manchester. Inevitably the ramblers, the toilers who 'had been long in city pent', lifted up their eyes to the hills every fine weekend. But in the years before the last war, those hills were not wide open to the wanderer. They were under grouse. As the grouse season opened officially on August 12th – the Glorious Twelfth to the shooting man – a cordon of keepers encircled the enticing wilderness of Kinder Scout.

There are grouse moors still flourishing all the

Right: Crossing from Derbyshire to Staffordshire on the 20 Stepping Stones over the River Dove in Dovedale. Its limestone gorge is called locally 'Little Switzerland'

Opposite: The Bishop of Lichfield officiates at the Tissington well-dressing ceremony on Ascension Day

Teesdale in the Pennines

way up further north in the long chain of the Pennines, and this bird of the curious call of 'come back-bek-bek-bek' and of the whirring flight as he starts from under your feet when you tramp through the heather, is one of the delights of the moorlands of Britain. The plump red grouse is the main target of the guns, as the beaters send them up towards the marksmen waiting in the butts. The shooting does not seem to harm their numbers for the grouse is a prolific breeder and many of them would be doomed to die from lack of food in hard winters if they were not 'thinned' – or so the shooting men stoutly maintain to the anti-blood sports lobby. The black grouse, which comes into

its own the further north you travel in the Pennines is larger than the red variety and has a far more interesting love life. The males gather on communal mating grounds known as 'leks', and here the blackcocks flap their wings and fluff out their feathers in mating displays and battle for the greyhens. The winner takes all, or at least as many as he can keep on his territory against the losers, who continue all through the Spring and Summer to hover hopefully on the fringes.

The ramblers of Lancashire did the same before the last war around the forbidden 'lek' of Kinder Scout, until the trespassing climbers organised themselves to fight what has passed into the walker's folklore as the Battle of Kinder Scout. I talked with one old hand recently who looked back nostalgically to the romantic days when he and his comrades used to plan commando-type operations to reach the summit. Two or three of them would show themselves on one side of the track leading up to the high ground and draw the keepers. Then the fastest man, hidden behind the rocks and trained for high-speed work over the deep tangled 'groughs', would race triumphantly for the top. Who won the battle? In the long run the ramblers; for, even before the war, the government in 1939 looked at the whole question of the public rights of way on the land and passed the Access to the Mountains Act. After the war, they went further. In the general feeling of euphoria as the gunfire died away, Parliament created the new series of National Parks, of which the Peak District was the first to be designated in 1950.

The concept of national parks did not originate in Britain. It came to us from America where in 1872 the US Senate set aside Yellowstone Park, an area which is as large as all seven English national parks put together. And British parks differ in essence from those set up in countries like the USA, Canada or Australia where there were still big areas of unsettled country. In Britain every inch of land already owned by somebody and to buy the whole area of a place like the Peak would embarrass the most recklessly spendthrift of governments. But although the land remains in private possession, or may be owned by such bodies as the Forestry

Commission or the National Trust, the Park authorities have the right to control all unsuitable developments and the duty to provide car parks, general amenities and generally oversee the growth of the Park. The system works well, although the pressure increases continually on these reserved areas. From time to time heavy industry proposes developments in the parks which seem diametrically opposed to the purposes for which the parks were set up. The big quarries and the concrete-making plants naturally want to continue to expand in the Peak. Rio Tinto Zinc were anxious to mine copper in one of the wildest parts of Snowdonia. The Park authorities have to balance the immediate needs of vital industries with the future need to preserve our national heritage of beauty in the countryside. The decisions they make do not please everyone.

The very popularity of the parks brings its own problems. The officials of the Park not only have to negotiate rights of way with the farmers and landowners. They also have to educate a town-bred public in the art of using these rights properly. Tension can grow between tourists and the men who have to make a living out of the land, if the tourists leave gates open or let their pet dogs worry the sheep and cattle. I, myself, am lucky enough to own a small patch of the coastline in the Pembrokeshire National Park, and I was delighted to give my permission for the coast path to go through to the thrilling views out to the great cliffs of Cemaes Head. I was a little upset one day to find a car had been driven through the fence on to the cliff edge and a family party were busy scattering their lunch rubbish around them. I naturally expostulated with them but was a little disarmed when the friendly father said, apologetically, 'Well, this is a National Park, you know, and it's now owned by the people, and we were just enjoying ourselves.' All ended happily with the family cheerfully picking up their litter and with me inviting them to return; but that little incident taught me a lot about farmers' fears and the problems facing the Park administration.

The Peak Park authorities, as befits the pioneer, have been working hard towards a solution to the

The moors above Haworth in Yorkshire, which Emily Brontë used as the setting for 'Wuthering Heights'

over-use of the park. They have reserved some areas, like the Goyt Valley, completely for walkers. They have instituted 'Sherpa' buses to take hikers to the start of their trail from car parks well out of sight of the beauty-spot to be visited. They have cleared a section of the disused Ashbourne to Buxton railway as a green track for pony-trekkers and walkers. They have shown that, in crowded Britain, only a system of National Parks can safeguard the wild and beautiful places, backed up by the vigilance of such voluntary and dedicated bodies as the Council for the Protection of Rural England and its fellow councils in Scotland and Wales.

Above: Turner's watercolour of a lonely dell in Wharfedale, an area much loved by the English watercolourists

Opposite: The River Ribble, which flows eastwards through the Pennines to the Lancashire coast at Preston

You have only to proceed to the next section of the Pennine Way to see what happened in the past when there was no National Park system to control development. The high moors remain impressive with their heathery wastes although Defoe went a little too far when he called Blackstone Edge 'the Andes of England'. The heads of lonely valleys are filled with reservoirs, but industry has crept up the lower course of those valleys from the Lancashire mill towns to the west and from the Yorkshire woollen towns to the east. The railways and the new arterial roads have all had to fight their way across this high central spine of northern England and haven't exactly left beauty in their path. But the great hills shake these encumbrances free and the last little town where you feel the breath of industry is Haworth. Its incredibly steep cobbled main street leads you up past the stone-built cottages with their slate roofs to the little square which contains the church, rebuilt with the exception of the tower, and the parsonage symbolically overlooking the grave-yard. You are now in a place of pilgrimage. Here the Brontë family lived from 1820 to 1861. Opposite you is the Black Bull Inn in which Branwell, the sisters' unhappy brother, drank himself to death. I first visited Haworth in January when the vestiges of snow still lay in the streets and the drifts were deep on Penistone Hill and Haworth Moor. The whole place seemed to have stepped right out of the pages of 'Jane Eyre', or better still, of 'Wuthering Heights'. I expected Heathcliff to come riding down any minute through this stern, uncompromising landscape, which so vividly retains the atmosphere of the Brontë novels. I confess it was with some sense of breathing a happier, brighter air that I then drove up into the Yorkshire Dales.

Even in mid-winter, I feel that these lovely

valleys, with their pastures set amongst the high hills, are happy places to be in. There are welcoming inns, deep woods and clear streams that seem to tumble over picturesque waterfalls especially to please the painters. There are falls in vast variety, from the 100-ft Hardraw Force in Wensleydale which is the highest single-drop waterfall in England, to the elegantly stepped Aysgarth Force lower down the dale. No wonder Turner and the English water-colourists returned again and again to the Dales. The main Dales are five in number, pushing deep into the Pennines from the fertile York plain like the probing fingers of a hand. The southernmost finger, the Aire, is unhappily the dirtiest finger since it has to run through the heavy industrial area around Leeds, but even the Aire redeems itself in its upper reaches where it cuts a wide path through the hills towards the valley of the Ribble coming up through Lancashire from the west. Here lies the celebrated Aire gap, the easiest way across the main Pennine chain. It was used by the Leeds and Liverpool canal, and earlier still by Cromwell, when he made his lightning dash through the mountains in 1648 to cut the invading Scots to pieces at Preston. North of Airedale comes seductive Wharfedale; then comes Nidderdale, moving up to the dark moorland climax of Great Wernside. The Ure Valley comes up from Ripon and is called Wensleydale in its middle reaches as a compliment to the little village of Wensley, where they first sold the splendid cheese which is the gastronomic glory of the Dale. There are other smaller dales, that branch off the Big Five. Dentdale must be the deepest of them.

Swaledale is the most northerly of the main valleys and always seems to me to be the wildest of them, mainly because I once bicycled over to it from Teesdale against a head-wind. I struggled up the road on to the moors to a welcome pause at Tan Hill which then had the highest inn in England at about 1,700 ft. Then came my reward – a long free-wheeling run off the moors down the road that almost tumbles into Keld, the topmost village of Swaledale. I had time to look across to Great Shunner Fell and the delightfully named Lovely

The 70-ft drop of High Force over the Great Whin Sill escarpment on the River Tees in Yorkshire, with Cronkley Fell in the distance

Seat. All the fells here are over the 2,000-ft level and in Autumn the heather dyes them a rich purple. They are tough walking, with patches of sphagnum moss, but the birds are your reward. The curlew calls, the grouse clatter away across the heather, and the redshank and the golden plover haunt the damp boglands. The streams tumble down the hillsides in white skeins of waterfalls in the stony clefts or 'gills', and the stone walls make subtle patterns against the green lower slopes. Through the meadows and woods on the valley floor, the Swale stream goes singing down the valley. As I bicycled down Swaledale, I wasn't simply riding through the splendid scenery but through the very character of the Yorkshire folk – strong and unyielding like their moors above, warm and loyal beneath like their dales.

Next day I walked the green track that leads from Keld over the slopes of Kisdon Hill to Muker; the Copse Way they call it, for until 1580 the nearest consecrated ground was 15 miles away at Grinton. If anyone died high up on the fells, the body was placed in a wicker coffin and dragged down on a sledge to Keld. It was then carried on the sturdy shoulders of the relatives through Muker, where they kept special glasses in the inn kitchen to refresh the mourners. There was much water in the streams as I returned and all night through my bedroom window at the inn I could hear the consoling roar of the fall of Cotrake Force.

I ended my cycle tour outside the dales themselves at a noble ruin which still seemed to belong to them in spirit and purpose – Fountains Abbey, which is the biggest, and some claim the most beautiful, of all the many ruined abbeys of Britain. It has rivals – Tintern set in the woods beside the encircling Wye or Melrose on the Tweed. Even in Yorkshire itself it must compete with Rievaulx in the Wolds, with Whitby perched on its headland above the grey North Sea, and Bolton, with the River Wharfe racing towards it through the strange, narrow rock-channel of the

Strid. Somehow Fountains out-towers them all. It is built on a grander scale and at the Dissolution it was the richest monastery in England. The great church may be a roofless shell and the refectory ruined, but the grass is still smooth and green in the cloisters and the whole plan of the building is intact. You can walk through the silent open passageways and imagine exactly how a monastery functioned in its most opulent days.

But as I loitered among these ruined splendours and long arcades, my mind went back to the early days of Fountains, to AD 1137 when the monks came from York to settle in what was then a remote spot out of the world, and adopted the stern Cistercian rule of prayer linked with hard work. They were agricultural pioneers, reclaiming the wilderness through sheep-farming on a grand scale. It was the same all over England and Wales at this generative time – the Cistercians, in their white robes of wool, went out into the wilderness and made it productive. In Wales they settled in Strata Florida in Cardiganshire and led their flocks out over the wild country south of Plynlimon. From Fountains the monks tamed the harshest moors of the Pennines. No wonder that the Cistercians were the order that won the affection and respect of the common people. But initial sacrifice brought corrupting success. The money from the wool-clip mounted and the numbers of the monks fell. They let out their moors to tenants and the cash that came from the sale of their products to the wool-hungry weavers of the Netherlands and Italy poured into the coffers of the monks. In the early Middle Ages England was the great wool-exporting country. The low-lying water-crossed plains at the mouth of the Rhine and the hot Mediterranean valleys around Florence were no good for sheep-rearing on a big scale. Europe needed wool, for silk was for the rich only and cotton hadn't yet appeared on the industrial horizon. The great centres of finance and culture in the Netherlands and Italy began their rise to power on the wool trade. It pleases me to think that some of the cash that commissioned Van Eyck and Giotto might have begun its career, as it were, on the back of a sheep up in lonely Swaledale! And I wonder, too, how many of the Dalesmen owe

Above: The River Swale at Richmond, a view from the Norman castle which dominates the town

Opposite: Kilnsey Crag in Wharfedale

their descent to the monks' first tenants. But by the time of the Dissolution of the Monasteries in 1538, Fountains had long lost its first splendid inspiration. Henry VIII sold it to Sir Richard Gresham in 1540 and the last abbot didn't hesitate to accept a pension, generous in those days, of £100 a year.

The abbey lands were a rich prize, for they stretched right across the Pennines into the remarkable country around Settle which forms such a contrast to the dark millstone grit country to

the east. Here the mountain limestone, which we met far to the south in the Peak, reappears with spectacular effect. Wharfedale runs up into it and holds many of its spectacular show-places like the great limestone cliff of Kilnsey Crag. You are still within the clutches of the old monks who made Kilnsey village their headquarters for their manor courts and gave the monastery's name to the 2,000-ft Fountains Fell. You walk on the old drovers' road of Mastiles Lane across the hills to Malham, where the humped bridge reminds you of

the packhorses that carried the wool away from this limestone wilderness to the outside world. Malham introduces you to the real reason for the limestone country's existence. It lies on the Craven Fault, part of the remarkable series of gigantic faults that, in Permian times, lifted up the underlying limestone 5,000 ft almost to the level of the millstone grit. All the features we have already met in the mountain limestone of Derbyshire reappear on an epic scale – including the vast underground cave systems which are a challenge to the experts. Malham Cove

Above: A view from Fountains Fell in Yorkshire of Pen-y-Ghent (2,273 ft)

Right: Aysgarth Force on the River Ure in the West Riding of Yorkshire. The series of waterfalls extends for half a mile

itself is a white, curved sheer cliff with the River Aire flowing out from its base. Two miles away, along the line of the fault, is the gorge of Gordale Scar.

Grouped around the head of Ribbledale are the three summits of the Pennine limestone land – Ingleborough, Wernside, and the most interesting mountain shape in the whole of the Pennine range, Pen-y-Ghent. Near Ingleborough and again behind Malham Tarn you can see examples of the strange limestone pavements formed by solution along the joints in the limestone. And everywhere the limestone walls make patterns over the smooth grassy uplands. Dry-stone walling is an art, and the technique varies throughout the hill country of Britain. Up in the Pennines, the 'dyker' builds his wall of two separate courses of flattish stones, leaning slightly inwards, and he fills the space in between, the 'heart', with smaller stones. Curiously enough, he piles the bigger stones uppermost to allow their weight to keep the whole structure

solid. In the Southern Uplands of Scotland they build the 'Galloway wall', with the top 2 ft more loosely piled so that light shows between the big stones. The Scottish dyker, so the theory goes, plays on the psychology of the sheep. They come to the wall, look at it, and decide that the whole thing is too rickety and dangerous to climb over. I do not know if the Swaledale and Wensleydale breeds are more hard-headed than the Scottish Blackface. Perhaps, like true Yorkshire folk, they refuse to be imposed on and therefore need solid walls the whole way up to keep them in. The Yorkshire sheep-farmer, like sheep-farmers all through Britain, relies not only on his walls but on his trusted sheep-dogs to manage his flock. The fascinating art of handling sheep-dogs seems to be peculiar to Britain and visiting Frenchmen or Germans are always amazed at our sheep-dog trials by the skill of the shepherd in getting the dogs to obey orders implicitly and by the intelligence of the dogs in understanding those orders over long distances. Not every sheep-dog is naturally gifted. The shepherd must select the most willing and quick-witted of the young dogs for the special training required. It is one of the pleasures of walking in the hills to come across a sheep-farmer rounding up his sheep, to hear his sharp whistles and then to see the dogs, like small black and white specks moving far, far up the steep hillside. A shout and a whistle and the two dogs crouch motionless as the sheep come to a gap in the wall. Another whistle and they race around in a circle and down comes the flock safely on to the low ground and the dogs come panting back to their master's heel with the look on their faces of a job well done. Indeed it always is, for sheep-farming in the high hills depends on this heart-warming partnership between man and dog. You can't whistle for tractors in country like the limestone crags of Pen-y-Ghent.

The sheep world is with you all through the final long miles of the Pennine Way. The path itself goes on to the Cheviot Hills but I feel that it ends outside the true Pennine country. I take the line of the Tyne Gap to be the terminal point of this 200-mile long splendour of dale and moorland and bright rivers running through deep, wooded valleys. Along its northern boundary the Romans built their wall, and I refuse to cross the 'limes' into the uncharted country beyond! I get my final Pennine excitement from the fine wall of hills that forms the eastern boundary of the valley of the Eden. This escarpment has been described as 'the most remarkable geological feature in England'. A great fault has dropped down the Pennine rocks and brought in the New Red Sandstone that forms the fine Eden valley that runs northwards to Carlisle. This valley has been, time and again, the route along which the Scottish armies invaded England. The last ill-fated army to march this way was that of Bonnie Prince Charlie in 1745. The Highlanders had crossed the actual border at the little river Esk just north of Carlisle with high hopes, led according to the old song by the famous hundred pipers:

'The Esk was swollen sae red, sae deep,
But shoulder to shoulder the brae lads keep,
Two thousand swam o'er to fell English ground,
And danced themselves dry to the pibroch's sound.'

Alas, they did not have much spirit for dancing as they retreated the same way to Scotland. All the way along the Eden valley they marched under the shadow of the 30-mile long escarpment marking the edge of what geologists have termed the Alston Block, a stretch of high lonely moorland which is of great, 'unchanged geological simplicity'. I rather like that word 'simplicity', for this is the quality that impressed itself on me as I walked on a crisp January morning towards the highest summit of the Pennines, Cross Fell, which rises just short of 3,000 ft. I had started my climb from the little hamlet of Kirkland, past the strange formations on the ground they call – for a reason I have never discovered – by the splendidly irrelevant title of the Hanging Gardens of Mark Anthony. I came out on to the light snow and I crunched my way to the highest top, after paying pious tribute to the lonely spot where the Tees rises. I looked across the deep trench of the Eden valley to the high summits of the Lakeland mountains, buried under deeper snow. Yes, the view had a stern elemental simplicity; it summed up, in one swift glance, the essential power of this great range of high moors that forms the worthy Backbone of England.

January with the Poets

Out of the grey air grew snow and more snow
Soundlessly in nonillions of flakes
Commingling and sinking negligently
To ground, soft as froth and easy as ashes
Alighting, closing the ring of sight. And
Silting, it augmented everything
Furring the bare leaf, blurring the thorn,
Fluffing, too, the telephone-wire, padding
All the paths and boosting boots, and puffing
Big over rims, like boiling milk, meekly
Indulging the bulging hill, and boldly
Bolstering the retiring hole, until
It owned and integrated all.

W. R. RODGERS

When chapman billies leave the street
And drouthy neebors neebors meet,
As market-days are wearing late,
And folks begin to tak' the gate;
While we sit bousing at the nappy,
An' getting fou' and unco' happy,
We think na on the lang Scots miles,
The mosses, waters, slaps and stiles,
That lie between us and our hame,
Where sits our sulky, sullen dame,
Gathering her brows like gathering storm,
Nursing her wrath to keep it warm.

ROBERT BURNS

On old Cold Crendon's windy tops
Grows wintrily Blown Hilcote copse,
Wind-bitten beech with badger barrows,
Where brocks eat wasp-grubs with their marrows
And foxes lie on short-grassed turf,
Nose between paws, to hear the surf
Of wind in the beeches drowsily.
There was our fox bred lustily
Three years before, and there he berthed,
Under the beech-roots snugly earthed,
With a roof of flint and a floor of chalk
And ten bitten hens' heads each on its stalk,
Some rabbits' paws, some fur from scuts,
A badger's corpse and a smell of guts.

JOHN MASEFIELD

February

February, to me, is a time of pause in the rhythm of the countryside. Winter seems reluctant to leave, although the first daring primroses are already out on the hedgerows of southern Britain. The name comes from the Latin, Februarius – the month of the feasts of purification or expiation, and indeed there is a feeling about this rather drab time of year of stopping to consider – and maybe to regret – all we have gone through in Winter, before we meet the first challenge of Spring in March.

The farmer's year naturally knows no such pause. In the lower and warmer parts of the country he is preparing for the spring sowing. In the hills the shepherd is keeping a wary eye on his ewes for the lambing season is not so far away. Farming tasks must be done even if the rain is falling remorselessly to earn the month its old nick-name of 'February Filldyke'. The old farmers had a string of proverbial sayings about February, as they had about every other month, and they rather welcomed a wet February:

> 'February brings no rain
> 'Tis neither good for grass nor grain.'

And again:

> 'All the months of the year
> Curse a good Februeer.'

But how much trust can you put in these old sayings? Modern meteorologists, with their carefully kept records, tend to cast doubt on most of them. In defence of these ancient sayings – especially of those connected with specific times of the year – we ought to remember that our calendar was changed by law in the mid-18th Century. Our continued use of the old method of reckoning had

'Rain, Steam and Speed', Turner's remarkable impression of a train crossing the viaduct over the River Thames at Maidenhead

200

put us 11 days out of line with the rest of Europe, which had already adopted the much more accurate Gregorian system. The ordinary man felt – as many people felt after the recent introduction of metrication – that, somehow or other, the experts had cheated him. There were riots in some places. They tramped through the streets shouting, 'Give us back our 11 days.' Of course, the whole thing was totally accepted within a few years, but those lost days may throw out of gear a lot of the old country sayings. Did our forefathers celebrate Candlemas Day, February 2nd, a week and a half later than we do? Is it now safe to say,

> 'If Candlemas Day be fair and bright,
> Winter will never have another flight;
> If Candlemas Day be clouds and rain,
> Winter is gone and will not come again.'

I'd like to believe it. I feel as Thomas Hardy did in his moving poem about the oxen, which were supposed to kneel in their stall in homage to the new-born Holy Child at twelve o'clock on Christmastide. And if, says Hardy, someone would invite me to go and see those gentle creatures kneel in their strawy pen:

> 'I should go with him in the gloom,
> Hoping it might be so.'

In the same spirit I will go on repeating:

> 'If there's ice in November that will
>   bear a duck
> There'll be nothing after but sludge
>   and muck,'

and calling February 'Filldyke', hoping it might be so.

In this month of pause, the country lover can have time to look around him and analyse the landscape. The trees are still dark skeletons without leaves. There is still a possibility of snow sprinkling the lower ground and outlining its features in white. The basic structure of this land of Britain shows through as in an X-ray plate; and the first thing that strikes you is how firmly man has put his imprint upon it. Of course, all the bones of the landscape have been there from immemorial time in the rocks, torn and twisted and sheered through the countless centuries. The ice was the last natural remoulder of the land on a big scale, and it melted at last to leave most of the country of Britain plastered with boulder clay. In geological time it is only yesterday, a mere 10,000–15,000 years ago, that the last permanent ice melted in the lonely corries of the Cairngorms and the returning grass, trees and bushes reclothed the raw landscape in consoling green. Soon in the wake of the vegetation came the great herds of wild animals, and in their wake came Man the Hunter. From that moment he became, in an ever-increasing measure, a shaper of our landscape.

Is there anywhere on the ground of Britain where man has not set his foot? Up until late Victorian times it was possible for both poets and guide-book writers to talk of the pathless wilds of Snowdonia or Skye. But then came the first rock climbers, the forerunners of a vast horde of crash-helmeted, sling-festooned enthusiasts who, in ten years' time, will have found and mastered the last foot of unclimbed rock in our mountains or along our sea-cliffs. There may be some lonely reefs and scattered rocks off the coast where the swirl of the breakers and the rise and fall of the ocean swell make it almost impossible to land from boats. The most outlying speck of rock that is now claimed as British is Rockall, far out in the Atlantic beyond remote St Kilda's. A party finally got on to it with difficulty not so long after the last war and hoisted the Union Jack. Between the lonely islet off Pembrokeshire which bears the Smalls lighthouse and gannet-haunted Grassholm lies the reef called the Barrels and Hats. The Hats never seem to show plainly but the Barrels show up as a dromedary-hump rock and a challenge to adventure. In 1955, the well-known naturalist, R.M. Lockley, managed to set foot on it from a boat and two more adventurers followed later, judging the moment as the swell lifted, to cling to the seaweed-covered lower rocks. Another lonely patch of the land of Britain had been trodden by the foot of man. Today a helicopter could probably do the trick in 20 minutes from a mainland base.

Britain underground may still offer possibilities for exploration – for the strange inexplicable pleasure of finding yourself in a place where no human being has been before you! Exploration of the vast caverns in the limestone areas of Britain goes on apace and the really difficult areas are still tough enough to be reserved for experts only. I have been taken down into one of the more testing caves of the Mendips and have had a glimpse of the problems involved. In my 'wet suit' I slid down water-courses disappearing into dark cracks in the rocks, or wriggled through 'letter boxes' that forced you to become an india-rubber man. The reward was the magical sight of the cascades of stalactites and stalagmites glittering in the beams of the lamps, the still, mysterious lakes stretching into darkness, the huge empty silent caverns floored with pure white sand. Below ground, there is certainly an untrodden, unaltered Britain. Above ground, it's another matter.

But if man has traversed nearly every square yard of the above-ground surface of Britain, are there any parts of it his hand has not altered or attempted to alter? I remember camping on the banks of the Kerkaig stream in the wide wilderness of Sutherland. The strange pyramid of Suilven lifted itself in splendour from its base of ice-scraped rocks. The long summer day was dying in the west with the resplendent colours you only get on the west coast of the Highlands. I sat outside the tent, the only human being, as far as I could see, in the whole of that wild country. A herd of deer, led by a majestic, antlered stag, came over the rocky ridge behind me – and then turned silently away and were lost amongst the rocks. This, I said to myself, was how it must have been not long after the ice melted – the world new-minted and untouched by man.

Yet, even in wildest Sutherland, man has been moulding this savage land for centuries to suit his needs. He has burnt the heather and bracken to get feed for his flocks. Long before that he burnt and cleared the forest. He has even been constantly changing the animals that graze the sparse grass he has left. The highland cattle that were the clansmen's main wealth disappeared from many of the glens when the lairds found, in the early 19th Century, that the sheep paid better. The 'clearances' gained a grim notoriety as the old Highland

crofters were driven off the land by the ducal owners and replaced with the more efficient lowland shepherds. The emigrant boats anchored in the lochs and the old clansmen went aboard with bitterness in their hearts and sad songs on their lips to make new Scotlands in Canada, Australia and New Zealand, far from 'the lone sheiling on that misty island'. There came a time when the sheep themselves were displaced. The rich took up the sport of deer-stalking, made popular by the Prince Consort, and huge areas of the Highlands became 'forest' once more. The very stag that I saw on that still summer's eve under Suilven was no descendant of the vast herds that roamed here after the Ice Age. His forebears were themselves introduced 150 years ago.

It is the same all over lowland Britain. This country owes most of its surface features to the enterprise, the inspiration and the meddling of man. There have been slow changes of climate which could have interfered with forest growth, rising and falling in the sea levels which could alter the coast line, meanderings of the rivers which can cut new paths. But while all these forces were at work through history, man has increased his power of controlling them. The landscape of Britain today is man's somewhat flawed masterpiece. Nature gave him the theme, and he has written the variations.

The first variation was agricultural. When the hunter gave place to the farmer and stock-keeper in what archaeologists called the Neolithic Revolution, man made his first visual impact on the surface of Britain. He cleared small patches in the woodland for his crops and led his cattle and sheep to graze down the bushes and tall grass on the chalk downs. Through the long centuries that saw Roman, Saxon, Dane and Norman succeed the Celts over so much of the land of Britain, this steady gnawing away of the original forest covering continued, and a pattern of agriculture emerged in the southern and eastern parts of the country known as the three-field system. The typical mediaeval village clustered around its church. About it were spread the wide open fields, divided into strips, tended by individual peasants under a system of rights and duties which became increasingly complicated as the years went on. In the background lay the forest. Its boundaries were steadily shrinking but a considerable area remained even 300 years ago. The villagers needed it for their firewood, their furniture and houses, and their pigs and cattle. The kings and great men needed it for their sport. Shakespeare could write about the Forest of Arden and his audience would have no difficulty in imagining vast tracts in their own countryside where outlaws could live happily 'under the Greenwood Tree'.

Epping Forest spread into Essex almost from the gates of London. Sherwood, Charnwood, Cannock Chase are now mere ghosts of themselves but 300 years ago they were still genuine forests where the deer ran wild. Apart from the forest, Shakespeare's countryside would have looked bare, bleak and shaggy to our eyes. Above all, we would miss the hedgerows. These enchanting banks of flowers, hawthorn and small trees wriggle all over our landscape and turn it into a vast garden. They are Britain's unique possession. With the exception of parts of Normandy, only too familiar to our armed forces during World War II, I know of no other part of Europe which is a coloured patchwork of flowering hedgerows. Over most of the great northern European plains, the landscape has remained mediaeval in structure if not in agricultural practice. The wide open fields are still there, as they were in Britain until towards the end of the 18th Century. There were no obstacles then to the manoeuvring of armies over our countryside in the Civil War. Prince Rupert could make his thundering cavalry charges and Cromwell's Ironsides could advance, stirrup to stirrup, in their controlled 'good round trot' without fear of hedges breaking up their formation.

The great change gathered momentum throughout the first half of the 18th Century – that sensible, inventive, highly practical, straightforward century which was prepared to tackle problems that previous centuries had tended to shirk. The population was increasing with the long internal peace and the growth of trade. New methods of agriculture and stock-breeding had

pointed the way to increased production from the land; but only if that land was better used. The three-field system was out of date and had to go, but the process was painful. The Enclosure Acts went steadily through Parliament and the vast mediaeval tangle of rights and duties was drastically cut or abolished. But for the poor peasant who had suddenly lost his cherished right of grazing his one cow on the village waste land, the Enclosure Acts meant tragedy. He repeated the bitter verse:

'The law locks up the man and woman
Who steals the goose from off the common,
But lets the greater villain loose
Who steals the common from the goose.'

In vain. 200 years ago the landscape of Britain, through the pain of the peasantry, took the pattern that we see today. From then on, all new developments have had to be fitted into this framework.

No sooner had the framework been established than it had to face its first test – a test which it passed with flying colours and which, today, has added a new beauty to the countryside. The Industrial Revolution had begun in Britain. We were, in fact, the world pioneers in mass production. In the foundries of Birmingham, in the coal fields of Durham and South Wales, in the Potteries and the Yorkshire and Lancashire valleys

Waterfowl wintering on Connaught Water in Epping Forest, which was a royal hunting preserve until Tudor times

the new products were pouring out from the factories and from Blake's 'dark, satanic mills'. They had to be transported to the ports and to London over an almost non-existent road system. The diaries of 16th- and 17th-century travellers are filled with stories of coaches stuck axle-deep in mud, and with lamentations about the 'execrable highways' of any part of Britain you care to name. True, road improvement was very much in the air as the 18th Century developed. The names of

A flight of locks on the canal at Oldbury near Birmingham, in the centre of Britain's canal system

safer methods of transportation if they were to capture the world. The ingenious answer to the problem came in the canals.

We ought to remember, however, that the canal idea was not pioneered in England. The French during their Golden Age under Louis XIV, had already constructed the grandiose Canal du Midi, linking the Mediterranean to the Gironde and the Atlantic. The Dutch had made the Netherlands a maze of canals. But there was one thing missing in all their enterprises a system of locks and reservoirs. The essence of canal structure – the things that made it flexible and superior to canalised rivers – was the provision of a long summit level fed by reservoirs, which would ensure an adequate supply of water flowing down through the locks at either end. A canal could thus climb over a slope that would defeat a river. The honour of constructing this pioneer type of waterway goes to Northern Ireland, where the Newry canal was opened as far back as 1745. It was 16 years later, in 1761, that the Duke of Bridgwater, with his engineer, the self-taught James Brindley, opened his celebrated canal at Worsley and thus started the Canal Age in England. Brindley was the man of the hour. People clamoured for his services, and swiftly a canal system started to grow through the Midlands and the North, and then out to London and the great ports. The Industrial Revolution, in its early years, floated upon water!

The canal engineers were the forerunners of the great railway engineers of the 19th Century and were equally daring. They were prepared to carry their waterways up over high passes or drive them in tunnels through the hills. The early canals were comparatively short and tended to follow the contours. Later on the engineers grew bolder. They cut corners and built great embankments, arguing that this saved money by saving time. One of the last canals built to follow the contours was the Oxford, which meandered elegantly through the lush countryside, losing money for its promoters at every gentle turn. The successful canals were far more enterprising in construction. The builders and contractors organised armies of workmen, the navigators – hence our word 'navvy' – who, by

Macadam and Telford did not really become known until after 1800, but the first turnpike schemes were already under way, taking up where the Romans had left off 1,500 years before. But while the turnpikes could speed the mail, they were not geared for mass transport of heavy or delicate manufactured goods. The products of the genius of Watt and Wedgwood, and of the host of enterprising new-style businessmen, needed far

sheer manpower, helped occasionally by the horse or the steam pump, drove tunnels like Standedge on the old Huddersfield narrow canal which ran for 5,456 yards through the Pennines, at times 600 ft below the surface. Or they built aqueducts such as Telford's masterpiece, which carries the Llangollen branch of the Shropshire Union acros the River Dee in a cast-iron trough supported on a series of arches 120 ft high. The great flights of locks at places like Tardebigge or Bingley are splendid architectural creations in their own right. The canals were constructed at a period of fine architectural tradition and so their lock-gates, their bridges, even the canalside pubs fitted pleasingly into the landscape. They were built to the right human scale.

Paradoxically, this scale, so pleasant to the modern pleasure tourists on the canals which still remain, proved the undoing of most of them once the Railway Age began. Brindley, for what seemed very good reason at the time, standardised the locks at a length of 72 ft 7 in and a width of 7 ft 6 in. This entailed in turn a narrow boat which could not carry a load of more than 30 tons. This became uneconomic as the competition from railways developed. The canals didn't die overnight. They went on doing useful work, and carrying certain types of cargo until our own day, when that fatal 30-ton limitation proved their death-knell as a serious commercial proposition. Brindley gave the canal life and ensured that it would lose it in the end!

Yet the later-day life on the canals has a strange fascination. As the competition from the railways intensified in the 1870s, the boatmen found it cheaper to take their families with them on to the narrow boats. They became a race of water gypsies with the narrow boats as their caravans, and, as with gypsy caravans, the wives contrived to make the whole family cosy in the narrow space of the cabin. The boats were now decorated with the famous Roses and Castles pattern and a form of canal art developed much prized today by canal fans. The life was tough. The boats had to be 'legged' through some of the tunnels, with the boatmen lying on their backs on planks placed on the bows of the boat and pushing vigorously with their feet. I tried this recently through a comparatively short tunnel on the Brecon and Monmouth canal and emerged with a new respect for the men who manned the narrow boats.

I must not give the impression that the canal in Britain is now a lost cause. The surviving canals have gained a new lease of life with the holiday-makers. There is a strong lobby urging the authorities to look again at their commercial value as the roads choke with ever-increasing traffic. Enthusiasts are restoring many of the abandoned waterways; and even in their ruin, the old canals can be things of rare beauty. I walked along the abandoned towpath of the Montgomery canal on a still summer's evening, where it winds among the green hills. A perch leapt among the water-lilies and left a shining circle on the still water. A moorhen jerked her way among the reeds and a kingfisher flashed under the old bridge. The traffic had long since gone, but the old canal had turned itself into a nature reserve. A last irony, the same thing is happening to the canals' deadly rival. Through the countryside now run the abandoned railway-tracks, where the wild flowers grow and the blackberries offer rich harvests in September. Brindley must be chuckling sardonically in the Shades!

The countryside had absorbed the canals and even made them into things of beauty. The railways were a sterner test. They demanded more from the landscape than the canals. A railway had to be level, not rising more than a few feet in a mile. It had to be segregated from the road and be as straight as possible, for the railway train was designed to be run at speed. The canal boat went at the pace of the horse that towed it and the waterway could afford a certain amount of turning. The railway could afford no sharp turns. The railway engineers had to attack the landscape on a scale even the boldest of canal builders had not visualised. Richard Trevithick ran the first steam-driven train in 1804 on a mineral line in South Wales from Penydarran, near Merthyr Tydfil, down to Abercynon, but it was George Stevenson's success on the Stockton and Darlington Railroad in 1825 and later on the

A frozen lock on a spur of the Grand Union canal at Rothersthorpe in Northamptonshire

The Oxford canal at Thrupp. Boating on Britain's inland waterways has become a major leisure industry in recent years

Liverpool and Manchester line in 1830, that started the Railway Age. As with the canals the first 20 years were tumultuous. The railway seemed to express the boundless confidence of the early Victorian age. The Victorians took the steam engine to their hearts.

Technically, of course, there had been railways before steam. Horses had dragged cars along wooden and later iron rails from comparatively early times. In 1603–4, the accounts of Sir Francis Willoughby's estate at Wollaton Hall, near Nottingham, mention a railway and such lines, operated by horse-power, became common in the colliery districts in the 18th Century. The oldest continually operated line in the country closed comparatively recently, a mere 20 years ago. This was the famous Swansea to Oystermouth railway, which ran for four curving miles around the shores of Swansea Bay. It ended its life as an electric tramway, but I remember riding on it as a boy, in open trams, with a tank engine puffing smoke into our eyes. We were proud to face all discomforts for we had been told at school that we were the inheritors of the longest continuous railway tradition in the world. Before the comparatively late arrival of steam, the carriages on the line were all horse-drawn.

There was even an experiment in the use of wind-power. The Cambrian newspaper reported in 1807:

'An experiment of a novel kind was made on the Oystermouth Tramroad yesterday to ascertain the practicability of a carriage proceeding to the Mumbles without horse, by the aid of the wind alone. Some Jolly Sons of Neptune rigged a wagon with a long-sail, and the wind blowing strong and as fair as could be wished, set out from our quay, and after clearing the houses dropped anchor at the end of the tramroad in less than three quarters of an hour, having come a distance of about $4\frac{1}{2}$ miles.'

The steam engine could easily beat both sail and horse in speed. Furthermore it could drag behind it carriages which could hold far more goods and passengers than the most well-equipped canal boat. It was the weapon by which the early Victorians would conquer the future. No matter if this early

enthusiasm – christened the Railway Mania – suffered a temporary collapse in 1849 with the failure of the companies of the great speculator, Robert Hudson. The all-conquering march of the steam engine could not be stopped. By the 1850s the countryside of Britain was criss-crossed with an unrivalled network of railways.

There had been opposition, of course, to the whole business of railway construction. A railway had to cut directly across land and required an Act of Parliament before construction could be undertaken. Landowners could make a company pay dearly for the privilege of crossing their land. The classic case is that of Lord Petre of Ingatestone Hall in Essex who, it is claimed, forced the Eastern Counties line to pay £120,000 for land worth £5,000 at the most. No wonder Colonel Sibthorp, whose voice was later raised with eloquence against the project of the Crystal Palace, thundered in 1844: 'All railways are public frauds and private robberies.' There was also alarm at the hordes of navvies that camped in the countryside as a railway was under construction. In May, 1848, it was calculated that 188,000 men were at work in constructing 3,000 miles of railway. Undoubtedly some of these settlements were wild and tough; but the navvies were a very special breed of men, proud of their own skill, and gave a fierce loyalty to a great, fair-dealing contractor like Thomas Brassey. However, after all the lamentation and oratory about the social dangers of railways and railway construction, it comes as a surprise to find that the temperance societies, in some places, actually welcomed them. Thomas Cook started his career as the pioneer travel impressario by organising a temperance excursion from Leicester to Loughborough; and the teetotallers of Cornwall, as they travelled on the West Cornwall line in 1852 sang this rousing chorus:

'Happy Camborne, happy Camborne,
Where the railway is so near,
And the engine shows how water
Can accomplish more than beer.'

The surprising thing however about all the sound and fury occasioned by the advent of the early railway lines is how little of it was concerned with

Above: The railway viaduct over the River Tweed at Berwick

Right: Winter in industrial Britain: factories at Brownhills, north-west of Birmingham

their physical impact on the landscape. All the debates centred around the financial and social problems the railways brought with them. Few people complained about the great masses of earth piled across the skyline to make the Wolverton embankment on the London to Birmingham line, or denounced as an eyesore the deep gash through the chalk the same company made at Tring, then the deepest cutting yet made in the earth of England. The enclosures, the canals and turnpike constructors had already conditioned the public's mind to radical alterations in the landscape. The embankments and cuttings were even admired for their beauty. When the railway cutting was made at Windmore Hill in Middlesex, the local doctor's daughter was enthusiastic in her description of the scene:

'The excavations were beautiful in colour, the London clay being a bright cobalt blue when first cut through, and changing with exposure to orange. There were strata of black and white flints and yellow gravel; the men's white slops and the red heaps of burnt ballast made vivid effects of light and shade and colour against the cloudless sky ... There were also dark wooden planks and shorings to add neutral tints, and when the engine came the glitter of brass and clouds of white steam were added to the landscape. On Sundays and holidays the men were many of them resplendent in scarlet and yellow, or blue plush waistcoats and knee-breeches.'

The railway engineers were hailed as heroes. Samuel Smiles used George Stephenson as one of his chief examples when he wrote his unctuous volume on 'Self Help'. Brunel was felt to be a national asset. Constructions like Kilsby Tunnel and Saltash Bridge were reckoned among the wonders of a Progressive Age. The artists also felt them to be

something special and Turner produced one of his greatest colour symphonies in celebration of the train racing through rain and sunshine over the new viaduct across the Thames at Maidenhead. It was when the railways had to penetrate into the upland areas of Britain that the protests began. An embankment or viaduct amongst the hills has to compete with and even defy the natural form of the landscape. Those quiet glorifiers of Nature, Wordsworth and Ruskin, were eloquent in their fury. Wordsworth began his sonnet on the Windermere to Kendal railway with the cri-de-coeur:

'Is there no nook of English ground secure
From rash assault?'

Ruskin poured out his scorn on the railway promoters who planned the line from Bakewell to Buxton over his favourite stretch of Miller Dale:

'Now every fool in Buxton can be in Bakewell in half an hour, and every fool in Bakewell at Buxton; which you think a lucrative process of exchange – you Fools Everywhere.'

Yet, with the passage of time, the railways seem to have fitted in to the mountain landscape as successfully as they did to that of the lowlands. Age has mellowed the cuttings through the rocks. Even the viaduct across Miller Dale now seems to be a thing of beauty. In fact, viaducts amongst the mountains are one of the pleasures of railway travel. I think of the thrill of looking out from the curving line on the trains approaching the noble bridge over the Tweed at Berwick, or the excitement of travelling among the girders high over the Firth of Forth. And how beautiful are the patterns cast upon the moors of southern Galloway by the low winter sun, from the arches of the now disused viaduct behind Gatehouse of Fleet.

The truth is that the early railway engineers and architects came on the scene in the last few years before the old traditions of architecture had been broken by the mass-production techniques of the mid and late Victorian period. The canal builders had had no difficulty in assimilating the elegant architectural conventions of the Regency, and it was the same with the early railway architects. They could build their viaducts with the same motives that had inspired the builders of the Roman aqueducts. They could place Doric columns at the entrance to their tunnels with confidence that they would not look out of place. They could build Gothic towers, as enjoined by the Act of Parliament, to harmonise with the towers of Conway Castle where George Stephenson's bridge crossed the wide river. Around the same period, Trinity House was constructing lighthouses around our coast and also inheriting the same

tradition of good, restrained elegant design that inspired the early railway architects. Later on, railway construction fell upon less happy days. But, at the beginning, all was confidence and optimism.

The engineers were cheered as they drove their line along the coast under the Old Red Sandstone cliffs of southern Devonshire, defying the stormy winter sea. When Sir William Cubitt was faced with carrying his line from Folkestone to Dover, he decided to blast away the 375-ft cliff of Round Down. He had to remove a cliff face 300 ft wide and 70 ft deep. He placed 19,000 lbs of gunpowder in the cliff and invited the directors and their guests to see one of the biggest explosions yet planned in Britain. He erected a marquee a mile away on a cliff top and there his guests assembled somewhat nervously. A warning shot was fired. A dead silence fell. Then with a shattering report, the whole cliff collapsed with the sort of noise that one

Right: The huge pylons which take electricity on the National Grid to nearly every part of the country

Opposite: A power station on the River Trent, with its lines of pylons radiating outwards, dominates the landscape on the Derbyshire-Leicestershire border

spectator felt, would 'herald the end of the world'.

Rather was it the beginning of a new world. With the spread of the railway network, not only the passengers but industry became more mobile. It was possible to build factories and operate them successfully outside the towns, and to exploit mineral deposits, especially coal, in comparatively remote areas. Through the fifties and sixties a new type of landscape came into being, a curious mixture of country and industry. The great industrial towns have conquered and buried parts of the country. Some have preserved little forgotten bits of it in their hearts, brushed and combed into municipal parks. But the dominant impression of places like Glasgow, Birmingham, Manchester and Leeds is of a totally man-made environment – trees and grass have long been mere tolerated survivors here. But the semi-industrial areas are different. You feel that the countryside is tolerating

strangers for a comparatively short period, and in a hundred years or so, they will be gone. After all, this has happened again and again in our history.

The Weald of Kent was once the centre of our iron industry. The great oak forests were ruthlessly cut down to supply charcoal for the smelter's furnaces. By the early 18th Century the end was in sight. The industry had to migrate northwards and westwards in search of coal as an alternative source of fuel, and never returned. In place of the furnaces, it was the trees which returned, and the woods grow again on the Weald to reclothe it in beauty. The early mining industry has left ruins amongst the hills that can look as romantic in their old age as ancient castles. In Cornwall the engine houses of abandoned tin-mines stand starkly against the moors, with the chimneys as gracefully built as the round towers of Ireland. Strangest of all is the Durham coalfield not far from Chester-le-Street.

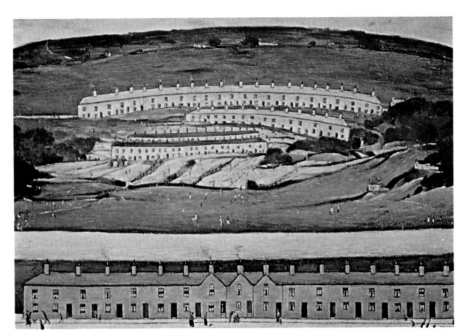

Left: L. S. Lowry: 'Hillside in Wales'. Lowry's evocative paintings of industrial Britain brought him international acclaim

Opposite: A carefully landscaped section of the M4 motorway near Yattendon in Berkshire

Right: The Forth road bridge, with the cantilevered railway bridge, opened in 1890, beyond it. The road bridge is $1\frac{1}{2}$ miles long and carries traffic from Edinburgh to the north of Scotland

Here the collieries, with their winding gear, stand – or perhaps I should say stood – in a dark, rolling countryside, and on a rocky knoll among them, yet dominating the landscape, rises (of all things) a sort of Grecian temple, with unfluted Doric columns, four-square and defiantly classical under the northern sky. This is the Penshaw Monument, dedicated in 1844 by the citizens of Newcastle to the first Earl of Durham, the great liberal politician ('Radical Jack') who became the first High Commissioner for Canada.

The colliery districts tend to produce these astonishing contrasts. Is there a stranger landscape than that of the South Wales mining valleys? In the deep chasms made by rivers like the Rhondda, the Afan, the Ogwr and the Garw, lie the mining villages, where the collieries struggle for space with the rows of terraced houses, the chapels, the welfare halls, the pubs and the Lucania billiard saloons, while above them lie the moorlands, now going under forest but still lonely and windswept. W.H. Auden, in the thirties, wrote that the Lancashire moss

> 'Sprouted up chimneys, and Glamorgan
>   hid a life
> Grim as a tidal rock-pool's in its glove-
>   shaped valleys.'

How wrong he was. Those isolated communities in the valleys developed a life of their own – intense, dramatic, salted with song and oratory. It was the same among the tin-miners of Cornwall and also in the strange china clay district of that county. Behind St Austell the shining white pyramids from the clay pits glitter like the volcanic cones on the surface of the moon.

All these areas – half town, half country – owe their early development to the railway. But they are not the last variations on the theme of the Natural Landscape of Britain. In our own day, two new developments now clamour to be fitted into the old framework. The first is the new motorway system.

It is tempting to feel that the motorway is the heir to the old turnpike road that brought in the golden age of the mail-coach at the beginning of the 19th Century. But the turnpike was, in essence, a surface improvement on the old road structure that went back to the Middle Ages. The advent of the motor-car meant that the turnpikes had to be straightened, widened and tinkered with on an ever-increasing scale, until, after the last war, it became obvious that Britain would have to do what Germany, Italy and the United States had already done – build special tracks solely for motor-driven traffic. The motorways were closer in concept to the railways than to the turnpikes. They were segregated from the other road system. They had limited access, and, like the railways, they were built for speed. But on a far bigger scale. A three-lane motorway, on either side, takes up immeasurably more room than a main-line railway. Can the landscape continue to accept them without serious damage to its aesthetic quality?

The same question-mark hangs over the second big-scale development of modern times – the creation of a national power grid linking all the electricity generating stations throughout the country. In many places, the generating stations themselves seem to have taken over the landscape. I drove on a misty February morning over the flat plains south of the Humber estuary where the waters of the Trent come to join those of the Yorkshire Ouse. The new power stations stood out over the level country like vast fortresses. From them the pylons stalked away carrying the slightly sagging lines in an impressive ever-diminishing perspective to the distant horizon. I could accept this new landscape clothed in February mist. But what happens when the pylons are 130 ft high, and go, as proposed, against the background of the South Downs?

Can we accept the motorways and the pylons as we accepted the canals and the railways? Or have we reached the point when the sheer scale of the new developments means the breaking of the mould into which our countryside has been cast with such beauty and success for over 10,000 years? These were the questions I asked myself, driving towards the Humber through the February mist. It will be many years before we know the answer. And when it comes, we may not altogether relish it!

February with the Poets

Come February rain!
Crocus, thrust tenderest steel again!
By cruel February is this acre freed,
In such an angry day shall every grain
Admit the winter rot or else succeed.

JOHN PUDNEY

There is a spot, 'mid barren hills,
Where winter howls and driving rain;
But, if the dreary tempest chills,
There is a light that warms again.

The mute bird sitting on the stone,
The dank moss dripping from the wall,
The thorn-trees gaunt, the walls o'ergrown,
I love them – how I love them all!

EMILY BRONTË

In the places of my boyhood
The pit-wheels turn no more,
Nor any furnace lightens
The midnight as of yore.

The slopes of slag and cinder
Are sulking in the rain,
And in the derelict valleys
The hopes of youth are slain.

And yet I love to wander
The early ways I went,
And watch from doors and bridges
The hills and skies of Gwent.

Though blighted are the valleys
Where man meets man with pain,
The things my boyhood cherished
Stand firm and shall remain.

IDRIS DAVIES

The hours of daylight must be lengthening now;
I walked among the frost and noticed how
The last softening snowdrops were in thaw;
Then, stepping between flecks of shadow, saw
The first collapse of crocuses begun,
Yellowy in small fritterings of sun.
Ridiculous with delight, I hurried home.

TED WALKER

Last Word

We have now completed our journey and followed the full cycle of the seasons around Britain. The Spring returns, and I turn back over the pages of our Countryside Companion with a slight sense of regret. Much of the beauty of Britain is here, but so much, of necessity, has escaped us. How can you enclose all the glories of our landscape between two book-covers? I would have wished to have shown the splendour of a lingering winter sunset over the lonely sands of Morecambe Bay, the grace of the 3,500 ft peak of Schiehallion rising above the autumn heather, the enticing almost feminine curves of the chalk downs near Shaftesbury – a hundred similar delights come to my mind and will occur to every reader of this book. We all have our favourites and must regret that they have been omitted. But we surely have included enough to justify the theme of our book – that all the varied richness of the world's landscape is here enclosed in one small island.

Yet there is a picture that I have deliberately excluded. It's the view that the fluttering hawk sees as he hovers over the outskirts of any big town in Britain. Below him the motorway runs relentlessly through the green countryside. On it, the Bank Holiday traffic crawls bumper to bumper, every car towing its own piece of mobile suburbia, a caravan, towards the hapless summer coastline. In the lanes the hedge-cutting machines employed by the local council are mowing down the flowers. The bull-dozers are laying out approach roads for the new factory on a 'Green' site. Another small part of Britain is disappearing under its carpet of asphalt and concrete. Here, in essence, is the problem facing the countryside today. Modern industry and modern agricultural practice demand big units. There is only a limited amount of space in our countryside. If we are too ruthless in exploiting it, the fragile landscape of Britain can crack under the strain. Sometimes, when I see the indifference of some of the planners and the public to the dangers threatening the rare beauty of the country scene, I am seized with a mindless rage. How much more traffic and concrete and asphalt will that hovering hawk see in twenty years' time – if indeed he, and his like, are there at all? I fall back on the practice of the old Welsh bards who were experts in the business of denouncing the spoilers of their country.

> Lord, let thy glaciers come again;
> Out from Snowdonia's fastness flow,
> Thy rivers of avenging ice,
> Remote, remorseless, cold and slow,
> To pile in one supreme moraine,
> Our godless Cities of the Plain.
>
> In snow-numbed silence let them move
> Through Birmingham and Coventry.
> Down every foul arterial road
> To sweep into the cleansing sea
> Pylon and pump and caravan,
> The muck that marks the Common Man.
>
> One rocky ark of refuge leave
> Above the icy winding sheet,
> Where, huddled in their rusting cars
> The shivering last survivors meet.
> There, Lord, if so Thy Mercy please –
> Leave them one space – to use their knees!

And then I am covered with contrition. From places like Birmingham come many of our leading conservationists, doughty champions who keep stern watch on the planners and who are ready to wage often successful battles against needless and careless so-called 'development'. More and more people are becoming aware that the price of landscape beauty is eternal vigilance. All is not lost. I have strong hopes that someone will be able to write an up-to-date sequel to this volume in 20 years' time, perhaps with that hovering hawk on the cover. I turn from the tradition of the old Welsh bards, with their gift of metrical vituperation, to the practice of the old Welsh preachers who were careful to conclude every sermon full of hell-fire with words of gentle comfort. I visualise a time when the glaciers of ugly development will melt again to reveal Britain still a 'green and pleasant land'.

At last, the warm reviving Spring
Shall make the prisoned waters run,
And over Earth's returning green
The trees cast shadows in the sun,
Till, through a soft caressive rain,
A man-free Eden blooms again.

No changing gears disturb the peace
Where, clear of oil, the waters lie,
And sweet the untransistored birds
Shall sing beneath a jet-free sky.
The whole bright world will bathe anew
In crystal, non-detergent dew.

Oh, might we enter, hand in hand,
New Adam and his fairer Eve,
Whom no forbidden fruit could tempt
Or serpent stupidly deceive;
For who would dare confess the crime
Of Eden lost a second time.

The checkered pattern of hedges and fields
in southern England

Further Reading List

I have intended this book to be one that you will wish to have with you as you travel about Britain, or to which you will turn in the winter when you are planning your journey. Today in a world of increasing leisure, more and more people are exploring the incomparable countryside of these immensely varied islands, many for the first time. The book is designed to draw their attention to the wide range of delights that await them. Inevitably it cannot be a detailed guide to all aspects of country life in Britain or a description of every part of the landscape. It is, as it were, an invitation to explore in greater depth the fascinating world that lies behind the holiday surface of Britain.

Good maps are, of course, essential and the Ordnance Survey maps of every part of Britain are incomparably the best. You will want to supplement them with a good gazetteer and here you can turn to the Shell Guides. The four volumes cover England, Scotland, Ireland and Wales. You are now armed with the method of getting around the country, but you will want to add to the purpose of your travels. A traveller who goes through a country without knowing something of its history is travelling blind. Today the shelves of our bookshops overflow with historical studies, biographies and novels, but a paper-back series like the 'Pelican History of England', with each period covered by experts, will give you an excellent introduction to modern research on the subject. Thames and Hudson publish popular 'Concise Histories' of Scotland and Ireland, both lavishly illustrated. You can supplement these general outlines with the volumes of the 'Portrait' series published by Robert Hale, which takes particular sections of the country and combines a guided tour of, for example, the Isles of Scilly or the Fens, with a pleasantly informal dash of history. For the social history of Britain, Sir George Trevelyan's volume is still fascinating reading.

The architecture of our villages next deserves attention, and I can recommend Thelma Nye's little 'Guide to Parish Church Architecture' which explains, in clear drawings, what you see before you when you enter, as all devoted countryside travellers always wish to do, the local village church. The great cathedrals and fine churches of our cities and towns may be more impressive, but the parish church can tell you a far more intimate and moving story of the life of the locality.

Then there is the structure of the land itself. Geology is a vast subject but there are three books that will help you to understand the way Britain has formed and changed through the long aeons of geological history. W. G. Fearnside's and G. M. B. Bulman's 'Geology in the Service of Man' is an excellent general introduction. L. Dudley Stamp's 'Britain's Structure and Scenery' is a classic exposition, as is Sir Arthur Trueman's 'Geology and Scenery in England and Wales'. This last volume is particularly useful for it explains in clear language and with simple drawings the exact structure of all the principal geological features of the country.

These few titles are only a foretaste of the range of publications that await you if you want to explore any special branch of countryside lore. Our generation has been fortunate in the way publishers have devoted their attention to producing cheap and easily portable guides to every aspect of life in Britain. For example, Fontana have just produced a series of 'Domino Guides', which are easy to slip into the pocket and will give you a guide to such varied subjects as the trees of Britain and the mushrooms and toadstools you will find in your country walks.

And, by the way, I hope this book will encourage you to leave your car and walk through the countryside. It is the only way you can really appreciate the subtlety of our landscape. The AA, with splendid impartiality, have encouraged their members to desert their cars and get to grips with exploring Britain, in a finely illustrated guide to a series of selected walks entitled 'No Through Road'.

Finally, may I recommend the joys of reading the accounts of the early travellers who have explored Britain and have written classical descriptions of their journeys. George Borrow's 'Wild Wales' is a gloriously robust tramp through the Principality in the 1850s and William Cobbett will take you on horseback through the yet unchanged agricultural scene of early Victorian England in his 'Rural Rides'. And who can resist the unconscious comedy of James Boswell as he describes how the bear led the formidable Dr Johnson through the wilds of Scotland to the lonely Hebrides?

If you have asked for the writings of these early travellers, this book has already achieved what it set out to do – to put you at the beginning of the happy road to the endless enjoyment and refreshment furnished by the landscape of Britain.

Acknowledgements

The Publishers would like to thank Robert Estall who took the following photographs:
15 bottom, 17, 20, 21, 33, 44, 45, 54 top, 57, 84–5, 93, 98–9, 102 left, right, 106 top, 107, 110 bottom, 127, 145, 148–9, 151, 158–9, 160, 164–5, 166–7, 168, 169, 175, 176 top, bottom, 178–9, 186, 187, 191, 204–5, 208 top, 210–11, 212, 219.

The Publishers also acknowledge the following:
Aerofilms Library: 22, 23; Malcolm Aird: 76–7, 89 bottom, 96, 138–9 bottom, 139, 142–3, 156–7, 161, 172; Barnaby's Picture Library: 34, 39; City Art Gallery, Leeds: 130–1, 190; John Cleare: 15 top, 40–1, 67, 69 top, 105, 111, 123, 133, 135, 138 top, 195, 206, 210, 213, 214, 215; G. R. Clifford Lomax: 72–3 top; Stephen Dalton: 25; D. M. and J. M. Dickinson: 137; Mick Hales: 2–3, 106 bottom; Sonia Halliday Photographs: 29; Eric Hosking FRPS: 13, 31, 85 bottom, 101, 109, 155, 171; G. B. Kearney: 174 top; The National Gallery, London: 92, 200–1; Norfolk Museums Service: 80–1; Spectrum Colour Library: 10–11, 36–7, 41 top, 48–9, 52, 53, 61 right, 68, 72–3 bottom, 75, 77 bottom, 83, 88, 103, 110 top, 118, 119, 142, 152, 153, 173, 178, 194; The Tate Gallery: 89 top, 122, 214; John Topham Picture Library: 7, 18, 30–1, 51, 54 bottom, 71, 74–5, 87, 90, 94–5, 108, 116, 120, 121, 125, 140, 141, 144 top, bottom, 174 bottom, 185, 188, 189; Victoria and Albert Museum, Crown Copyright: 24; A. Worth: 56, 60–1, 114–15; Peter Wrigley: 32, 41 bottom, 84 bottom, 126, 134, 182–3, 193, 196, 197, 208 bottom; ZEFA: 65, 69 bottom.

The publishers have made every endeavour to obtain permission from the copyright owners of all copyright material used.

Acknowledgement is made to the following:

The extract from 'August for the people and their favourite islands' by W. H. Auden is reprinted by permission of Faber & Faber Ltd from *The English Auden: Poems, Essays and Dramatic Writings 1927–1939* and by permission of Random House, New York; Patricia Beer and Hutchinson & Co. (Publishers) Ltd for an extract beginning 'A heavy frost last night' from *Selected Poems*; Sir John Betjeman, John Murray (Publishers) Ltd and Houghton Mifflin Co. for an extract from 'Upper Lambourne'; the extract from 'The Country Bedroom' is taken from Frances Cornford's *Collected Poems* by permission of the publishers Cresset Press; Mrs. D. Morris for an extract from Idris Davies' 'In the places of my boyhood'; The Executors of the W. H. Davies Estate, Jonathan Cape Ltd and Wesleyan University Press for permission to reproduce extracts from 'Early Spring' and 'The Green Tent' from *The Complete Poems of W. H. Davies*, Copyright © by Jonathan Cape, Ltd; A. P. Watt and Doubleday & Co. Inc. for permission to reproduce an extract from Rudyard Kipling 'Puck's Song' from *The Definitive Edition of Rudyard Kipling's Verse*; Laurie Lee and The Hogarth Press for an extract from 'The Three Winds' from *The Sun My Monument*; The Literary Trustees of Walter de la Mare and the Society of Authors as their representative for an extract from 'Sotto Voce': The Society of Authors as the literary representative of the Estate of John Masefield and Macmillan Inc., New York for an extract from 'On old cold Crendon's windy tops', from *Reynard the Fox*, Copyright 1919 by John Masefield, renewed 1947 by John Masefield; William Blackwood & Sons Ltd for an extract from a poem by Moira O'Neill; John Pudney and The Bodley Head for the extract beginning 'Come February Rain' from *Almanac of Hope*; The extract from 'Ireland' is taken from W. R. Rodgers' *Collected Poems* © Oxford University Press 1971 and is reprinted by permission of Oxford University Press; The Trustees for the Copyrights of the late Dylan Thomas for the extract beginning 'It was my thirtieth year' from *Collected Poems* published by J. M. Dent & Sons Ltd and New Directions Inc.; Ted Walker and Jonathan Cape Ltd for permission to reproduce an extract from 'February Poem' from *The Night Bathers*; Miss Ann Yeats, M. B. Yeats, the Macmillan Company of London and Basingstoke and Macmillan Inc., New York for extracts from W. B. Yeats' 'The Wild Swans at Coole' and 'The Circus Animals' Desertion' from Collected Poems of W. B. Yeats, Copyright 1940 by Georgie Yeats, renewed 1968 by Bertha Georgie Yeats, Michael Butler Yeats and Anne Yeats; Geoffrey Winthrop Young and Methuen & Co. Ltd for an extract from 'The Cragsman' from *Collected Poems*.

Index